Teaching Music in Secondary Schools

The Open University *Flexible* Postgraduate Certificate of Education

The readers and the companion volumes in the *flexible* PGCE series are:

All of these subjects are part of the Open University's initial teacher education course, the *flexible* PGCE, and constitute part of an integrated course designed to develop critical understanding. The set books, reflecting a wide range of perspectives, and discussing the complex issues that surround teaching and learning in the twenty-first century, will appeal to both beginning and experienced teachers, to mentors, tutors, advisers and other teacher educators.

If you would like to receive a *flexible* PGCE prospectus please write to the Course Reservations Centre at The Call Centre, The Open University, Milton Keynes MK7 6ZS. Other information about programmes of professional development in education is available from the same address.

Teaching Music in Secondary Schools
A reader

Teaching Music in Secondary Schools: A reader introduces and explores a broad range of contemporary issues and key ideas and will provide a useful background for those teaching and training to teach this exciting subject.

The book is concerned with the bigger picture of music education. Divided into three sections to help structure reading, it covers:

- Using music technology
- Progression and continuity
- Involving world musics in the curriculum
- The development of children's musical imagination
- Music psychology
- Valuing children's efforts in composing
- The history of music education
- Different approaches to music education in other European countries

The *Teaching in Secondary Schools* series brings together collections of articles by highly experienced educators that focus on the issues surrounding the teaching of National Curriculum subjects. They are invaluable resources for those studying to become teachers, and for newly qualified teachers and more experienced practitioners, particularly those mentoring students and NQTs. The companion volume to this book is *Aspects of Teaching Secondary Music: Perspectives on practice.*

Gary Spruce is a Lecturer in Education at the Open University and has responsibility for the Open University *flexible* PGCE, Music course.

Set book for the Open University *flexible* PGCE, Music course EXN880.

Teaching Music in Secondary Schools
A reader

Edited by Gary Spruce

London and New York

First published 2002
by RoutledgeFalmer
11 New Fetter Lane, London EC4P 4EE

Simultaneously published in the USA and Canada
by RoutledgeFalmer
29 West 35th Street, New York, NY 10001

RoutledgeFalmer is an imprint of the Taylor & Francis Group

© 2002 Compilation, original and editorial matter,
The Open University

Typeset in Goudy by Bookcraft Ltd, Stroud, Gloucestershire
Printed and bound in Great Britain by Biddles Ltd,
Guildford and King's Lynn

British Library Cataloguing in Publication Data
A catalogue record for this book is available from the British Library

Library of Congress Cataloging in Publication Data
A catalog record has been requested

ISBN 0–415–26233–X (hbk)

ISBN 0–415–26234–8 (pbk)

Contents

Illustrations

Figures

Table

Abbreviations

ACCAC	Qualifications Curriculum and Assessment Authority for Wales
AQA	Assessment and Qualifications Alliance
AVCE	Advanced Vocational Certificate in Education
BTEC	Business and Technology Education Council
CGLI	City of Guilds of London Institute
CSE	Certificate of Secondary Education
DENI	Department of Education Northern Ireland
DfEE	Department for Education and Employment
EBD	Emotional and behavioural difficulties
ENC	English National Curriculum
GCE	General Certificate of Education
GCSE	General Certificate of Secondary Education
GNVQ	General National Vocational Qualification
NACCCE	National Advisory Committee on Creative and Cultural Education
NCVQ	National Council for Vocational Qualifications
NVQ	National Vocational Qualification
OCR	Oxford, Cambridge and RSA Examinations
QCA	Qualifications and Curriculum Authority
RAMP	Research into Applied Musical Perception
RSA	Royal Society of Arts
VET	Vocational Education and Training

Sources

Where a chapter in this book is based on or is a reprint or revision of material previously published elsewhere, details are given below, with grateful acknowledgements to the original publishers. In some cases chapter titles are different to the original title of publication; in such cases the original title is given below.

Chapter 3 This is an edited version of an article originally published in *Music Education and Research* 1(2), Carfax Publishing, Taylor & Francis Ltd, Basingstoke (1999).

Chapter 6 This is an edited version of a chapter originally published in Spruce, G. (ed.) (1996) *Teaching Music*, Routledge, London. Original source: Mills, J. (1992) *Music in the Primary Years*, Cambridge University Press, Cambridge.

Chapter 8 This is an edited version of a chapter originally published in Spruce, G. (ed.) (1996) *Teaching Music*, Routledge, London. Original source: *British Journal of Music Education* 6(9), Cambridge University Press, Cambridge.

Chapter 9 This is an edited version of a chapter originally published in Spruce, G. (ed.) (1996) *Teaching Music*, Routledge, London.

Chapter 10 This is an edited version of a chapter originally published in Spruce, G. (ed.) (1996) *Teaching Music*, Routledge, London. Original source: Walker, R. (1988) *Imagination and Education*, Open University, Milton Keynes.

Chapter 14 This is an edited version of a chapter originally published in Spruce, G. (ed.) (1996) *Teaching Music*, Routledge, London. Original source: Swanwick, K. (1994) *Musical Knowledge*, Routledge, London.

Chapter 15 This is an edited version of an article originally published in *The British Journal of Aesthetics* 40(1), Oxford University Press, Oxford (2000).

Foreword

The nature and form of initial teacher education and training are issues that lie at the heart of the teaching profession. They are inextricably linked to the standing and identity that society attributes to teachers and are seen as being one of the main planks in the push to raise standards in schools and to improve the quality of education in them. The initial teacher education curriculum therefore requires careful definition. How can it best contribute to the development of the range of skills, knowledge and understanding that makes up the complex, multi-faceted, multi-skilled and people-centred process of teaching?

There are, of course, external, government-defined requirements for initial teacher training courses. These specify, amongst other things, the length of time a student spends in school, the subject knowledge requirements beginning teachers are expected to demonstrate or the ICT skills that are needed. These requirements, however, do not in themselves constitute the initial training curriculum. They are only one of the many, if sometimes competing, components that make up the broad spectrum of a teacher's professional knowledge that underpin initial teacher education courses.

Certainly today's teachers need to be highly skilled in literacy, numeracy and ICT, in classroom methods and management. In addition, however, they also need to be well grounded in the critical dialogue of teaching. They need to be encouraged to be creative and innovative and to appreciate that teaching is a complex and problematic activity. This is a view of teaching that is shared with partner schools within the Open University Training Schools Network. As such it has informed the planning and development of the Open University's initial teacher training programme and the *flexible* PGCE.

All of the *flexible* PGCE courses have a series of connected and complementary readers. The *Teaching in Secondary Schools* series pulls together a range of new thinking about teaching and learning in particular subjects. Key debates and differing perspectives are presented, and evidence from research and practice is explored, inviting the reader to question the accepted orthodoxy, suggesting ways of enriching the present curriculum and offering new thoughts on classroom learning. These readers are accompanied by the series *Perspectives on practice*. Here, the focus is on the application of these developments to educational/subject policy and the classroom, and on the illustration of teaching skills, knowledge and understanding in a variety of school contexts. Both series include newly commissioned work.

This series from RoutledgeFalmer, in supporting the Open University's *flexible* PGCE, also includes two key texts that explore the wider educational background. These companion publications, *Teaching, Learning and the Curriculum in Secondary Schools: A reader* and *Aspects of Teaching and Learning in Secondary Schools: Perspectives on practice*, explore a contemporary view of developments in secondary education with the aim of providing analysis and insights for those participating in initial teacher training education courses.

Hilary Bourdillon – Director ITT Strategy
Steven Hutchinson – Director ITT Secondary
The Open University
September 2001

Introduction

If this book were to have a subtitle, it might well be 'Ways of thinking about music'. For, although only the first chapter explicitly addresses this issue, many others have, as a kind of subtext, an awareness that: 'the way in which we think about music – our understanding of its nature and purpose – is most significant for our role as music educators. Our conception of what music *is* is a crucial factor in defining what we consider important subject knowledge to be, and by implication affects how we design our curriculum, what we teach and the way in which we teach it' (Spruce: Chapter 1).

This theme is continued in Chapter 2 where, following a brief overview of the changes in British music education over the last hundred years, Stephanie Pitts demonstrates how 'a clearer understanding of the past can inform our perceptions of contemporary music education'. She demonstrates this by considering from a historical perspective two perennial issues in music education: the teaching of notation and the place of popular music in the curriculum.

In Chapter 3, Lucy Green considers how certain sociological concepts can aid our understanding of various issues in music and music education. In the abstract to the original article (Green 1999) she describes how the chapter focuses on two main areas: first, ' the organization of musical activities – the production, distribution and reception of music by a variety of social groups'; and second, the social construction of musical meaning' – what music means, how it addresses those meanings and how those meanings are reproduced, contested and changed' (op. cit.) The chapter concludes by looking at how the concepts discussed can 'inform research in the sociology of music education'.

It is important that music teachers are aware of musical and pedagogical traditions other than their own and 'whether we in England may have something to learn from the systems and strategies adopted elsewhere'. In Chapter 4, Janet Hoskyns considers music education from a European perspective. She begins by looking at a number of music education ideologies, demonstrating how these map onto both western European traditions of schooling and reflect national traditions of education and schooling. She goes on to examine how tensions between the music curriculum and what is considered 'worthwhile knowledge' and between music outside and inside the classroom are resolved in a number of European countries, concluding that 'the ways in which this occurs are very variable and varied across the European continent'.

In the second section of this book, we look at music learning and musical develop-ment from a number of perspectives. Alexandra Lamont in Chapter 5 considers ways in which music psychology can assist our understanding of children's musical learning. Drawing on her own research and that of others, she examines the processes of *musical enculturation* – how innate capacities (those children are born with) develop according to the culture in which they grow up as well as their 'rapidly changing cognitive systems'. She makes the important point that although 'Conven-tional pedagogical wisdom states that passive experience is not the best way to learn … it is clear that "passive" experiences do have a role to play in developing musical understanding', and that music teachers need to take account of this in their teaching.

Evidence from Ofsted inspections suggests that music teachers in secondary schools tend to underestimate children's musical experiences and achievements at primary school. This then results in the standards achieved in Year 7 being lower than in the final year of primary school. In Chapter 6, Janet Mills discusses the musical development of children during the primary phase, describing what many experience and the level of attainment that might be expected of them. Continuing this theme, Helen Coll in Chapter 7 considers the issues of transfer and transition in music education. Drawing on Ofsted evidence, Government publica-tions and recent research, she draws parallels between issues of transfer and transi-tion in music and in other subjects. She considers the assumptions some secondary school music teachers make about primary school music and how these assump-tions translate into practice. She concludes by looking at some strategies for effec-tive transfer and transition.

Chapter 8 deals with aspects of music and special needs. Yvonne Packer high-lights the difficulties relating to the provision of music education in schools for the emotionally and behaviourally disturbed. She argues the case for 'the inclu-sion of music within a programme of special education … and recommendations are made as to how music may be made more accessible within this context'.

Assessment lies at the heart of teaching. As Keith Swanwick (1979) says, 'to teach is to assess'. It is therefore of critical importance that the role of assessment is clearly defined and issues relating to assessment are clarified. In Chapter 9, Gary Spruce considers assessment in the arts from the perspective of the assumed need for objectivity. He looks at the relationship between the arts and the sciences and the relationship between objectivity and criteria-related assessment, concluding with a discussion of the principles that might underpin the formulation of an effec-tive assessment model for the arts.

One of the main aims of music education must be the fostering of children's imaginations. However, how do we recognize musical imagination in children? Why do we frequently fail to encourage and celebrate children's musical imagina-tion as we do their creativity in art and writing? How do we react as individuals and society to manifestations of musical imagination in children and adults? Do we agree what imagination and creativity actually are? These questions are addressed by Robert Walker in Chapter 10. Drawing on musical examples from many different styles and cultures, he questions accepted ideas about the nature of musical creativity, particularly as it applies to children's compositions.

The third section of this reader looks at four musical contexts, beginning with an overview by Paul Wright of ICT in the music curriculum. In this chapter, Wright not only looks at specific applications for ICT in music but how ICT impacts upon the nature of music and our perception of it. He considers a range of hardware both discretely and as part of a 'set up'. He concludes by examining how ICT can be integrated into planning for music learning and considers where ICT might lead music education in the future.

Composing is a relative newcomer to the Music curriculum. The associations that composing has with 'great' music of the past result in what Ted Bundy in Chapter 12 describes as 'unwarranted assumptions about what makes someone a "real" composer'. He considers why it is that our particular culture is so unwilling to accept children's composition in the same spirit as we do their work in art. Drawing on the work of, amongst others, Paynter, Ross and Gammon, he argues for greater emphasis on creativity to make the music curriculum 'a vital and meaningful experience that fosters creativity and innovation'.

World musics are an established part of the music curriculum for most schools. The present National Curriculum, for example, has across all Key Stages the requirement that children study 'a range of live and recorded music from different times and cultures' (DfEE/QCA 2000). Music departments' schemes of work regularly include modules or topics based on, for example, Indian music and Balinese gamelan. Anyone spending a few days in a typical secondary music department will observe children listening to, composing and performing music from a wide range of styles and cultures. In Chapter 13, Malcolm Floyd raises fundamental issues concerning our attitude towards music from other cultures, particularly as they appear in the school curriculum. Developing some of the issues raised by Spruce in Chapter 1, he argues that considering music exclusively 'in terms of its structures and modes of operation ... is insufficient, and allows for the unauthorised appropriation of techniques, timbres and, perhaps most perniciously, samples without permission'. This raises issues of musical ownership and musical meaning which Floyd considers in the context of the music of the Masai of Kenya and northern Tanzania.

In Chapter 14, Keith Swanwick says both the best and worst teaching he has seen has been by instrumental teachers. He argues that the best instrumental teaching is by those teachers who see 'their job as teaching music through an instrument and not just teaching the instrument'. For, as he says in typically robust fashion, 'Getting people to play an instrument without musical understanding – not really "knowing music" – is an offence against human kind'. Drawing on research and observations of instrumental teachers at work, he explores the benefits of varied practice strategies, the use of metaphor in instrumental teaching and the benefits to be gained by teaching in groups. The overarching theme of the chapter, though, is that instrumental lessons should always be *musical encounters*.

Finally, in 'The art of improvisation and the aesthetics of imperfection' (Chapter 15), the book, in a sense, comes full circle. Andy Hamilton considers improvisation in the context of an hegemonic aesthetic in music as 'works', operating on the presumption of 'classical masterpieces as the touchstone of artistic excellence'. Focusing primarily on jazz and other popular musics, he attempts to correct the 'many pervasive misunderstandings of improvisation'.

Reference

Swanwick, K. (1979) *A Basis for Music Education*, Slough: NFER-Nelson

Section 1

What is music and music education?

1 Ways of thinking about music

Political dimensions and educational consequences

Gary Spruce

> More important than economic benefits were the social improvements which reformers believed could be achieved through education. Schooling would bring a sober morality to the destitute and 'godless' urban poor and impose a social authority over the working-class child where the working-class family had failed ... their desire was to counteract the spread of radical ideas through education of working-class children and later adults in the benefits of middle-class morality and bourgeois political economy.
>
> (Green 1990: 52–3)

Introduction

Government education policy over the last twenty years has significantly reduced teachers' and schools' autonomy over curriculum structure, lesson content and, by implication, teaching methodology. The Education Reform Act (1988) through the National Curriculum established 'the first statutory curriculum in the history of British education' (Docking 1996: 1). For the first time, the subjects to be taught in maintained schools and, in many cases their overall content, were determined at national government level.

The National Curriculum Council (a quasi-government body) was established to consult and make recommendations as to the broad style and content of each subject. Many of their initial recommendations were controversial, running counter to prevailing educational orthodoxies. Moreover, they were perceived by many as an attempt to impose upon schools a narrow, politicized and nationalistic subject perspective, the purpose of which was to return education to its traditional role as a means of constructing a 'political discourse through which the authority of the state and traditional social values can be restored' (Quicke 1988).

In music, the debate focused upon whether the Programmes of Study should reflect and support the music classroom as a place where children engage with music experientially as performers and composers, or signal a return to music education as 'music appreciation' of a European canon of high art music. The former view prevailed. The music Programmes of Study prescribed two Attainment Targets, performing and composing, and listening and appraising, with the proportion of time to be spent on each weighted 2:1 in favour of performing and composing. Within these broad boundaries, the content of the Programmes of Study was relatively non-prescriptive.

The autonomy which music seemingly enjoys was not granted to most other subjects. The 'content free' nature of the music National Curriculum allows music teachers much greater flexibility over subject content and pedagogical style than that enjoyed by colleagues in other subject areas. Music teachers' primary obligation is to provide a context in which children engage with a wide range of music as performers, composers and critical listeners. Within these broad boundaries, the content of the Programmes of Study is relatively non-prescriptive.

Such freedom has potentially many positive aspects. It allows music teachers to devise a curriculum that reflects the interests, aspirations and social and cultural backgrounds of their pupils. The diversification of teaching styles that naturally proceeds from such freedom is promoted by what Government agencies identify as examples of good practice. For example, both the Ofsted publication *The Arts Inspected* (1998) and the late School Curriculum and Assessment Authority's (SCAA) *Optional Tests and Tasks* (1996) reflect the varied nature of much contemporary music classroom practice. Consequently, children's experience of 'school music' can vary significantly both within departments and, particularly, between schools.

However, it is clear that autonomy and diversity have not resulted in universal quality music teaching and learning. Even *The Arts Inspected* (1998), whose essential purpose is to celebrate and extend good practice, warns against complacency: 'It would be wrong to suggest that all is well with music in schools ... for every lesson or school that is above average, roughly one falls below' (Ofsted 1998: 60). Recent research from The National Federation for Education Research (Kinder *et al.* 1995 and 2000) suggests that many pupils are dissatisfied with their school music education – at least that part of it which takes place in the classroom. It is evident therefore that musical *activity* and diverse repertoire are not sufficient to guarantee quality music teaching and pupil satisfaction. As Shulman says, we need to give 'careful attention ... to the management of *ideas* within classroom discourse' (Shulman 1987: 919) and in considering these ideas to take account of the historical, philosophical and, particularly, the political and cultural legacy that we take into the classroom.

What I will argue in this chapter is that the way in which music is perceived – the understanding of its nature and purpose – is critical to the way in which it impacts upon curriculum design, what we teach and the way we teach it. Consequently, this determines whether children receive a purposeful and rich musical experience that 'puts the child at the centre of the experience, engaging with music from the inside' (Pitts 1998: 32).

I will suggest that, despite radical developments in musical classroom pedagogy and increased diversity of repertoire, our understanding of what music *is* and what constitutes worthwhile music has remained significantly unchanged over the last hundred years; furthermore, that this understanding is rooted in a conception of music that has its genesis in the late eighteenth century and which is fundamentally politically constructed; finally, that the main aim of this political 'construction' has been to maintain social and cultural hegemonies through low art/high art distinctions that are assumed to articulate and reflect class divisions. Music, I shall argue, has operated as a tool of social stratification with western art music identified with the upper and middle classes – the bourgeoisie – whilst popular musical forms are typically associated with the working class. Consequently, the bourgeoisie, by virtue of their identification with art music, confirm their higher social status whilst, circularly, art music is perceived of as being inherently superior through its identification with the higher social status of its consumers. The traditional role of music in the curriculum has been to reflect and reinforce the social stratification articulated by this musical hierarchy, reflecting Brian Simon's argument that since its inception, English state education has served to 'preserve social stability and reinforce emerging social hierarchies' (Simon 1987: 106).

Traditional authority and music stratification

The sociologist Max Weber (1864–1920) argues that there are three ideal types (pure forms) of authority. Firstly, *charismatic authority* which is fundamentally leader-based and depends upon the power of personality. Secondly, *traditional authority*, which 'rests upon a belief in the "rightness" of established customs and traditions' (Haralambos and Holborn: 502). Finally, *rational–legal authority* which is established through law and operates conditionally upon society's acceptance of that law as being legitimate.

Of these three types, *traditional authority* is arguably the most effective, being rooted in the consent of the 'silent majority'. Moreover, consent that is derived from an acceptance of such authority as self-evident, pre-ordained, universal in application and, consequently, not open to question or debate. In a musical context, tonal music has acquired the mantle of traditional authority, in that:

> established rules and conventions, however arbitrary, come to seem right and proper, not to be tampered with or lightly disregarded. People who know nothing of formal music theory can instantly identify a 'wrong' note, and they often react to one just as they would if some other sort of social rule had been violated. The rules themselves are simply taken for granted, known but not noticed, and often they only become objects of our attention only when they are violated.
>
> (Martin 1995: 9)

Traditionally, there has been similar unquestioned acceptance of the superior status of western art music as the highest form of tonal music and, by implication, those musical procedures and values which it is perceived as exemplifying. Fundamental to these procedures and values is the notion of art music shaping itself 'in accordance with self-constrained abstract principles that are unrelated to the outside world' (Leppert and McClary 1987: xii). Music's meaning is understood as being expressed entirely in terms of the relationships of musical elements to each other rather than through mediation with the (social) context of its performance. High status music is *autonomous* music.

The ideology of musical autonomy

The ideology of musical autonomy is deeply rooted in the aesthetic of western art music. High art music is understood as being exemplified through musical 'works' – music as 'object'. Music thought of as 'object' is perceived as being essentially 'complete' like a painting or sculpture. It does not require an external justification for its existence. A contemporary expression of this view is made by Roger Scruton (1997) when he writes: 'the experience of art is available only if we forget the use. We must consider the work of art as an end in itself' (Scruton 1997: 375).

The ideological hegemony exerted by the notion of music as autonomous works, fully concords with Weber's notion of *traditional authority* as authority perceived of as self-evident, timeless and universal. However, 'musical autonomy' is none of these things. It is in fact a concept that has its roots in the late eighteenth century and developed primarily as a means by which the emerging bourgeoisie could identify with the old aristocracy and draw a clear distinction between themselves and the working classes.

Prior to the late eighteenth century, a musical 'product' (inasmuch as that term is appropriate) was deemed to have been achieved at the point of performance, not through its notation. Musical production being defined by performance has implications for the way in which the relationship between composer and performer is conceptualized. First, given that production is defined as being 'performance', the composer would typically be responsible for the entire process from composition to realization. Consequently, the distinctive roles of composer and performer, which we now tend to take for granted, were much less clearly defined. As late as 1802 'Prince Nicholas II of Esterhazy had to agree with Haydn that "it would be very difficult – especially in the case of new works – to perform music without the personal direction of the composer"' (Goehr 1992: 191).

Second, as music was not considered as an object but as an event, musical ownership did not exist in the way we now understand it. What was marketable was not an 'object' but the skills that enabled a music event to take place.

Third, given that the musical product was defined by its performance and not the production of an object, musical performance would be motivated primarily by external exigency. Music was composed and performed for church, state or entertainment occasions. Composers were part of the fabric of society and were employed to produce music to order. There was no rationale for the production of music for its own sake, for any value music had was purely in terms of fulfilling a particular social function.

Musical production prior to the late eighteenth century was inextricably linked to social context. The notion of going to a particular place specifically and exclusively to listen to a musical performance was contrary to the way in which music was conceived of as functioning within society. This is not to suggest that music was not listened to attentively. Rather, that such attentiveness would result from the context in which it was being performed (for example a religious service) and the text that was set, rather than in order to construe an inner meaning from the relationship and interplay of the musical parts. Indeed, the sublimation of music to the setting of morally and spiritually uplifting texts was considered to be the highest function to which music could aspire:

> it was believed that the words of a text captured music's meaning much more adequately than sounds by themselves; sound and dance movements were usually relegated to the status of accompaniment either to a text or an 'occasion' which would provide them by association with meaning. The use of words, however, was often considered essential to any musical occasion if that occasion was to be regarded as edifying, truthful, and thereby respectable. The immediate implication of this belief was that music without words ... [had] insufficient moral import and, therefore, was probably of very little import at all.
>
> (Goehr: 128)

Instrumental music was thus considered to be of lower status, suitable only as prelude or interlude to vocal performances or as accompaniment to dancing and eating.

Finally, as music was understood as existing only in performance and not as autonomous 'object', the perception of the function of notation was significantly different from the way in which it has been perceived since the end of the eighteenth century. Notation simply provided the broad parameters that enabled a performance to take place – indeed primitive printing techniques allowed only such limited uses. The realization of the notation through performance would be informed by stylistic understanding, tradition and, frequently, the involvement of the composer–performer. Notation did not, for example, in many instances specify tempo, dynamics or even instrumentation. It was not, as it became in the nineteenth century, a means of attempting to codify every aspect of music in order to create an objectified and definitive version.

So what then happened to so dramatically change our perception of music's nature and function? At the end of the eighteenth century there occurred what Wolff refers to as: 'the developing and problematic relationship between the bourgeoisie and the working class ... the effort made by the new ruling class to control the working class and legitimate its own rule' (Wolff in Leppert and McClary 1987: 6). In order to legitimize social stratification, the bourgeoisie needed to demonstrate their inherent superiority through the construction and application of Weber's traditional (or self-evident) authority type. One way in which this was achieved was through identification with the emerging notion of 'art' as an autonomous, non-utilitarian construct capable of being appreciated only by those of refined sensibilities.

In order for music to act as a tool of social stratification it had to fulfil two interrelated criteria. First, access was controlled so that the music identified with the middle and upper classes was accessible only to them. This was achieved firstly by moving art music to places specifically designated for its performance (away from the theatres, coffee houses and market places and into concert halls), then charging for admission at prices prohibitive to all but the bourgeoisie and aristocracy.

Second, in order to legitimize restriction of access, there developed the notion of musical 'ownership'. This required a reconceptualization of the nature of music and its relationship to other disciplines. Music had traditionally been part of the medieval quadrivium with arithmetic, astronomy and geometry – disciplines rooted in the Platonic notion of theoretical discourse. Such a conception of music obviously made the notion of ownership inappropriate. For it is axiomatic that in order for anything to be owned it needs to be complete, be open to transference – it needs to be objectified.

It is at this point that the notion of the musical score takes on a significance that it had hitherto not obtained. Notation in the form of a musical score came to be seen as giving physical form to the music, thus providing the means by which it could be marketed and sold. Music was reconceptualized from theoretical discourse to membership of the object-arts such as painting and sculpture. Music and the musical score were perceived as virtually synonymous. Musical meaning was considered to reside in the score as a codification of the interplay and relationship between musical 'elements' such as rhythm and harmony and texture. Music, as exemplified through the score, was now perceived as a fully autonomous object not required to refer outside of itself to any social context in order to make its meaning. Consequently, as musical meaning resided in the object of the score, meaning must be what the composer intended it to be. Music, which once reflected the nature and proportions of the universe (the music of the spheres), now reflected the human dimension of its creator – the composer. Thus developed the distinctive roles and hierarchical relationship of the composer as creator of musical meaning, the performer as realizer of it and, below, a sub-hierarchy of listeners. This subhierarchy constructed upon listeners' ability to listen attentively, analytically and aesthetically to the music in order to construe accurately the composer's intentions. Music is considered as a language in which 'a practiced judge easily distinguishes true ideas from mere cliches' (Hanslick in Dahlhaus 1989: 121).

The distinction between autonomous high status music and socially-situated popular music had two further consequences. First, instrumental music, which was previously the poor relation of vocal music, became pre-eminent as the purest form of autonomous music, having no reference outside of itself, not even to text.

> the very idea that instrumental music lacked both referential significance as well as concrete and specific content, the very idea, in other words, that had led to the rejection of such music as unworthy, turned out to be the key for finding this music its long-sought-after respectability.
>
> (Goehr: 153)

Second, there emerged the distinction between the 'aesthetic' and 'utilitarian' with higher status accorded to the former. Art music is valued for its *lack* of a utilitarian function, for its logical working-out of autonomous procedures and its transcending of social context. Popular music, judged by the same criteria, is seen as being inherently inferior by virtue of its reliance on social context and consequent lack of autonomy. Popular music expresses an overt relationship with, and reliance upon, the culture and social context within which it exists.

Thus was conceived the distinction which was to articulate the division between high and low status music – its autonomy. Bourgeois art music is confirmed as intrinsically superior and, by association, so are its consumers. It may well be, as both Blacking (1987) and Elliot (1994) point out, that the notion of musical autonomy is fallacious: art music is equally as dependent upon a social and cultural context as any other music. However, the fact that western art music is *perceived* as independent of social context has served to perpetuate the notion of this music – and the musical values of abstractness and completeness which it articulates – as being inherently superior. By this argument, to be a consumer of western art music is to demonstrate membership of the upper and middle classes.

Music education, autonomous music and 'high status' knowledge

If one accepts Brian Simon's (1987) argument that a traditional function of education is to articulate and reinforce social divisions, it is unsurprising that western art music, as a reflection of bourgeois values, formed the bedrock of curriculum music lessons during much of the last century. There is a sense, of course, in which the presence of classical music as the hegemonic musical style within the curriculum is sufficient of itself to articulate its superior status. However, equally significant is the way in which the values and procedures of western art music reflect the characteristics of *all* high status subject knowledge, which itself reflects bourgeois norms and values. For it is in this way that music in the curriculum finds common purpose with other subjects.

High status subject knowledge

Young (1999) argues that if knowledge is to be an effective tool of social stratification, it must fulfil three conditions. These are:

1   that it can be compartmentalized and made portable in order to be appropriated and transferred into educational contexts such as schools;
2   that it is capable of being engaged with on an individual level;
3   that it can be easily and objectively assessed.

Four consequences emerge from these conditions having been met:

1   First, situating knowledge in arenas specifically designed for learning (such as schools) results in the *decontextualization* of knowledge from its social context.
2   Second, in order that social decontextualization can occur, knowledge undergoes a process of abstraction existing independently of any practical application. Such abstraction and decontextualization

[disregards] an individual's social experience … and … restricts the kind of connections which the individual can establish and ratify with the natural and social world.

(Goody and Watt 1962 in Young 1999)

3   Third, literacy is elevated over oracy as the most appropriate form for knowledge. For *literate knowledge* can be objectified, abstracted, access to it controlled, engaged with on an individual level and, perhaps most importantly, used as an instrument of authority.
4   Fourth, the abstraction, decontextualization and objectification of knowledge enable power elites through schools and teachers to define what is and is not legitimate (dominant) subject knowledge.

If knowledge is to be a tool and means of social differentiation, it must also be perceived as being legitimate. As Weber says,

> men and women typically obey not because of coercion or custom or material gain but because the organizing and exercise of power are based upon consent and thus acquire authority.

(Weber 1978)

Part of the process of legitimization is demonstrating that knowledge can be objectively assessed at the level of the individual. Consequently, higher status is accorded to those subjects which can be characterized as possessing objectifiable bodies of assessable knowledge (for example mathematics and sciences) whilst the knowledge body of other subjects (typically the arts) is 'schooled': transformed in order that they too can be objectified and assessed. Assessment then typically occurs through written tests (literacy) in controlled contexts (exams) which assess abstract knowledge on an individual basis.

Young (op. cit.) thus concludes that the dominant characteristics of high status knowledge are:

- unrelatedness of academic culture to common experience;
- abstract knowledge;
- individualization – avoidance of group work and emphasis on individual assessment;
- literacy – emphasis of written over oral.

There is a clear relationship here between the characteristics of autonomous western art music and that of high status subject knowledge as defined by Young. Both seek to transcend social context through autonomy, objectification and abstraction. The clear demarcation of the roles of composer, performer and listener emphasizes the importance of the individual over the collective, thus allowing for stratification and selection. The emphasis on the 'score' as embodiment and objectification of musical meaning emphasizes the literary notion of 'music as notation'. Finally, the role of the performer in accurately realizing the score and the notion of an 'educated' listener provides opportunities in an educational context for 'objective' assessment.

Having established the parallels between dominant subject knowledge and high status music, the important issue now is to consider the impact this has upon the music curriculum. My suggestion is that the values and ideologies of western art music are perceived as being so self-evident that, even when music of other styles, genres and cultures is the focus of attention, the superior nature of western art music continues to be asserted. This is achieved through 'schooling' all music so that it reflects the values of western art music and the characteristics of all dominant subject knowledge.

I want to develop this argument by considering four broad phases of music education which, although presented here as being chronological, were never discrete concepts of music education but rather dominant ideologies at a particular point in time. The first, typically described as the traditional approach, prevailed during the first half of the twentieth century, focusing upon what Pitts describes as music education as a means of initiating children into an 'adult phenomenon' (Pitts 1998: 32). The second, associated with the 1960s, is the so-called creative or progressive phase. This combined the musical principles and techniques of the avant-garde with a refocusing of the educational process away from the musical object towards the learning child. The third phase is more nebulous and difficult to define but covers the 1970s and 1980s, beginning with the years leading up to *Music in the Secondary School Project* at York University through to the beginnings of the music National Curriculum. Finally, contemporary music education, the aim of which can perhaps be characterized as developing children's knowledge of music as a way of knowing and understanding the world through engagement with the musical materials of a wide range of musical styles as performers, composers and listeners.

The traditional approach

It is undeniable that the 'traditional' model of music education was primarily concerned with inducting children into the aesthetic of western art music. Its purpose was, as Plummeridge says, to introduce 'children to the "great masters" whose works represent the highest accomplishments in the "world" of (Western) music' (Plummeridge in Philpott 2001: 8). However, although its ultimate aim was to perpetuate of the hegemony of western art music, its pedagogy was not (as it has sometimes been characterized) entirely restricted to children sitting passively in appreciation of 'great' music. The approaches were more diverse and could be broadly typified as:

- music 'appreciation', including information about composers and their works;
- music theory;
- whole class singing sometimes supported by the teaching of solfeggio.

All of these activities were teacher directed and to a great extent occurred discretely. They were not considered as linked activities but rather as distinct means of initiating children into the values and procedures of western art music. As such, they all demonstrate characteristics of dominant subject knowledge.

Western art music, as the exclusive focus of listening activities, articulated its superior status whilst the focus on the biographical details of composers reinforced the hegemony of the composer and his (*sic*) 'special' nature.

Music theory was taught as an abstract concept rarely being related to any specific usage. To 'know' the names of the notes and the values of discrete rhythmic units was considered to be of value in itself. Theoretical knowledge thus conformed perfectly to the requirements of high status knowledge: it was abstracted and unrelated to practical application, emphasized literate knowledge and provided a means for objective assessment which could act as a legitimization of that knowledge. Practical application of the knowledge was reserved for an elite who played instruments.

The school song repertoire of this period provides an interesting example of the schooling of music to make it articulate bourgeois values through conforming to the values and procedures of art music and high status knowledge. Songs tended to be of two types. The first was the eighteenth- and nineteenth- century 'national air', mainly celebrating military exploits and the dominance of the British Empire. A typical collection was *The National Song Book,* copies of which were to be found in most schools until well into the second half of the twentieth century. The second, and more interesting, category, was the folk song. Whereas national airs overtly articulated a political message of national unity to which all might subscribe, the folk song – as it appeared in the school music curriculum – reinforced class divisions.

As Georgina Boyes (1993) has pointed out, the emergence of the folk song revival at the end of the nineteenth century has traditionally been presented as an act of resuscitation by the liberal middle classes of an endangered cultural heritage. However, those involved in this revival, although ostensibly concerned with the preservation of a tradition, came to the task with pre-determined notions about what defined good and bad music. Indeed one of the initial motivations of the revival movement was a fear that the 'purity' of the folk song was in danger of being contaminated by the 'vulgar' songs of the music hall (Boyes 1993: 64). Such concerns were then inevitably reflected in the way in which the songs were intro- duced into the school curriculum – their rationale and pedagogical use.

In arguing for the inclusion of folk songs into the school music curriculum, Cecil Sharp, the leading light of the revival movement, articulates, albeit unconsciously, three linked issues that were to exercise music educators for much of the twentieth century:

1   the notion of a musical hierarchy with 'good' music as a force for moral improvement;
2   the notion of a musical hierarchy where music of lower status could be used as a way 'into' art music rather than valued on its own terms;
3   a perceived tension between 'quality' music and 'accessibility'.

> The ideal song should satisfy two conditions. It should, of course, be music of the highest and purest quality. But this is not enough. It must also be attractive to children and be easily assimilated by them. Many ... of the songs that are now sung in our elementary schools satisfy one or other of these requirements;

few satisfy both. Good music is often dull to children, difficult to sing and difficult to understand; whilst the music which is immediately attractive to them is often little better than rubbish. These considerations point to the folk song as the ideal musical food for very young children. Folk songs most certainly belong to the category of good music; they are natural, pure and simple ... not only would the musical taste of the nation be materially raised, but a beneficent and enduring effect would be produced on the national character.

(Sharp in Boyes 1993: 45–6)

Sharp was highly selective of those songs that he accepted into the canon of the folk song and consequently included in his collection of folk songs for schools. He allowed only those songs that reflected an idealized view of rural England – a 'Merrie England' and 'land of lost content' – and routinely altered the words in order to achieve this. The message of the songs Sharp accepted into the canon of 'folk' is the immutable and timeless nature of social stratification and the essential dignity in accepting one's social position. The more politically charged industrial ballads – which were no more or less a part of the oral tradition than the rural song – were ignored.

Musically, the folk songs were 'schooled' so that they exemplified, albeit across a smaller canvas, the values and procedures of bourgeois art music. Products of an essentially oral tradition with many 'variants' were objectified through notation and turned into musical objects. Although, as A.L. Lloyd says, 'illiteracy as a condition of musical folklore has been exaggerated ... whenever singers could write, they have inclined to commit songs to paper as an aid to memory' (Lloyd, 1967: 25), Sharp, from the vantage point of an upper-middle-class male, was able to dictate the dominant version of any song. The dominance of the particular version was then asserted by notating (objectifying) the song and publishing it, often in his collections for school use. In doing so, the status of the notated form changed from simply one 'version' of many (for example those written down for publication through broadside ballads) to the status of 'definitive form'. The distinction was lost between musical notation as a *post-facto* recording of a particular performance occasion and musical notation when, as in the case of much art music, it mediates with the compositional process to form a definitive version. Moreover, although keen to preserve the original melody of the song without editorial improvements, Sharp failed to acknowledge the limited ability of notation to codify many aspects of song's performance – particularly vocal nuance. Moreover, Sharp's accompaniments added little to the song other than to imply functional harmonic conventions that the song often did not possess. Fundamentally what Sharp did was to appropriate folk song as a means of reasserting bourgeois musical values. As Boyes says of Sharp, 'A national art music was his first goal [and] making vernacular arts fit bourgeois aesthetics was the basis of his career and the guiding spirit of the revival which he built around it' (Boyes 1993).

Sharp's treatment of the English folk song thus fully concords with Young's (ibid.) notion of dominant curriculum subject knowledge as socially decontextualized and abstracted in order that it can assert bourgeois aesthetics. However, removing traditional music from its social context, locating it in the classroom and using it as a means of entry into the world of classical music was not unique to English folk song or English classrooms. Kodály, for example, although celebrating the inherent worth of Hungarian traditional music through using it as the basis of his *Choral Method,* nevertheless adopts a hierarchical position towards it in relation to western classical music: 'The music of the people "can be lifted out from beneath the rubbish heaped on top of it, and a higher art built upon it"' (in Crofton and Fraser 1985: 85). Perhaps, as Small says when writing of Kodály, there is a strong case for arguing that he and Sharp were, albeit unconsciously, involved in 'the exploitation of the old cultural forms of peasantry perhaps for the purpose of preserving middle-class nostalgia for an ancient and stable European social order which never did exist' (Small 1987: 349).

The 'progressive' approach

Orff-Schulwerk

The progressive movement in music education is typically dated from the emergence of a group of composer–educators during the 1960s: figures such as Peter Maxwell Davies, Brian Dennis, George Self and R. Murray Schafer. However, the educational climate which allowed their ideas to flourish was arguably created by the publication in the early 1950s of Carl Orff's *Music for Children* developed from his *Schulwerk. Music for Children* was key in establishing the principle of children experiencing music directly and, to an extent, creatively, prior to becoming concerned with its notation and codification.

The *Schulwerk*'s focus on rhythmic and melodic ostinati, pentatonic and modal melodies and drones, reflected Orff's own very particular and individual compositional style, characterized by Kater as: 'diatonic tonality; a primitive, *Volkslied* character; monorhythmic sequences' (Kater 1995: 1–35). What Orff's music typically does (at least from *Carmina Burana* onwards) is to challenge the traditional western aesthetic balance and relationship between melody, harmony and rhythm and to elevate one element (usually rhythm) to a dominant, often hegemonic, role. In the *Schulwerk*, traditionally atomistic but contributory parts to a musical whole – for example rhythmic motifs and melodic ostinati – are treated discretely.

Unfortunately, the materials of the *Schulwerk* tended to become detached from the philosophy that underpinned their development and which are critical to their successful use in the classroom – fundamentally, 'that music should be thoroughly integrated with movement, dance and theatre as well as with speech, song and instrumental sound (Sadie (ed.) 1980). They had an appeal for those teachers looking for materials that would address the demands of the 'experiential' classroom quickly and easily without the necessity of addressing fundamental issues concerning the importance of musical style and culture. Consequently, the *Orff-Schulwerk* came to mean (at least in the United Kingdom) simple musical ideas (usually ostinato rhythms and pentatonic melodies played on chime bars) combined in whole-class performances to create a kind of generic tonal music.

However, the music resulting from the arbitrary combination of discrete musical atomizations divorced from any stylistic or social context was essentially neutral – it had neither inherent nor extra-musical 'meaning'. Performed on instruments which would only ever be encountered in the classroom, the music based on the *Schulwerk* became possibly the ultimate in decontextualized music. It articulated an autonomous classroom music culture allowing no connections with the child's social and musical world, such that:

> outside music had become variously experimental, minimalist, pop and rock … while inside some musical classrooms the music subculture often seemed to be based on materials of pentatonic scales and sounded nothing like music anywhere else in the world, let alone students' lives.
>
> (Swanwick 1994: 166)

A consequence of this stylistic neutrality, its lack of social resonance and its intrinsic association with 'school music', is that it ultimately failed to sustain children's interest beyond the early years. It did not support the child's musical development further than what Swanwick (1988: 76) describes as the 'sensory and manipulative phases' to the point where children recognize and become interested in musical conventions and style (Munsen 1986 in Colwell 1992: 499).

As Fletcher (1987: 34) puts it: 'the rather basic structuring of the music and the severe limitations of the "Orff" instruments had (and still have) very much less appeal to self-conscious secondary children'.

Music education and the avant-garde

The progressive ideal of the 1960s reinforced the emerging ideology of music education as providing opportunities for children to engage directly with music as composers and performers. However, it sought to replace the rather socially neutral Orff-based music with musical activities that would provide opportunities for children to externalize their own creative impulses and feelings through surface engagement with the techniques of the prevailing avant-garde music. There was a coming together of the relative freedom offered by avant-garde techniques and the notion of music as a means of self-expression. The teacher's role changed from that of a possessor of pre-determined knowledge to be passed on, to one who facilitated children's creative exploration through engagement with musical materials.

Although avant-garde music is generally considered to be the very antithesis of the Romantic aesthetic, it embodies ideals which clearly identify it as art music and is thereby reflective of bourgeois values. Its tendency to emerge from contexts specifically designated for its development, such as Darmstadt and IRCAM, emphasize its autonomy and social decontextualization. Moreover, much avant-garde music of the early post-war years sought to rationalize, through serialism, not only pitch but other aspects of musical organization such as rhythm and dynamics, thus articulating a philosophy of musical autonomy and music-as-object as great as any Romantic symphony. Also, it typically occurs in places specifically designated for the purpose of its performance; either traditional concert halls, electronic studios or converted spaces such as London's 'Round-house', and the traditional hierarchy of composer–performer–listener remains intact, or the role of the performer is dispensed with through the use of electronics or computer-based technology.

Musical reaction to this highly organized form of composition came in two ways: first, through the use of aleatoric elements and second, through the emerging mini-malist school. In the case of aleatoric music, the score (in whatever form it exists) does not claim to direct the performer towards one definitive way of performing the music and consequently the notion of music as object is challenged. However, as Smith Brindle says, in many works which contain aleatoric elements, 'the notation … is given with considerable exactitude, so that though the ordering and performing-style of sections may vary, the listener may well find recurring and recognisable elements in each performance' (Smith Brindle 1987: 73). Meaning was still perceived as being embodied in the score and articulated through the musical materials.

The musical principles upon which the progressive ideal of music education was based – broadly speaking those of the avant-garde – were as far removed from pupils' own musical experiences as the symphonic processes of the nineteenth century symphony and less recognizable to them as 'music'. For, to engage with aleatoric musical sound as in George Self's *New Sounds in Class* (1967), or to accept, as R. Murray Schafer proposed, the natural aural environment as potential musical material, was to stretch to the limit what children were prepared to recognise as music based on their own experiences. Furthermore, to understand music in such terms required a high degree of conceptual understanding of what was an innovative reorganisation and redefinition of the surface musical sound world. Consequently, as Lucy Green has pointed out, the avant-garde was also relatively unpopular with teachers: 'many did not teach it, or only did a little of it, because they self-avowedly did not know much about it and were not, therefore, familiar with its style' (Green 1988: 69).

Minimalism, on the other hand, is the great survivor of the sixties' avant-garde in education. Some time after it has ceased to be a significant force in contempo-rary western music, it still features in many music departments' schemes of work, prompted perhaps by its inclusion in popular published teaching materials. Its general appeal perhaps lies in what Polin describes as its 'objectivity, almost anonymity, in the use of pure sound alone. Music freed itself from artistry and taste, by excluding expression, drama, psychology … little happens that is musical, allowing nothing but the auditory experience of sound' (Polin 1989: 227).

Much like the *Schulwerk*, minimalism is arguably socially neutral and, unlike Romantic music which simply *aspires* to the claim of social transcendence, it can be argued that minimal music actually *achieves* this state. It articulates no meaning other than through the relationship of its materials. It is, as interpreted by its critics, 'music directed towards a specific public – listeners who prefer to avoid the stress and turmoil of "music of our time", or intend to evade our times altogether …

Inevitably such music must have an attractive surface sheen, and this is most often the most perceptible element' (Smith Brindle 1987: 194).

The nineteen-seventies and eighties: towards a rational–legal authority in music education

The Schools Council Inquiry 1 (1968), which identified music as one of the least popular subjects in the secondary school curriculum, resulted in radical changes to surface classroom music practice.

As I hope to have demonstrated, however, many of the principles that have underpinned the development of the music curriculum since then were established in the years preceding the publication of the report, particularly the principle of children practically engaging with musical sound through performance and improvisation/composition. Moreover, as I have also indicated, many of these 'new methods' continued to reflect the values and processes that delineate high status music knowledge. In addition, as Rainbow (1991: 329) has pointed out, in the case of the *Orff-Schulwerk* and the 'Kodály Concept', their decontextualization from, respectively, their original philosophical and social underpinning resulted in limited effective influence. Most failed to be embraced by teachers – they failed to acquire the status of an educational orthodoxy. The fundamental challenge therefore was to develop an approach to music education that would gain widespread support amongst teachers, pupils and government. There needed to be created an orthodoxy reflective of Weber's notion of 'traditional authority' which would support the experiential approach to music education.

It is arguable that the development of music education over the last forty years can be described as a striving for the establishment of a (semantically contradictory) new traditional authority. However, by definition, 'traditional authority' cannot be externally imposed but can only emerge from within a social grouping. The best that can be done externally is, through using the tools of charismatic and rational–legal authority, to create the conditions most efficacious to the establishment of a traditional authority model. Thus, one way of understanding the developments in music education (and perhaps all education) during this time is through the way in which charismatic authority and rational–legal authority were used by different groupings to establish such conditions.

Following this idea through, the sixties, seventies and early eighties can be described as the 'charismatic' period, where innovations were identified with particular personalities such as John Paynter. However the success of these methods depended to a great extent upon the 'charisma' being carried through into the classroom by a kind of music-teacher-as-apostle. There were great successes where teachers were committed to the approach and understood the supporting rationale and philosophy, for example those teachers involved in the development and piloting of ideas and materials in the *Music in the Secondary School Project* under John Paynter at the University of York. However, the problem with charismatic authority is that, by definition, it cannot be demonstrated by everyone. Therefore, when teachers did not bring 'charismatic' authority to their teaching and/or were not aware of the underpinning philosophy of the materials or methodologies, these materials and methodologies simply became a new way through which traditional musical values continue to be expressed.

If new and radical methods of music teaching were occurring successfully in only a few high profile and predominantly *state* comprehensive schools, they could be ignored either as a temporary and irrelevant aberration from the norm or, more problematically, as reflective of one particular stratum of the highly stratified English educational system. The association of models of music education and musical genres with particular schools and their social intake was particularly dangerous for the cause of music education, in that it provided the opportunity for a reassertion of a class-based hierarchy of musical styles.

This became a particular issue with the introduction of popular and non-western music into the curriculum as *music worthy of consideration on its own terms*. As such, music often expressed few of the values and musical processes of autonomous art music; it became associated with particular types of schools and social groupings.

To caricature only slightly, popular music, for example, was perceived by some as appropriate only for working-class, low-achieving, disaffected boys in inner city comprehensives. Lucy Green, drawing on a case study carried out by Graham Vulliamy, writes:

> His case study showed that teachers ... acted on the grounds of unspoken assumptions that involved treating 'working-class' pupils as less musical and pop as less valuable ... They played pop more with low streams and tended anyway to use it mainly to keep children quiet or as a treat at the end of a lesson.
>
> (Green 1988: 58)

The divisions between high art and other musics were further articulated through the parallel exam systems of O level and CSE. CSE – the exam originally created for primarily working-class children in secondary modern schools – allowed popular and world musics, whilst O level music continued to reflect high status music knowledge both in terms of its content and, most significantly, its methods of assessment. Whereas CSE allowed coursework and teacher assessment as well as, in some cases, the devising of the syllabus by schools (Mode 3), O level was assessed through written, timed examinations in formal conditions – abstracted and socially decontextualized knowledge. O level's focus on analytical listening and musical historical knowledge could lead to it being perceived as being mainly concerned with the creation of a new generation of consumers of art music and the perpetuation of bourgeois musical values.

When presented in the context of socially-stratified examination systems, popular music presented no challenge to the hegemony of western art music. Indeed it affirmed the bourgeois belief of art music as accessible only to those of intelligence and sensitivity and that these characteristics were observable primarily through class divisions. A threat to the hegemony of art music appeared only when, in the eighties, non-art music sought emancipation and legitimization through rational–legal authority.

In educational contexts rational–legal authority is articulated through quasi-legislation – such as examination syllabuses and HMI reports – as well as through parliamentary decree. In the early 1980s, the main piece of quasi-legislation was the introduction of the GCSE examination. The *raison d'être* of GCSE was to create an examination which would cater for far more children than the 60 per cent provided for by the parallel CSE and GCE systems. However, if certification was to be extended to the majority of young people, then it followed that assessment contexts and methods needed to be appropriate in order to enable all pupils to demonstrate skills and knowledge. Written examinations and formal examination contexts were not always the most appropriate means of doing this. Thus, for a brief time at least, coursework, the demonstration of practical skills, and oral as well as written forms of communication, were accorded a legitimacy that they had never previously possessed. This provided the context in which performing and, particularly, composing, could become significant parts of the music examination syllabus.

Of arguably greater import however was the emancipation of musical styles implied by the GCSE music criteria:

> we must avoid exclusivity, giving the impression that only a few traditions of music are acceptable. And it is important to recognize the context in which the differentiated assessments are to be made, allowing each candidate the opportunity to respond to music with which he or she has a particular sympathy.
>
> (SEC 1986: 22)

Popular and non-western music styles were no longer the defining characteristics of a low status examination but were being accepted into the mainstream of music education. Furthermore, the focus of the syllabus on performing and composing meant that the pedagogical issues presented by the inclusion of these activities (as well as stylistically diverse repertoires) could no longer be avoided – at least at GCSE level. Teachers had, up to this point, been under no compulsion to teach music as a 'practical' subject or include a range of musical styles in their teaching.

The GCSE criteria questioned how 'music' and 'musical' were to be thought of and consequently how they were to be assessed. In doing so, the GCSE challenged not only the pedagogical beliefs of those teachers whose ideas were rooted in the procedures of art music, but also perceptions of how 'appropriate knowledge' was to be defined. Indeed, through phrases such as 'allowing each candidate the opportunity to respond to music with which he or she has a particular sympathy' (op. cit.), there was the implicit suggestion that appropriate and valuable knowledge could be defined by the needs, aspirations and interests of the pupil rather than imposed externally. As such, GCSE music represented a fundamental challenge to the notion of education as 'an initiation into existing forms of worthwhile knowledge and understanding' (O'Hear 1991).

Such a challenge to the hegemony of art music and its associated pedagogy inevitably provoked a negative reaction, particularly from the selective and private sectors. As a consequence of this, one examination board took advantage of the flexibility offered by the GCSE music criteria as to how the three areas of the syllabus (composing, performing, listening) could be weighted, and, through to 1992, offered two syllabuses. The Mode A syllabus reflected the O level's emphasis on western classical music and theoretical knowledge, whilst Mode B embraced musical diversity and children's engagement with music as performers and composers as well as listeners. The rationale for this distinction was that 'for some candidates, certain aspects of the traditional approach may be essential as well as enjoyable' (MEG 1990: 3).

The GCSE criteria certainly represented a challenge to the principle of autonomous art music being exclusively representative of high status subject knowledge. Furthermore, the publication of the HMI document *Music from 5–16* in 1985 provided a quasi-rational–legal framework for the teaching of music across the entire compulsory education age range in an experiential way. However, the dual syllabus at GCSE, the unreconstructed nature of A level examinations and the continuing focus of universities and conservatoires on, respectively, academic study and the development of performance skills, meant that mixed messages were being sent out. Moreover, the monitoring of the implementation of the recommendations contained in *Music from 5–16* was erratic owing to the small number of music HMIs, and in any event lacked the force of statute. If music education was to progress towards a traditional authority model which articulated democratic beliefs about the purpose of music education, then it needed the support of pure rational–legal authority.

Contemporary music education: establishing a rational–legal authority model

The opportunity to establish a rational–legal authority for music education came with the Education Reform Act (1988) which introduced the music National Curriculum in 1992. The music National Curriculum in combination with GCSE provided a rational–legal model of music education extending from 5–16 which emphasized the experiential nature of music education. This nominally created a context in which a 'traditional authority' model might emerge reflecting similar values.

There is no single answer as to why this cannot yet to be said to have succeeded; or why, after such radical developments in pedagogy and curriculum content, pupil satisfaction should be so poor relative to other arts subjects. However, perhaps one significant reason is that, despite a commitment from the outset to cultural and stylistic diversity – 'Pupils should perform and listen to music in a variety of genres and style from different periods and cultures' (National Curriculum 1992) – the National Curriculum continues the tradition of articulating the processes and values of art music as being the most appropriate for school music knowledge.

I have considered the way in which this occurs in some detail elsewhere (Spruce 2001). However, a brief consideration of the broad issues may serve to exemplify what I mean. The National Curriculum legitimates music education as 'activity' rather than appreciation of aesthetic capital. The National Curriculum in its first two versions (1992 and 1995) defines these activities as composing, performing and listening and appraising. However, as Nicholas Cook (1998) says, such distinctions imply perceptions, presumptions and musical hierarchies which reinforce the hegemony of bourgeois-defined high status music. As I made clear earlier, these distinctions (particularly between composing and performing) are neither timeless nor self-evident in the case of art music and are inappropriate ways of understanding many musical genres and cultures; jazz, for example. It may well be that curriculum documents from the GCSE criteria of 1986 through to the first revision of the National Curriculum nine years later contain exhortations to integrate these activities, but the fact remains that 'the taxonomy of composing/performing/appraising ends up perpetuating the very distinctions it was meant to erase' (Cook 1998: 16).

Furthermore, these distinctions have been perpetuated through the way in which music is assessed, particularly in public examinations. The necessity of being seen objectively to assess pupils leads inevitably not only to disaggregation of musical activities but often further disaggregation within the activity itself (see Chapter 9). In assessing performance, technical aspects are often considered separately from considerations of style and 'performance presence' and consequently given greater weight.

The importance western music attaches to the realization of notation derives directly from the bourgeois notion of musical meaning residing in the score as an objectification of the composer's intentions. The hegemony of the musical object as represented by the score continues to exert tremendous influence on the way in which music is taught. It may well be, as Major says, that the aim of curriculum music is for children to work with the materials of music, to 'make concepts (elements) such as pitch, duration dynamics, tempo, timbre, and texture central to the learner's musical knowledge and understanding' (Major 1996: 184). However, we need to be aware that conceptualizing music in such terms is arguably to continue to articulate a particularly western aesthetic way of perceiving music. Certain 'concepts' such as pitch and duration have greater value in western art music in that they are the ones most easily codified and objectified and thus contribute most significantly to the ideology of musical autonomy. Therefore the emphasis which is given in educational contexts to pitch and rhythm implicitly articulates the superiority of music which exemplifies and emphasizes these aspects over those musical genres which rely more on, say, timbre and texture – aspects which are perhaps less easily codified through staff notation.

The most recent revision of the National Curriculum goes some way to addressing these issues with its one Attainment Target of 'knowledge, skills and understanding' (DfEE/QCA: 1999). It attempts a culturally inclusive language of 'creating and developing musical ideas' and 'controlling sounds through singing and playing'. But its very inclusivity means that its terminology is open to interpretation exclusively in terms of a western music aesthetic. Consequently, the decisive factors remain the assumptions, beliefs and understanding of music that the teachers take with them into the classroom.

Conclusion

The Schools Council Inquiry of 1968 acted as a catalyst for a fundamental reappraisal of the nature and purpose of music and music education and the development of radically new methods of classroom practice. However, such developments were slow to win acceptance, only achieving the status of 'common practice' through the rational–legal authority of GCSE and the National Curriculum.

In the interim period, however, previous practice was somewhat caricatured. There was, rightly, the rejection of the classroom as a surrogate concert hall where children sat in rows in passive appreciation of 'great' music, and activity was at best whole-class singing and at worst the copying of information about music. However, this quickly became interpreted as meaning that the only acceptable activities were performing and composing. The greater weight given to performing and composing in the first two versions of the music National Curriculum (1992 and 1995) reinforced this idea. Furthermore, to 'develop understanding of music from different times and places' in Attainment Target 2 (listening and appraising) underplayed the importance of social context to an understanding of musical practice. A consequence of this plus the segregation of listening and appraising from composing and performing could result in the latter continuing to be conceptualized in the 'autonomous' terms of the western art music aesthetic resulting in the implicit undervaluing of popular and world musics.

My argument here is that, in creating a context that recognizes the inherent worth of musics of other genres and cultures, the role social context plays in articulating musical meaning needs to be recognized and integrated into music teaching. I am not here proposing a return to copying down information about composers, drawing instruments or producing 'projects' on pop singers outlining their life, loves and what they enjoy for breakfast. Rather, in a context of a curriculum which espouses cultural diversity, there needs to be a recognition that music and its social context are interdependent and that this interdependence should be reflected in the way in which music is taught.

Through understanding the social dynamics of musical 'production', children (and teachers) might recognize the many ways in which music is understood, experienced and created. This need not be a dry exercise but one that impacts positively upon children's musical experience and teachers' pedagogy. It can be used to create a context in which skills such as improvisation and learning music aurally – characteristics of many musical genres – achieve emancipation with performance from notation – characteristic primarily of western art music but dominant in the curriculum. This would then give equal status to the skills of, for example, rock musicians who typically learn 'cover' versions aurally from recordings, using notation only as a structural *aide-memoire*. Similarly, when working on original material, rock and pop musicians often compose in groups, blurring the lines between composer(s) and performers, the separation of whose roles is such an important part of the western music aesthetic. Through acknowledging the many ways in which music is perceived, experienced and created, a *traditional authority* model could result, embracing the 'music for all' and 'sound before symbol' philosophies.

Philosophies which have underpinned music pedagogy over the last thirty years, but which perhaps have yet to be seen through to their logical conclusion.

Note

1   The circumstances surrounding the creation and implementation of the first music National Curriculum are fascinating and complex but cannot be dealt with here. Vincent (1992), Swanwick (1992), Shepherd and Vulliamy (1994) and Philpott (2001) deal with this from different, and invariably interesting, perspectives.

References

Blacking, J. (1987) *A Commonsense View of All Music*, Cambridge: Cambridge University Press.

Boyes, G. (1993) *The Imagined Village: Culture, Ideology and the English Folk Revival*, Manchester: Manchester University Press.

Colwell, R. (1992) *Handbook of Research on Music Teaching and Learning*, New York: Schirmer Books.

Cook, N. (1998) *Music: A Very Short Introduction*, Oxford: Oxford University Press.

Crofton, I. and Fraser, D. (1983) *A Dictionary of Musical Quotations*, London: Croom Helm.

Dalhaus, C. (1978) *The Idea of Absolute Music*, The University of Chicago Press.

DES (1992) *Music in the National Curriculum (England)*, London: HMSO.

DFE (1995) *Music in the National Curriculum*, London: HMSO.

DfEE and QCA (1999) *The National Curriculum (Music)*, London: HMSO.

Docking, J. (ed.) (1996) *National School Policy*, London: Fulton Ltd.

Elliot, D. (1994) 'Rethinking music: first steps to a new philosophy of music education', *International Journal of Music Education*, 24.

Fletcher, P. (1987) *Education and Music*, Oxford: Oxford University Press.

Goehr, L. (1992) *The Imaginary Museum of Musical Works*, Oxford: Oxford University Press.

Goody, J. and Watt, I. (1962) 'The consequences of literacy', *Comparative Studies in History* 3

Green, A. (1990) *Education and State Formation*, London: The Macmillan Press.

Green, L. (1988) *Music on Deaf Ears*, Manchester: Manchester University Press.

Haralambos, M. and Holborn, M. (1995) *Sociology Themes and Perspectives*, London: Collins Educational.

Harland, J., Kinder, K. and Hartley, K. (1995) *Arts in Their View*, Slough: NFER.

Harland, J., Kinder, K. Hartley, K. *et al.* (2000) *Arts Education in Secondary Schools: Effects and Effectiveness*, Slough: NFER.

Kater, M. (1995) 'Carl Orff im Dritten Reich,' *Vierteljahrshefte für Zeitgeschichte* 43, 1 (January 1995): 1–35.

Leppert, R. and McClary, S. (1987) *Introduction to Music and Society. The Politics of Composition, Performance and Reception*, Cambridge: Cambridge University Press.

Lloyd, A.L. (1967) *Folk Song in England*, London: Lawrence and Wishart.

Martin, P. (1995) *Sounds and Society*, Manchester: Manchester University Press.

Major, A. (1996) 'Reframing curriculum design', *British Journal of Music Education*, vol.13 no

Midland Examining Group (1990) *GCSE (Music) 1992*, Cambridge: MEG.

Munsen, S.C. (1986) 'A description and analysis of an Orff-Schulwerk program of music education (improvisation)', unpublished doctoral dissertation, Urbana: University of Illinois.

Ofsted (1998) *The Arts Inspected*, London: HMSO.

O'Hear, A. (1991) 'Out of sync with Bach', *The Times Educational Supplement*, 22 February

Philpott, C. (ed.) (2001) *Learning to Teach Music in the Secondary School*, London: RoutledgeFalmer.

Pitts, S. (1998) 'Looking for inspiration: recapturing an enthusiasm for music education from innovatory writings', *British Journal of Music Education*, 15(1): 25–36, Cambridge: Cambridge University Press.

Polin, C. (1989) 'Why minimalism now?' in R. Leppert and S. McClary (1987) *Introduction to Music and Society. The Politics of Composition, Performance and Reception*, Cambridge: Cambridge University Press.

Quicke, J. (1988) The 'New Right' and education, *British Journal of Educational Studies*, 26(1).

Rainbow, B. (1987) *Music in Educational Thought and Practice*, Aberystwyth: Boethius Press.

Sadie, S. (ed.) (1980) *Grove's Dictionary of Music and Musicians*, London: Macmillan.

Schools Curriculum and Assessment Authority (1996) *Music Optional Tests and Tasks*, London: HMSO.

Scruton, R. (1997) *The Aesthetics of Music*, Clarendon Press.

Secondary Examinations Council (1986) *Music GCSE: A Guide for Teachers*, Milton Keynes: Open University Press.

Self, G. (1967) *New Sounds in Class*, London: Universal Edition.

Shulman, L. S. (1987) *Knowledge and Teaching: Foundations of the New Reform*, Harvard Educational Review 57 (1): 919–40.

Shepherd, S. and Vulliamy, G. (1994) 'The struggle for culture: a sociology case study of the development of the national music curriculum', *British Journal of the Sociology of Education*, 15(1).

Small, C. (1987) *Music of the Common Tongue*, London: Calder Publications.

Simon, B. (1987) 'Systemisation and segmentation in education: the case in England', in D. Muller, R. Ringer, and B. Simon, (eds) *The Rise of the Modern Educational System*, Cambridge: Cambridge University Press.

Smith Brindle, R. (1987) *The New Music. The Avant-Garde since 1945*, Oxford: Oxford University Press.

Spruce, G. (1996) 'Assessment in the arts: issues of objectivity' in G. Spruce (ed.) *Teaching Music*, London: Routledge.

Spruce, G. (2001) 'Music assessment and the hegemony of musical heritage' in C. Philpott and C. Plummeridge (2001) *Issues in Music Education*, London: Routledge.

Swanwick, K. (1988) *Music Mind and Education*, London: Routledge.

—— (1992) *Music Education and the National Curriculum*, The London File: Papers from the Institute of Education: Tufnell Press.

—— (1994) *Musical Knowledge*, London: Routledge.

Vincent, A. (1992) 'Behind the scenes of the National Curriculum' in *Music File*, Series 4 Issue 2, Mary Glasgow Publications.

Young, M. (1999) 'The curriculum as socially organised knowledge' in M. McCormick and C. Paechter (eds) *Learning and Knowledge*, London: Paul Chapman.

Weber, M. (1978) *Economy and Society*, G. Roth and C. Wittich (eds), Berkley: University of California Press.

Wolff, J. (1987) 'The ideology of autonomous art', in R. Leppert and S. McClary (1987) *Introduction to Music and Society. The Politics of Composition, Performance and Reception*, Cambridge: Cambridge University Press.

2 Finding the future in the past

Historical perspectives on music education

Stephanie E. Pitts

Introduction: why study the history of music education?

For those embarking on a teaching career, it is almost instinctive to engage in historical research. New teachers will look back at their own music education, whether for inspiration or out of a determination not to replicate apparent shortcomings, and will compare contemporary practice with what they remember from their own school days. For some, this comparison will be made within a few years of completing their own secondary education, for others it might be rather longer, but whatever the reality, changes in perspective, policy and practice can make it feel like a lifetime ago. This informal investigation of the past is the first step in evaluating the changes that have contributed to the development of music education. It highlights the essential features of the best research in history of education: it is concerned with people, and the stories they have to tell about the experience of teaching and learning music; with ideas, and the way that individuals have shaped their practice to reflect their views about music and about education; and with evaluation, as the best practice of the past informs the directions of the future.

If every new teacher brings this wealth of historical information to their first classroom encounter, it is clear that many more riches can be found amongst the published and archive materials that document centuries of change in music education. Systematic research in this area has expanded in recent years, and ready access to the history of music in education since 800 BC (Rainbow 1989), discussion of music in nineteenth-century schools (Cox 1993) and developments in the twentieth century (Pitts 2000a) is now available. This chapter will present a brief overview of changes to British secondary school music teaching within the last century, before considering a number of examples in detail to show the connections between historical and contemporary thought. It will attempt to demonstrate how a clearer understanding of the past can inform our perceptions of contemporary musical education, and shape our ambitions for its future. It also aims to communicate something of the commitment and inspiration that is abundant in many of the published ideas of the twentieth century, as the writings that will be discussed here offer one of the most reliable and interesting routes towards appraisal of contemporary teaching, with the potential to stimulate thought and reflection amongst teachers of every level of experience.

Music education in the twentieth century: an overview

Generalizing about developments in music education is a dangerous business, as it can often obscure the vibrancy of individual accounts, or give the impression that change occurred simultaneously in all secondary schools across the country, which is of course very far from being the case. Nevertheless, it is helpful to have a framework for discussion, within which more detailed consideration of the motives for and outcomes of change can take place. Broadly speaking, then, the history of music education in the twentieth century can be summarized within the following stages.

1900–35

The beginning of the twentieth century was a time of limited and utilitarian secondary education, where rote learning and firm discipline characterized schooling for those who could afford to attend. Music was largely confined to singing, learning sol-fa and staff notation, and listening to the works of the 'great composers'. Teachers and inspectors such as MacPherson (1922; 1923), Somervell (1931) and Scholes (1935) were amongst those who promoted the more systematic teaching of music, placing emphasis on children's acquisition of musical knowledge through singing and listening. This was intended to prepare children for a life of amateur music-making or attentive listening, and music was seen as having a civilizing influence upon young people. The tendency for music listening to dominate the curriculum was supported by the technology of the time, as gramophone records and radio broadcasts became increasingly accessible, both in school and at home.

1935–55

At the outbreak of World War II, arts education was in a state of flux, as listening and singing continued to dominate the music curriculum, whilst art, dance and English teachers began to adopt more adventurous and creative approaches. Music remained caught between a desire for academic credibility and excellence in performance – typified by the GCE O Level syllabus introduced in the 1950s – and a growing recognition that composition could have an important role in children's musical education. Successful school music was most often to be found outside the classroom, as extracurricular orchestras, choirs and opera productions thrived (Smith 1947), greatly influenced by the classical performing background of the majority of teachers. A diversity of practice existed, as some schools lacked specialist resources and teachers, whilst others flourished through the enthusiasm of particular individuals.

1955–80

The inconsistency of facilities and direction for music education became more problematic as the changing educational climate began to focus more closely on the needs of the adolescent (Ministry of Education 1963). While some teachers and writers aimed to sustain the careful training of previous decades (Rainbow 1956/71), a new generation of composer-teachers was advocating a more exploratory approach to music education by giving composition a prominent place in the curriculum (Schafer 1965; 1967; 1969; Paynter and Aston 1970). A perceived conflict between 'traditional' and 'progressive' methods was emerging, as new ideas were welcomed by some teachers and resisted by others. Accompanying the practical developments in music education was an increased tendency to theorize about its nature and purpose, with Swanwick (1979) amongst those seeking a 'conceptual framework' within which to evaluate classroom practice.

1980 and beyond

The final decades of the twentieth century saw the continued growth of theoretical and practical innovations in music education, assisted by the introduction of the General Certificate of Secondary Education (GCSE) in the mid-1980s. The trinity of composing, performing and listening was established as the foundation of the examination syllabus, providing official credence for the only recently-accepted innovations of the classroom. A growing interest in world and popular musics also broadened the scope of music teaching (Farrell 1990; Sorrell 1990), and technology became more affordable, resulting in keyboards and synthesizers in the majority of secondary schools. Political influence on education was greatly increased during this time, and the National Curriculum in its various revisions (DES 1992; DfE 1995; DfEE 1999) prompted debate amongst professionals and passionate support for music education in the media. Theorizing and research made use of psychological and philosophical developments (Odam 1995; Green 1988; 1997), so contributing to the continuation of thinking and innovation in music education into the new century.

Reasons for change

Looking back over the past century, the development of music education seems to be an evolutionary process, with each generation adopting the best practice of the time and building on it according to contemporary values and aims. This view is supported by the attempts within GCSE syllabuses and National Curriculum drafts to capture all the elements of previous decades in a balanced approach to music teaching. However, such global schemes only make sense with hindsight, and educational change can perhaps be explained more logically as a series of reactions to the opportunities and ideals of different times. Influences at this more immediate level are numerous: the advent of new technology, whether the gramophone or the electronic keyboard; the catalyst of major political events, from world wars to changes of government; shifts in educational climate and policy, as with the fluctuating interest in child-centred teaching; and changes in the musical world, such as the growing awareness of world music and the discovery of minimalism. Far from being the insulated communities they are sometimes portrayed as, schools are subject to all these social, political and cultural influences, as they touch the lives of teachers and pupils alike.

Advances in technology or changes to the school leaving age, important though they are, cannot of themselves generate a new perspective on the place of music in the curriculum. Practical changes need to be supported by a clear rationale if they are to be sustainable, and the history of music education has seen a succession of different, often equally convincing, answers to the fundamental question: 'What is music education for?' (Pitts 2000b). For early twentieth-century teachers, music was seen as part of the cultural heritage being passed down to the next generation, and indeed that view can still be defended, provided that the definition of 'cultural heritage' reflects the social changes of the past hundred years. Similarly, the mid-twentieth-century preoccupation with teaching musical skills and knowledge retains its validity, especially when combined with the later interest in composition to create a curriculum that is more exploratory and less didactic than that of the 1950s. We have much to learn from the past, not just in the sense of avoiding previously made mistakes, but also in capturing the enthusiasm for music education that radiates from the pages of some of these almost forgotten texts. In order to illustrate the direct relevance of historical thinking to contemporary practice, the next section of this chapter will look at two examples in detail, making connections between past and current thinking on significant questions in music teaching and learning.

Historical perspectives on contemporary questions

Is it important to teach notation?

Whether and how to include staff notation in Music teaching is a question that has occupied teachers throughout the past century, and continues to generate considerable debate. A readily measurable indication of musical knowledge, notation, is seen by many contemporary teachers as a valuable tool with which to equip pupils, yet difficulties arise in the secondary school when some children possess advanced knowledge acquired during instrumental tuition, whilst others are unfamiliar with conventional pitch and rhythm representations. There are many possible practical and pedagogical solutions, yet there is remarkable similarity across the generations as writers have considered the fundamental balance that is at stake between aural and visual approaches to music. Yorke Trotter (1914) and Mainwaring (1951), for example, both argued forcibly that musical experience and aural understanding should precede the learning of notation:

> The study of notation should come after, and not before, the feeling for music has been developed. The child must first have the effect in his mind before he knows the symbols that should be used to express that effect.
>
> (Yorke Trotter 1914: 76)

> Proceed from sound to symbol, not from symbol to sound.
>
> (Mainwaring 1951: 12)

Despite the different contexts in which these educators were publishing their ideas, there is an implicit frustration with current practice in each one, and a determination to place the active, practical experience of music at the heart of learning. Yorke Trotter's contemporaries were concerned with the relative merits of sol-fa and staff notation, but he looks beyond that for a deeper rationale, aware of the risk that children 'will know a great deal about the art but will in no sense be ... artists [themselves]' (Yorke Trotter 1914: 4). Within the context in which he was working and writing, Yorke Trotter's views are ambitious and far-reaching, and have retained their relevance because of their musical and educational integrity (cf. Pitts 1998). Nearly forty years later, music education had changed considerably, but lacked 'a generally accepted aim', leading Mainwaring to observe that 'without such an aim teaching tends to drift and flounder' (Mainwaring 1951: 1). If it seems surprising that his solution is so close to Yorke Trotter's, suggesting little fundamental change in thinking, it is still more chastening to find a more recent publication asserting the priority of musical experience over knowledge in remarkably similar terms:

> Thinking in sound, imagining sound, constructing possible sounds in the head and improvising music all have to be established as skills before the symbols for these things are learnt. When we eventually use the symbols we have already to know how they will sound.
>
> (Odam 1995: 4)

Between them, these three writers draw on a rich background of musical thought: Yorke Trotter's ideas are rooted in aesthetics and philosophy (cf. Yorke Trotter 1924), Mainwaring's reflect his interest in music psychology, whilst Odam incorporates neurological thinking to consider the balance of the left and right brain hemispheres in music learning. Yet their generational and academic differences are resolved in their shared commitment to the centrality of musical experience and enjoyment. Each writer is able to stand back from the immediate concerns of teaching to contemplate the implications and ideals of current thinking, and to propose a direction for music education that might otherwise have been obscured. This is one of the most important lessons the past has to teach us: that contemplation, reflection and idealism, unfashionable though they may be in today's educational climate, are of the greatest importance in developing practice in music education. Reading Yorke Trotter may not tell us how to help the Year 9 child who still cannot understand crotchets and quavers, but it does demonstrate that the questions concerning teachers need to be broader and more searching if professional and musical growth is to be sustained.

What place does popular music have in the curriculum?

Whereas historical evidence on the teaching of notation demonstrates a connection of ideas across changing circumstances, an understanding of why popular music still occupies a somewhat insecure place in the curriculum is more closely linked with social, technological and educational developments. When early drafts of the National Curriculum caused some vociferous protest for being 'out of sync with Bach' (O'Hear 1991), it was clear that the use of a wide variety of musics in the classroom had not been universally accepted, despite the innovative practices that had been developing in the preceding decades (Vulliamy and Lee 1976–80). Once again, the real questions were hidden beneath the surface details, and discussion of whether Beethoven was superior to the Beatles obscured the more central dilemma of whether music teaching should be about imparting established repertoire or exploring stylistic and cultural differences.

Pop music first found its way into secondary school classrooms in the late 1960s, when teachers were faced with the increasingly urgent challenge of responding to the growing youth interest in pirate radio broadcasts and pop recordings. A disparity between 'home' and 'school' music was nothing new: Scholes quotes a teacher of the 1930s who expressed the hope that music appreciation lessons would encourage children to 'persuade mother to buy a gramophone record other than a jazz tune' (Scholes 1935: 234). The hierarchy of musical validity in evidence then was still placing classical music above contemporary tastes in the 1960s:

> To use pop music as a 'light relief' at the end of term is a fairly common habit and a poor one for it inclines once more to the cultural divisions: it admits that the teacher feels the pressures that adolescents can apply via popular music, and yet indicates that the teacher will not consider it seriously *as* music. If it is to be used at all it must not be as a 'let out', but as a *way in*.
>
> (Swanwick 1968: 113)

Whilst Swanwick recognizes the problems of relegating pop music to the status of a fun end-of-term activity, his proposal that instead it should be a stepping-stone towards the classical repertoire marks a shift of emphasis, but not of attitude. A cautious approach to the widening of musical resources in the classroom remained typical, although teachers who embraced the pop music 'revolution' more wholeheartedly were able to take advantage of the new Certificate of Secondary Education (CSE) Mode III examinations, constructing their own syllabuses to reflect the interests and expertise of staff and pupils (Farmer 1979).

The debate over the place of pop music in the curriculum was not easily resolved, closely connected as it was with the long-established dominance of the western classical tradition and its associated cultural and musical values. Expanding definitions of music in the curriculum were soon to be further challenged by an increasing awareness of world musics, which offered greater scope to those teachers who were committed to exploring the materials of musical invention, whilst presenting an additional threat to those determined to retain the traditionalist stance. Early, naive attempts to teach world musics suffered from the same tendency to 'reduce all music to a western standard' (Farrell 1990: 3), showing that pop music had not questioned that assumption as thoroughly as it might have done. Resources and recordings were increasing all the time, but, without a clear sense of purpose for their use, effective teaching and learning using pop and world musics were still dependent on the enthusiasm and expertise of individual teachers.

Contemporary discussions of the place of popular and world musics in the curriculum can help to resolve the remaining challenges for practising teachers, and this is not the place to rehearse those arguments in detail (see Chapter 13). However, a historical perspective goes some way to explaining why uncertainty still exists, given that early attempts to include a variety of musics in the curriculum were for the most part made in reaction to localized opportunities, rather than through widespread conviction about their role in a broad and balanced music curriculum. Similar doubts have been raised about electronic keyboards, which have gone through the same process of being absorbed into the secondary classroom with 'no philosophy, and no Vaughan Williams or Orff ... to support their presence' (Salaman 1997: 143). The value of all these resources and ideas in contemporary music education is almost beyond dispute, but it is still true that their historical pedigree is dubious, and their use demands careful thought by today's teachers. Whilst the history of education can be seen in many ways as an evolutionary process, the need remains for individual teachers to engage with the challenges that have occupied previous generations, and to teach from a sense of conviction, rather than accepting current practice unquestioningly. 'Believing in what we teach is what it is all about' (Paynter 1997: 18), and development in music education can only be sustained if each new generation of teachers considers afresh the purpose and practicalities of music education. The effective use of pop music is only one of a multitude of questions that teachers face, but it is helpful if these apparently everyday concerns can be considered within a wider picture of what music means in education, and how its aims can best be implemented in the classroom.

Reluctant revolutions

The pace of change in British education over the past fifteen years has been immense, with new approaches to examinations at 16+ and 18+, multiple versions of the National Curriculum, and new policies on inspection, accountability and management. Almost the only unifying feature is that all these changes have been imposed from outside the school, sometimes with consultation, but more often with the threat of deadlines and external evaluations to speed up the process. It is understandable that many otherwise excellent teachers are weary or suspicious of change, as they feel under pressure to generate measurable and ever-improving results, and have little time to consider the importance and direction of music in the curriculum. Nevertheless, the history of music education shows that the most inspiring changes in thought and practice have been generated by teachers who use their awareness of the weaknesses of contemporary practice to propose and demonstrate innovative solutions. It is vital, now more than ever, that ideas and enthusiasm for music education are kept alive in schools, and not swamped by the seemingly endless paperwork.

Changes imposed from outside the school in the fashion of recent political interventions were much less frequent before the Education Reform Act of 1988, and indeed British education was often referred to as a 'secret garden', beyond the control of those outside the profession. Nevertheless, tremendous changes took place over the course of the twentieth century, generated by innovative ideas and new solutions to the challenges of teaching music. Keeping pace with change is notoriously problematic, in education as in many areas of life, and it is quite understandable when teachers who have developed a successful style through their own experience or ideas are reluctant to adopt new practices, especially if they are not fully convinced of their validity. It is rare for this kind of struggle to be recorded, but Salaman (1983) was generous in documenting his uncertainty about embracing the ideals of 1970s education, when composition and discovery became prominent in the music curriculum:

> Swirling impressions of unconnected strictures and exhortations filled my mind. It seemed that moral values were being attached to many aspects of music education, that group work, avant-garde procedures, invention, the integration of the arts and self-expression were 'good' while more traditional concerns such as notation, tonality, metre, method, singing and information about music were 'bad'.
>
> (Salaman 1983: 65)

Salaman, along with like-minded colleagues across the country, realized that the role of the music teacher was changing, and that the highly commended performances that had been the mark of a musically successful school could not compensate for classroom learning that was not similarly alive and engaging. Expected, as most music teachers still are, to fulfil a teaching role and a more public 'Kappellmeister' role (ibid.: 1), Salaman sought to transfer the energy and enjoyment of his rehearsals into his class lessons, formulating a set of guiding principles to evaluate whether musical learning was occurring. The urgency to question classroom practice was particularly acute during the period Salaman is describing, but the fact that those particular challenges are historical does not make them any less relevant to contemporary teachers. Accepting received wisdom, however carefully considered and articulated, is no substitute for the individual exploration of central questions in music education, which every teacher needs to tackle afresh.

Of course, not all change in education is perceived in a positive light, and resistance to the prominence of composing in the curriculum was expressed particularly strongly by those who had met with considerable success in the 'Kappellmeister' role that Salaman had discarded (ibid.: 10). Fletcher, for example, bemoaned the 'limited usefulness' of a composition-based curriculum, which he claimed had devalued the status of music in schools:

> Few thinking musicians would ever have suggested that conscripting groups of thirty children on no other criterion than similarity of age, and placing them in a restricted space in an authoritarian institution for two prescribed periods of forty minutes every week, was an ideal or even feasible way of developing musical understanding and activity. It is only because of the fact that musicians have had to brace themselves to this seemingly inevitable task that the sorts of noises which emanate from classrooms are seen to have anything to do with music at all.
>
> (Fletcher 1987–9: 39)

With hindsight, it is easy to see Fletcher's view as reactionary, stemming from a misunderstanding of the purpose of composing in the classroom, which was never to turn children into professional composers, as he assumes (ibid.: 41), but to allow them to engage with the materials of music in a creative and independent way. Fletcher will not have been alone in his views, of course, and nor will this have been the only point in music education history at which there was some hostility to ideas that were otherwise gaining public and professional credibility. This makes the careful reading of historical and contemporary texts even more important, with the ability to evaluate and compare ideas proving an essential skill for teachers seeking inspiration in published works.

Publications are by no means the only source of ideas in education, and indeed it is likely that only a small proportion of academic research reaches practising teachers and can be said to have any direct effect. The immediate pressures of examination syllabuses, parental expectations, and inadequate resources do much to work against experimentation in the curriculum; and, on the other hand, supportive colleagues, access to influential figures and ideas, and the perceptions and needs of pupils all operate at a local level to encourage change and development. The essential ingredient in a vibrant curriculum, now as throughout the history of music education, is the individual teacher's willingness to question his or her own practice, formulating a view of what is important in music education, and communicating that through professional practice. This vibrancy and commitment is, contrary to the prevalent political view, more important than the finer details of curriculum content, as the children involved in education will be far more aware of their teacher's enthusiasm for their subject than of the theories and directives that lie behind the lesson plan.

> We come to understand what it is to behave musically by being with people who display musicality in their own actions ... People catch the flavour of music and learn to think musically by being involved in a variety of pursuits over a period of time.
>
> (Plummeridge 1997: 26)

This contemporary vision of a 'musical dialogue' (ibid.: 26) between teachers and pupils has resonance with many ideas of the past: Yorke Trotter's concern with the child's 'inner nature' (1914: 134), Mainwaring's insistence on 'active and interesting musical experience' (1951: 48), and Paynter and Aston's search for 'a truly liberal education, alive with the excitement of discovery' (1970: 3). Educational thinking can embrace many perspectives, with the single, vital aim of ensuring a lively, progressive and practical music education for all children.

Conclusions: the importance of professional thought in music education

The enormity of the music teacher's task reveals the disadvantages of the evolutionary nature of music education history, as new ideas have been taken up in addition to, rather than instead of, previous aims. In practical terms, this means that the demands on teachers can seem unreasonable, as they strive to balance breadth of musical experience with depth of understanding, and aim to foster in their pupils an enjoyment of music that is founded on knowledge and critical awareness. Things were certainly simpler when the 'masterworks' of music were unambiguously defined and focusing on the lives of the 'great composers' had educational validity, but thinking and practice have moved a long way in the last century, and the dilemmas facing today's teachers reflect the complexity of the musical, social and educational world they work in.

It might be tempting to conclude from the historical evidence that music education has now arrived, and that the practice of 2000 is greatly superior to that of 1900. Whilst it is true that the pupils of today would find the music lessons of 100, 50 or even 20 years ago alien to their current experience, a commitment to musical learning and enjoyment has underpinned best practice across the century, and the similarities, as well as the differences, between past and present can be useful starting points for thinking about the future. The classrooms of today have greater resources and offer wider opportunities than did previous decades, but the enduring challenges of music education remain, and must be tackled within every new context that occurs. In an age when political directives threaten to stifle innovative thinking in education, it is increasingly important that teachers should reflect on the purposes and direction of the musical education that they offer. Relying on a published scheme of work is an approach with some practical merits, but there is a danger that the acceptance of someone else's thinking on music teaching will prevent the development of new ideas and limit the spontaneity and enthusiasm that has always contributed to best practice in music education. Day-to-day decisions about how to respond to pupils and their particular needs must be set in the context of clear beliefs about, and belief in, music education.

There are many effective routes to thinking about music education, but this chapter has demonstrated that published texts from the past represent a particularly rich source, as they capture the enthusiasms and priorities of previous decades in a way that encourages reflection on contemporary practice. An understanding of the way in which changes of the past have come about can lead to a greater critical awareness of the present, by lifting debate on music education out of the familiar context and offering fresh comparisons with the challenges of the present. The many passionate and committed writers of the past century still have much to offer their professional descendants, as a respect for music education history can help us be evaluative of the present, and ambitious for the future.

References

Cox, G.S.A. (1993) *A History of Music Education in England 1872–1928*, Aldershot: Scolar Press.

Department for Education [DfE] (1995) *Music in the National Curriculum: England*, London: HMSO.

Department for Education and Employment [DfEE] (1999) *Music: The National Curriculum for England*, London: DfEE/QCA.

Department of Education and Science [DES] (1992) *Music in the National Curriculum: England*, London: HMSO.

Farmer, P. (1979) *Music in the Comprehensive School*, Oxford: Oxford University Press.

Farrell, G. (1990) *Indian Music in Education*, Cambridge: Cambridge University Press.

Fletcher, P. (1987–9) *Education and Music*, Oxford: Oxford University Press.

Green, L. (1988) *Music on Deaf Ears: Musical meaning, ideology, education*, Manchester: Manchester University Press.

—— (1997) *Music, Gender, Education*, Cambridge: Cambridge University Press.

MacPherson, S. (1922) *The Musical Education of the Child*, London: Joseph Williams.

—— (1923) *The Appreciation Class: A Guide for the Music Teacher and the Student*, London: Joseph Williams.

Mainwaring, J. (1951) *Teaching Music in Schools*, London: Paxton.

Ministry of Education (1963) *Half Our Future* [*The Newsom Report*], London: HMSO.

O'Hear, A. (1991) 'Out of sync with Bach', in *Times Educational Supplement* 22 February: p. 28.

Odam, G. (1995) *The Sounding Symbol: Music Education in Action*, Cheltenham: Stanley Thornes.

Paynter, J. (1997) 'The form of finality: a context for musical education', in *British Journal of Music Education*, 14(1): 5–21.

Paynter, J. and Aston, P. (1970) *Sound and Silence: Classroom Projects in Creative Music*, London: Cambridge University Press.

Plummeridge, C. (1997) 'The rights and wrongs of school music: a brief comment on Malcolm Ross's paper', in *British Journal of Music Education* 14(1): 23–7.

Pitts, S. E. (1998) 'Looking for inspiration: recapturing an enthusiasm for music education from innovatory writings, in *British Journal of Music Education* 15(1): 25–36.

—— (2000a) *A Century of Change in Music Education: Historical Perspectives on Contemporary Practice in British Secondary School Music*, Aldershot: Ashgate.

—— (2000b) 'Reasons to teach music: establishing a place in the contemporary curriculum', in *British Journal of Music Education*, 17(1): 33–42.

Rainbow, B. (1956/71) *Music in the Classroom*, London: Heinemann.

—— (1989) *Music in Educational Thought and Practice: A Survey from 800 BC*, Aberystwyth: Boethius Press.

Salaman, W. (1983) *Living School Music*, Cambridge: Cambridge University Press.

—— (1997) 'Keyboards in schools', in *British Journal of Music Education* 12(2): 143–9.

Schafer, R. M. (1965) *The Composer in the Classroom*, Toronto: BMI Canada.

—— (1967) *Ear Cleaning: Notes on an Experimental Music Course*, Toronto: BMI Canada.

—— (1969) *The New Soundscape*, Toronto: BMI Canada.

Scholes, P. A. (1935) *Music, The Child and The Masterpiece*, London: Oxford University Press.

Smith, W. J. (1947) *Music in Education*, London: Faber & Faber.

Somervell, A. (1931) *The Three R's in Music (Reading, Writing, Rhythm)*, London: Boosey & Co.

Sorrell, N. (1990) *A Guide to the Gamelan*, London: Faber & Faber.

Swanwick, K. (1968) *Popular Music and the Teacher*, Oxford: Pergamon Press.

—— (1979) *A Basis for Music Education*, Slough: NFER-Nelson.

Vulliamy, G. & Lee, E. (eds) (1976–80) *Pop Music in Schools*, Cambridge: Cambridge University Press.

Yorke Trotter, T. H. (1914) *The Making of Musicians*, London: Herbert Jenkins.

—— (1924) *Music and Mind*, London: Methuen.

3 Research in the sociology of music education

Some introductory concepts

Lucy Green

Introduction

Recent global changes in communications and demography, affording unprecedented diversity in the range of music which is produced and consumed in any one place, are going hand in hand with increasing interest by music education researchers in sociological methods, as well as related areas such as ethnomusicology. In this article I aim to present some fundamental sociological concepts, suggest ways in which these concepts can be helpful in thinking about music in general terms, and then focus on some of the possible applications of sociology with reference to music education. Finally, I will briefly indicate the potential breadth of future research in this area. The discussion is by no means intended to represent a definitive method, but rather, it concentrates on some particular ways in which sociology can be illuminating in the study of music education. My perspective and examples focus on the situation in England, and will therefore differ in detail from those in other countries. However, as all countries in the world are socially organized in some way or other, the principles and methods suggested would be pertinent to many other countries. In fact, international comparative research could be very illuminating.

The social organization of musical practice

Here, I will examine two concepts – groups and practices. For each one, I will very briefly attempt to explain its meaning and significance in general sociological terms,[1] then relate it to the sociology of music.

Groups

One area that interests sociologists of many kinds is the organization of society in terms of groups. Three of the most well-researched groups are those of social class, ethnicity and gender, and these will be my main focus; but other groups abound, including those of age, religion, nationality, subculture and many more. In some ways, at a macro-level, we can understand society as being made up of different groups such as these. At the same time, each individual is always a member of several groups at a time. Membership is neither simple nor permanent. For example, a person may move from one social class to another, a person may have mixed ethnicity, but may identify more with one ethnic group than another; a person may be androgynous or transsexual. Nonetheless, in all such cases it is impossible for anyone to altogether avoid standing in some relation to the social groups of class, ethnicity and gender, as well as others.

In the sociology of music, we observe that different social groups relate to music in different ways.[2] As examples I will take the three areas already mentioned, of social class, ethnicity and gender. In the case of social class, more middle-class people tend to go to classical concerts or learn to play classical instruments than working-class people. In the case of ethnicity, the majority of reggae musicians in Britain during the 1970s and 1980s were Afro-Caribbean; in London at the beginning of the 1990s many young South Asian people were listening to music which was a fusion of Asian and Euro-American pop; those who attend the opera are overwhelmingly white. In the case of gender, throughout the history of western classical music, the vast majority of composers have been men; in some societies, women commonly play certain instruments such as the piano, but rarely play others such as the drums; some types of popular music are enjoyed predominantly by young girls, others by boys. In similar ways other social groups, such as religion, age, nationality or subculture, have a correlation with different types of music.

Practices

The other area that interests sociologists is the practical ways in which people go about surviving together, or go about reproducing the conventions of their society through history. It is helpful to conceive of these practices in a threefold way, as production, distribution and consumption. First, production includes the production of commodities, of utilities, and of cultural objects amongst other things. In the case of music, sociological questions about production include: how is music composed, improvised, or performed; what other productive activities does music entail, such as sound engineering; is music produced by individuals working in isolation, by groups, by professionals, amateurs, adults, children, or other categories; where is it produced – in a solitary room, a recording studio, the streets, or the neighbours' garage? Second, questions about distribution are concerned with the ways in which commodities and other objects are sent around the society. Who sends them, and who has access to them? In the case of music, this includes asking: how does music get from the musician to the audience (through live performances, records, cassettes, CDs, videos, radio or TV)? How is music passed on from generation to generation (by notation, copying, printing, computer processing, or aural methods)? Who passes it on (family, friends, musicians or schoolteachers)? Third, the area of consumption, often called reception where cultural commodities are concerned, calls for enquiry into how commodities are used and who uses them in what situations. In the case of music, questions are asked such as: do people listen to music, dance to it, use it for background, or study it; do they use it for work or leisure; do they buy it as scores or recordings; do they hear it live, or do they make it themselves; do they use it in concert halls, in their homes, in dancehalls, at raves or in classrooms and lecture theatres; and who uses what music in these different types of situations?

The sociology of music, then, is interested in social groups and their relations to musical production, distribution and reception. I will refer to this area as 'the social organization of musical practice'.

The social construction of musical meaning

Sociology is not only about which social groups produce, distribute and consume commodities, cultural objects and other things; it also asks what those things mean to us. In so doing, it must also enquire into how people come to agree or to disagree about these meanings, how we reproduce old meanings, and produce new ones. Similarly, the sociology of music enquires into the meanings of the music which social groups produce, distribute and consume; what those meanings are, and how they are constructed, maintained and contested. A fundamental aspect of the sociology of music is a commitment to look at both the social organization of musical practice, and the social construction of musical meaning. Otherwise, the sociology of music will miss some of the most important and interesting characteristics of the very thing it purports to study.

A great deal of work has been done over many centuries on the subject of musical meaning, and this is not the place to review this work in its own right.[3] The aim here is to discuss some aspects of musical meaning with specific reference to sociological questions within the field of the sociology of music education. In order to pursue this aim, I will first present a brief résumé of my understanding of musical meaning, deriving from my previous work in the sociology of music education.[4]

I wish to outline a theoretical distinction between two aspects of musical meaning. The first aspect operates in terms of the interrelationships of musical materials, or, to put it simply, in terms of the sounds of music. In order for a musical experience to occur, musical materials must be organized in such a way as to have relationships, and these relationships must be perceived in the mind of the listener. For example, the musical materials might give rise to the listener's sense of whole and part, opening and close, repetition, similarity and difference, or any other pertinent functional relationships. These relationships will normally accrue within any particular piece of music, but they will also arise from the listener's previous experience of a number of pieces of music that together make up a style, sub-style or genre. The organization of the musical materials acts to construct what I will call 'inherent musical meanings'. These are 'inherent' in the sense that they are encapsulated within the musical materials, and they are 'meanings' in the sense that they are perceived to have relationships.

To put it another way: inherent meaning arises when, for example, one 'bit' of musical material leads us to expect another 'bit', or one bit reminds us of another bit that occurred earlier on, or one bit contrasts with another bit. Then we can say that one bit refers to another bit, or one bit has significance in terms of another bit, or in loose terms, one bit *means* another bit. Inherent meanings are neither natural, essential nor ahistorical; on the contrary, they are artificial, historical and learnt. Listeners' responses to and understanding of them are dependent on the listener's competence and subject-position in relation to the style of the music. The listener must have some previous experience of listening to this kind of music, and must be familiar or competent with the style of the music, in order to conceive some inherent meanings. If the listener is not familiar or competent with the style, few meanings will be conceived.

For example, a student in a class on twentieth-century music was played the opening of 'Mondestruncken' from Schoenberg's *Pierrot Lunaire*. She declared that she was unfamiliar with this type of music, that she did not like it, and that it sounded chaotic and random to her. She had failed to notice that the melodic fragment at the beginning is repeated and varied numerous times throughout the piece; therefore the music could not be chaotic or random. If she had been more familiar with this kind of music, she would have stood more chance of noticing this organization, or, in other words, of conceiving some inherent meanings.

A piece of music whose materials are highly meaningful or very rewarding to one individual might be relatively meaningless or lacking in interest to another. There are thus multiple possible inherent meanings arising from any one piece of music. To summarize, whereas the materials of music physically inhere, the inherent meanings of music arise from the conventional interrelationships of musical materials, in so far as these interrelationships are perceived as such in the mind of a listener.

Whilst this aspect of musical meaning is necessary for musical experience, it is only ever partial, and can in reality never occur on its own. We have become accustomed to the idea that the social or cultural images of performers make an important contribution to their commercial survival. It would be surprising, for example, to see a 1960s record cover of Beethoven piano sonatas showing the pianist Vladimir Ashkenazy wearing nothing but a pair of Bermuda shorts; and a 1960s record of the Beach Boys would seem incongruous if they were dressed in suits and ties. But the manipulation of performers' images is not a mere marketing strategy. Clothes, hairstyle or posturing on the sleeves of recordings are all details of a broader aspect of any music: its mediation as a cultural artefact within a social and historical context. Not only the context in which the music is produced and distributed, but also the context of its reception affects our understanding of it. These contexts are not merely extra-musical appendages; they also, to varying degrees, form a part of the music's meaning during the listening experience. Without some understanding of music as a social construction, we would ultimately be unable to recognize any particular collection of sounds as music at all. When we listen to music, we cannot separate our experience of its inherent meanings entirely from a greater or lesser awareness of the social context that accompanies its production, distribution or reception. I will therefore suggest a second aspect of music meaning, qualitatively distinct from the first, which I will call 'delineated meaning'. By this expression I wish to convey the idea that music metaphorically sketches, or delineates, a plethora of contextualizing, symbolic factors.

It is not possible to hear music without some delineation or other. We do not always have to be conscious of delineation, but it is always going on in our minds, as an integral element of our listening experience. In everyday life, it comes to us in various unnoticeable ways. For example, a piece of music might cause us to think about what the players were wearing, about who listens to this music, about what we were doing last time we heard it, if we have ever heard it before. In a live concert, we might in some way identify with, or recoil from, the subcultural values which we believe the audience holds in common. Some of these thoughts and beliefs will be so closely connected to the music, and so readily accepted by all members of the society, that we can say what the music has come to mean, or delineate those meanings at a conventional level. Other delineations result totally from individual identity. As with inherent meaning, listeners construct the delineated meanings of music according to their subject-position in relation to the music's style.

In simple terms, the difference between the concepts of inherent and delineated meaning is as follows: with inherent meaning, both the musical 'sign' and the object being referred to are made up of musical materials; with delineated meaning, the 'sign' is made up of musical materials, but the object being referred to is made up of non-musical elements.

Central to the conception of music as including both inherent and delineated meaning is an insistence on the irrevocable interface between the two types of meaning, such that neither can exist without the other impinging its own presence. This is not to imply that both types of meaning always co-exist to the same degree, or that we are always *conscious* of both, or even either, of them. On the contrary, it is the very ability of each kind of meaning to become obscured that has caused a great deal of discussion and disagreement about music. The point of distinguishing between the two types of meaning is that, although they cannot exist without each other, each operates very differently in the way that it affects the formation of social groups around music, and the way that it impinges upon musical experience.

Holistic musical experience

I now wish to consider how these two aspects of musical meaning co-exist in musical experience.

At the top of the chart in Figure 1 are the two types of musical meaning, both of which must be in operation, as I have suggested, during any musical experience. It is helpful to understand our responses to each aspect of musical meaning in terms of polar extremes. These are expressed as extremes for the purposes of analysis: in practice, of course, everyone will experience a variety of subtle shades in their responses. First, I will consider inherent meaning. At one extreme, we can have a highly affirmative response (joined to 'inherent meaning' on the chart by a solid line). This will occur when we are very familiar with the style or the particular piece, we feel we understand its nuances, and we are carried along securely or plea-surably in its ebb and flow. At the other extreme, there is what I call 'aggravation' (joined on the chart by a dotted line). Like the Schoenberg student above, we do not understand the music, we are unfamiliar with its style, we cannot make any sense of it and we cannot respond to its internal similarities, differences, continuity or changes. Second, I will consider delineated meaning. At one extreme we have a

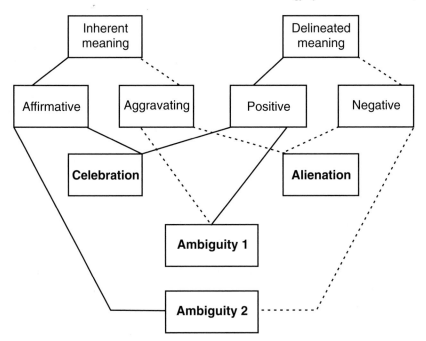

Figure 3.1 Two types of musical meaning

Source: Adapted from Green (1988, p. 138; 1997, pp. 134, 251).

positive response (solid line) when we feel the music in some way expresses our feelings, supports our position in society, when we identify with the music because it delineates our social class, our clothing, our political values, or whatever. At the other extreme we have a negative response (dotted line) when we feel the music delineates social or political values of which we disapprove, or social groups from which we are excluded.

The quality of the experience of music's inherent and delineated meanings can sometimes correspond. 'Celebration' (joined up by two solid lines) is experienced when affirmation by inherent meanings is accompanied by positive inclinations towards delineations. In contrast, 'alienation' (two dotted lines) is experienced when aggravation by inherent meanings is accompanied by negativity towards delineations. But sometimes the two aspects of musical meaning are in contradiction with each other, and this will engender an experience of what I call 'ambiguity'. There are two types of ambiguity deriving from these categories. In 'ambiguity 1', the experience of inherent meaning is aggravating, but that of delineated meaning is positive. For example, we can think of a person who is totally unfamiliar with the inherent meanings of Mozart, has never played or sung Mozart, who dislikes the music and hears it as frilly and superficial: this person is aggravated by the inherent meanings. But at the same time, she can nonetheless love the delineations in terms of the operatic plots, the social event of going out to the opera with friends, and so on: this indicates a positive inclination towards delineations. In 'ambiguity 2', it is the other way around: experience of inherent meaning is affirmative, but that of delineated meaning is negative. In such a case we can think of the Mozart opera-goer who is totally familiar with the inherent meanings, being a pianist and singer who has performed Mozart for many years: thus she is affirmed by the music's inherent meanings. But, simultaneously, she is critical of the operatic plots, she dislikes going to the opera because she thinks the rest of the audience is 'stuffy', and is forced to go to the opera to keep up family appearances: this person is negative towards the delineations.

Not only do our responses to inherent and delineated meanings sometimes conflict, but the one is able to overpower and influence the other. On one hand, if we are already negative to music's delineations, we are unlikely to be affirmed by its inherent meanings, and in some cases unlikely ever to get ourselves in a position to become sufficiently familiar with its inherent meanings for affirmation to take place. For example, if a listener is convinced that women cannot compose, then the delineation that a particular symphony was composed by a woman might prevent that listener from being affirmed by the inherent meanings. There is evidence to indicate that this has been the case many times in history, and it is one reason why some women have composed using male pseudonyms. On the other hand, if we are unfamiliar with the style of the music, and therefore aggravated by its inherent meanings, we are predisposed to being negative about its delineations. For example, my grandmother used to say, 'all pop music sounds the same' (that refers to its inherent meaning), 'and I can't *understand* why anyone should want to watch those scruffy long-haired boys mouthing it into a microphone' (that indicates antipathy to its delineations). In short, attitudes towards one aspect of musical meaning can overpower and influence our attitudes towards the other. It is in this area, concerning the interaction between inherent and delineated meanings, that some of the most challenging issues for music education arise.

The sociology of music education: practice, meaning and musical experience

One of the questions that seems most compelling in the sociology of music concerns how the social organization of musical practice and the social construction of musical meaning are reproduced over history. One of the areas that seems very provocative in the sociology of music education involves asking what role the school plays in that reproduction. I wish to approach this area through two pathways.

First, if we look at the social organization of musical practices in schools, we see a number of patterns. As mentioned at the beginning, the following description pertains to English schools, which will differ in detail from schools in other countries. However, the *fact* of musical patterning and its capacity to be discerned in schools is likely to pertain to most countries. The patterns emerge in terms of pupils' groups including social class, ethnicity and gender, as well as nationality, age, religion, subculture and other categories. Children from these different groups tend to be involved in different musical practices. For example, in terms of social class: middle-class children are much more likely than working-class children to play orchestral instruments in schools; working-class children are much less likely to take music options at school and to go on to study music at university or conservatoire; even though children from all classes enjoy listening to popular music, middle-class children are more likely to respond positively to the delineations of classical music in the classroom, and they are also more likely to be familiar with, and therefore affirmed by, classical music's inherent meanings. Regarding ethnicity: very few Asian or black pupils take the British 18+ music exam (A level), and even fewer go on to study music in higher education; South Asian children in parts of London listen to quite a lot of Asian popular music, whereas children in all-white, rural schools may never have heard any of it. With relation to gender: girls are much more keen on singing in choirs and playing classical music on keyboards, guitars and orchestral instruments than boys; boys are much more interested in the realms of technology and popular music; girls show signs of lacking confidence in composition, whereas boys appear to excel at it. Religion, age, subculture and other social factors are also discernible as significant influences in pupils' relationships to music in school.

Second, I suggested earlier that the sociology of music should look not only at the social organization of musical practices, but also, vitally, at the social construction of musical meaning. It is helpful, when coming to understand the different musical practices of different groups of pupils in schools, to address the pupils' as well as the teachers' concepts of what the music means. This will help to reveal some reasons *why* pupils from different groups engage in certain musical practices, why they avoid others, and *how they respond* to music in the classroom. It will also contribute to increasing the self-understanding of teachers: our values, our aims, and our unspoken assumptions and expectations not only in relation to our pupils' but also in relation to our own musical abilities and interests. Finally, it may help us to understand why teachers can find it very hard to make any changes to the musical tastes and practices of many pupils.

If we re-visit the chart of musical experience above, we can categorize the probability that in classrooms, some pupils will be celebrated by the music which the teacher presents to them, whereas other pupils will be alienated, and for others, musical experience will be ambiguous. The reasons for pupils' experiences being celebratory, alienated or ambiguous are not just to do with innate musical ability, but are also the result of the pupils' social background and membership of a variety of different social groups. Familiarity with inherent meaning and attitude towards delineated meanings will partly derive from the listening habits, the values and the cultural norms of their class, ethnicity, gender, age, religion, subculture and so on. If pupils are aggravated by music's inherent meanings, the teacher's task would seem to be simple: make them more familiar, teach them something about the music's inherent meanings, and slowly they will begin to understand it – perhaps even to like it. But how difficult it can be to do this, if the pupils are also already negative to the delineations of the music!

I will give one example of what I mean here, drawn from my recent research on gender (Green 1997). As I have already indicated, it is mainly girls who sing and play classical music in schools. But not only that, for in interviewing pupils, I have found that classical music takes on delineated meanings that correspond with its practices – that is to say, classical music in schools to a large extent *delineates femininity,* and more radically, effeminacy. By the same token, popular music, and practices such as playing the drums and electric guitar, *delineate* masculinity, and beyond that, *machismo.* Thus for girls and boys, the delineations of different types of music in various situations can be problematic. As teachers we may wish to 'remove the problem' and encourage all pupils to enjoy music as a whole: for example, giving additional opportunities for girls to play the electric guitar, encouraging more boys to join the choir. But for many pupils themselves, there may be a very different agenda. Girls do not necessarily wish to 'act like boys' and may not feel comfortable engaging in musical activities that consciously or unconsciously are generally regarded as masculine within their peer group, just as many boys do not wish to engage in activities which are seen as 'feminine'. Teachers' sensitivity to and respect for the depth and highly personal nature of pupils' responses can only be beneficial in dealing with such situations.

Past research has shown that for many years a number of music teachers in England have been wary of 'intruding' on children's culture, particularly in relation to popular music (see, for example, Green 1988; Vulliamy 1977a,b). However, not all teachers have experienced such doubts, and recently, partly as a result of major changes brought about by the GCSE syllabus (introduced in 1986) and the National Curriculum (from 1992), more and more teachers are incorporating popular music, even current charts music, into their lessons. (Concrete evidence of what appears to be a sea-change here has been made available to me very recently by some questionnaire research that I am currently engaged in.) The benefits of such a change, involving the breaking down of barriers between teachers and pupils, are by no means under question here. But what I would like to suggest is that sociological concepts and methods of research can, again, help to reveal certain aspects of the complexities involved. The example above, of girls' and boys' wishes, suggests that pupils' constructions of delineations can make it very difficult for teachers to change or challenge pre-existing musical practices. The next example illustrates what a hard task it can be to really 'reach' some of the musical delineations that circulate in children's culture independently of the school.

This example, taken from recent research for an MA dissertation (Alden 1998), focuses on ethnicity. Alden interviewed children in a mixed-race, inner city London primary school in which about 70 per cent of pupils spoke English as a second language. He was familiar with the school and had been a teacher there previously. He asked the pupils about their musical tastes and the kinds of music they listened to at home. When the pupils were talking to him in large, mixed-race groups, a picture emerged of a listenership that was almost entirely committed to charts music such as that broadcast on the BBC television programme *Top of the Pops* or BBC Radio One. But when he interviewed Asian children in single-ethnicity groups, Alden was presented with a very different picture. He states 'although they were familiar with "pop" music and sometimes listened to *Top of the Pops* they were all very clear that Hindi film music was the substance of their experience at home and they stated that this was their preferred music' (p. 84). They also told him they enjoyed listening to local radio stations broadcasting Hindi popular music.

Having discovered this side of these pupils' tastes and practices, Alden then conducted another large-group, mixed-race interview. He asked pupils to work together at devising a curriculum and resources that they would like to have for music in their school. Their suggestions included only mainstream popular forms and instruments associated with such music, as well as some of the classroom percussion instruments they were already familiar with. During discussion afterwards, the Asian pupils in the group were silent. 'I pointed out that pupils in the school listened to a much wider range of music than that which had been suggested and asked if this range should be included. Even with such a clear lead, there was no voice strong enough to say "yes"' (p. 88). On asking the pupils separately why they did not speak up, Alden found they attributed the cause explicitly to peer pressure (p. 85).

In a school such as this which had an anti-racist policy and a multicultural curriculum, in which Alden observed lessons and curriculum materials involving music from around the world, including the rehearsal of a Hindi song for assembly on the very morning of the interviews, the home listening habits of some pupils nevertheless appeared to be something about which they were, to all intents and purposes, ashamed, embarrassed and secretive.

The power of musical delineations is such that it can override even the best of intentions on the part of teachers: pupils have their own delineations, their own desires and their own agendas in relation to music, and these can be reinforced by the school, or they can remain in a cultural sphere which is separate from the school. Musical delineations are not just heard, but they are adopted as symbols of social identity. Whether you play music, sing it, or listen to it, compose it, study it or teach it, music can be taken on and worn rather like a piece of clothing, to indicate something about your class, ethnicity, gender, your sexuality, religion, subculture, political values and so on. It can be worn by pupils as a public expression within the school, which may reveal or may indeed conceal part of the pupils' private identity or, alternatively, musical 'clothing' may be worn only in the privacy of the home or other situations beyond the school. Particularly in the case of children and adolescents who are searching for identity as new adults in a changing society, music can offer a powerful cultural symbol, which aids in their adoption and presentation of a 'self'.

It is music's delineations that offer this symbolization, but it is in the musical experience as an undifferentiated whole, in which delineated and inherent meanings come together as one unified apperception, that the deepest power of music resides. When we play, compose or listen to music, we do not normally analyse our experience, or declare: 'Oh, yes, that's a delineation, and that's an inherent meaning'. On the contrary, the two appear as one. Therefore delineations appear to arise, not from the social context of musical production, distribution and reception, but mysteriously, from within the music itself. Delineations thus come to us with the impact of apparent, immediate truth. It is then in musical experience itself – in the apparent unquestionability of how things are and of who we are – that the music classroom's most powerful and most deep-rooted reproductive mechanisms lie. These mechanisms arise not only from what is in the curriculum, nor only from the way it is included, but also from what is not included.

When, as teachers, we require our students to engage in musical activities, we are often requiring them to engage in music whose delineations may correspond to or may conflict with their self-images, their social backgrounds, their public or private identities, values and desires. This correspondence or conflict must go beyond the delineations, to affect each student's musical experiences as a whole. Therefore, when we think we are measuring and enhancing students' musical ability with relation to inherent meaning, it may be worth enquiring whether musical ability can be adequately represented in such terms. Teachers can only benefit from being aware of the complex web of musical meanings with which we all negotiate, and of the intrinsic relationships between students' social groups, their musical practices, and their overall musical experiences. In this way, we are less likely to label students 'unmusical' without first considering the deep influence of social factors on the surface appearance of their musicality; and we are more likely to respond sensitively to students' genuine convictions about what music means, what it is worth and what it is to 'be musical'.

Some implications for further research

Sociological methods and concepts within the field of music education represent a goldmine for research, which could be done by teachers whilst they are in service as well as by academics and professional researchers. Even though, as I mentioned at the beginning of this article, a growing amount of such research is already being done, there is still much that is left open. Interviewing not only pupils but teachers about their musical tastes, observing them in their interactions with music, connecting such work, for example, to their lives at home, their possession of musical instruments or recordings, their involvement in community music events, their parents' musical practices and tastes, all these areas are wide open for investigation. And this is before we throw social class, ethnicity, gender, age, religion, nationality, subculture and other factors such as intra- and international geographical and historical differences into the balance.

For example, to take just one of the areas I have mentioned as an axis, and revolve some of the others around it: we know that pupils are musically differentiated by gender in several ways. But is this the same for middle-*class* girls and boys as it is for working-*class* girls and boys? Is it the same for different *ethnic* groups? At what *age* does it become manifest? At what age is it most extreme? Is involvement in a *subculture* a factor; for example, does subcultural involvement increase or decrease the likelihood of girls playing drums and boys playing violins? What effects do *parental tastes* and listening habits have upon girls and boys? There are issues of locality and internationality to be considered too: for example, are girls and boys in urban areas likely to be more or less differentiated than those in rural settings? Do similar situations persist in different countries? Once such a process of revolving various sociological factors around one central factor is started, it becomes clear how very many questions and conjectures there are yet to be explored.

Acknowledgements

I would like to thank Andrew Alden for permitting me to refer to his dissertation. A shorter version of this chapter was originally delivered as a Keynote Lecture in the Fifth Annual Conference of the Brazilian Association of Music Education at Londrina, July 1996, and it is published in Portuguese as 'Pesquisa em sociologia da educacao musical' ['Research in the sociology of music education'], *Revista da Associacao Brasileira de Educacao Musical*, 4, 1997, pp. 25–35.

Notes

1 The sociological literature is obviously enormous. For anyone new to the field, an excellent introductory text is by Anthony Giddens (1994).
2 Regarding the sociology of music, I strongly recommend Peter Martin (1995).
3 For standard background texts relating to the twentieth century, see Langer (1955) and Meyer (1956); for recent helpful discussions (mainly with reference to popular music) see Middleton (1990), Walser (1993), Moore (1993) and Brackett (1996); and for a helpful sociological critique, Martin (1995).
4 The discussion of musical meaning below derives mainly from Green (1988, 1997). For early seminal work in the sociology of music education, see Vulliamy (1997a, b).

References

Alden, A. (1998) 'What does it all mean? The National Curriculum for Music in a multi-cultural society', MA dissertation, London University Institute of Education.

Brackett, D. (1996) *Interpreting Popular Music*, Cambridge and New York: Cambridge University Press.

Giddens, A. (1994) *Sociology*, London: Routledge.

Green, L. (1988) *Music on Deaf Ears: musical meaning, ideology and education*, Manchester and New York: Manchester University Press.

—— (1997) *Music, Gender, Education*, Cambridge and New York: Cambridge University Press.

Langer, S. (1955) *Philosophy in a New Key*, Harvard: Mentor Books, New American Library, Harvard University Press.

Martin, P. (1995) *Sounds and Society: themes in the sociology of music*, Manchester: Manchester University Press.

Meyer, L.B. (1956) *Emotion and Meaning in Music*, Chicago and London: University of Chicago Press.

Middleton, R. (1990) *Studying Popular Music*, Milton Keynes: Open University Press.

Moore, A. (1993) *Rock: the primary text*, Buckingham: Open University Press.

Vulliamy, G. (1977a) 'Music and the mass culture debate', in J. Shepherd, P. Virden, T. Wishart and G. Vulliamy (eds) *Whose Music: a sociology of musical language*, London: Latimer New Dimensions.

—— (1977b) 'Music: a case study in the new sociology of education', in J. Shepherd, P. Virden, T. Wishart and G. Vulliamy (eds) *Whose Music: a sociology of musical language*, London: Latimer New Dimensions.

Walser, R. (1993) *Running with the Devil: power, gender and madness in heavy metal music*, Hanover, NH: Wesleyan University Press.

Section 2

Music learning and musical development

4 Music education

A European perspective

Janet Hoskyns

European music education does not exist as a discrete entity, but the existence of music and education as fundamental privileges and entitlements in the twenty-first century mean that we should at least understand the influences which make music education what it is today. The influence of national, international, musical and schooling traditions has had significant effects upon the curriculum which is presently taught in English schools and other educational institutions.

The creation of a European Community and associated harmonization of qualifications, economic systems, etc., has not yet fully permeated compulsory education and teaching, in the way that it has done in other professions, e.g. law or medicine. The notion of subsidiarity (that local matters should be decided at the most appropriate local level) has prevailed in almost all aspects of education systems across the European continent. The Commission of the EC (1994) Maastricht treaty, article 126, provides an opportunity for a harmonized European school curriculum, but also leaves to individual nations the responsibility for education in their own country. This appears to be politically expedient, but the school curriculum and schooling traditions remain the responsibility of the states and regions in which they are located. There are opportunities for exchanges of staff, students and pupils to promote European co-operation and understanding but harmonization of the school curriculum is unlikely to occur.

Since each country within the European Union has its own regional and national systems for educating its citizens, it would be difficult, even if it were desirable, to produce a European education system, with all the paraphernalia which that entails.

There is, nevertheless, a will amongst educators to manage the development of a European Dimension so that 'Each national educational culture will retain much of its own distinctiveness, which will add to the richness of Europe and to enhanced consumer choice' (McLean 1990: 117–18). However, a European education system is not envisaged.

For teachers and pupils, it is important to know about how music is learned and taught in neighbouring states, and from time to time to consider whether we in England may have something to learn from the systems and strategies adopted elsewhere.

This chapter looks at types of music education, schooling traditions (drawn from the work of McLean 1990) and makes some comments about the traditions which have been adopted in various regions and countries of Europe. The chapter also examines examples of intercultural European projects in music education in order to highlight some of the positive learning which can take place in and through music.

Music education

Music education is a process in which a human being becomes aware of and sensitive to music, develops understanding of its function and meaning, and enjoys being involved with it in a discriminating way. Kestenberg spoke of 'the thesis of artistic creation and … the antithesis of technical musicianship, we shall now aim at uniting the two in a synthesis, culminating in music education' (1953: 56). It is a process which should stimulate and encourage the development of the imagination as well as the emotions and intellect. It is not limited to any one mode of making, performing or listening to music. Neither is it confined to knowing about music, in sensory, intellectual or other ways. Rather, music education conforms to Grafton and Jardine's (1986: 219) definition of education, in that it exhibits conscious cultural traditions, educational ideologies and a curriculum.

Cultural traditions

European music's cultural traditions are in the making, performing and recording of music, from vernacular, art music and other styles and genres. The existence of definite European musical characteristics, which can be traced back to Judaeo-Christian origins, or even further to aspects of Greek classical culture, suggests that the cultural traditions are firmly entrenched. Since the early middle ages, as the Holy Roman Empire established itself, music has played an important part in both religious and secular activities. Those who needed to use music were trained in singing, reading and performing, so formal music education has a long history and many traditions. (See Rainbow, B. 1989, for comprehensive information about the culture and traditions of music education since 800 BC.) As an important aspect of European cultural life, music should and does have a distinctive contribution to make to the education of European citizens.

Music education – educational ideologies

However, the traditions of music education are complex and diverse. To assist our analysis, it is helpful to subdivide music education into three categories: music education; musical education; and education through music.

1   Music education is the overarching member of the trio. It is the way an individual gains understanding of the nature of music. It may be acquired by formal tuition or absorbed informally through listening to and participating in musical activities. It is the process by which one gains knowledge of music, in its broadest sense. This category masks divisions, which occur between a number of concepts of what music

education really is. Greek and Roman concepts of music education were entirely different from those of the twenty-first century; nevertheless, it was important.

2   Musical education develops musical knowledge and understanding through concentrated tuition and experience. It involves induction into the world of performing, composing, arranging and directing and can lead to a highly developed professional understanding of what it means to be a musician (Paynter 1982: 91). It is the main preserve of specialist music schools, conservatoires, *musikhochschulen* and university music faculties, and it encompasses the passing on of the accepted cultural heritage in that particular area of music.

3   Education through music. Paynter (1982: 89) refers to the process where music is used as the tool for educating, but the results may not be evident in a musical form. Using music as a tool to educate the emotions or to facilitate thinking or movement are examples of education through music. The expected outcome is someone who has a greater sense of well-being through understanding or knowing about music, rather than through being a high-level executant performer or analyst. This area forms the basis for music in the primary school curriculum in the UK, some parts of Germany, Holland and Spain.

These three definitions offer some clues as to the educational ideologies which underpin much music education in the western world and in Europe in particular.

A music curriculum

The curriculum is different in manner and kind for virtually every state, region or examining organization in Europe. In fact England and Wales are unusual amongst European states in having a *National* Curriculum. Most regions and countries of the EU have very different systems and practices in music education, which are most frequently related to the schooling traditions and the place of music within that educational framework. Music, as a subject or way of knowing, is viewed differently in different places and times. Historically, the Greeks treated it as a science, the Christian church of the Holy Roman Empire found music was useful to encourage devotion, humanists in the sixteenth and eighteenth centuries imbued it with rational qualities and tried to ensure it was unembellished. As an academic subject discipline, music continued to be included even after the collapse of the Holy Roman Empire.

'Music's place in higher education remained firm after the foundation of universities' (Rainbow 1989: 37). There were professors of music at Bologna in 1450 and from the thirteenth century in Salamanca University. The use of the 'Guidonian' hand and techniques of 'solmization' (singing using syllables such as sol, fa, etc.) to train choristers to pitch notes accurately were introduced during the eleventh century. So music education has been a part of some curriculum in Europe since the Roman Empire. Sometimes this education was concerned with the training of particular performers, choristers or priests, and sometimes it formed a significant part of the school or university basic curriculum.

Western European traditions of schooling

In historical terms, McLean (1990) identifies three traditions of schooling: the encyclopaedic, the humanistic and the naturalistic, which cover most of the education systems of EU countries. These relate both to curriculum style and philosophy.

Broadly, encyclopaedism is the tradition in which the French education system has been located during the last century. It is valued for its rationality and emphasis on philosophy and mathematics. Artistic education tends to be seen as occurring outside the main business of schooling, as a recreational extra, or something used to encourage young children to participate.

The humanist tradition can be seen in the educational systems of the ancient universities of England and in the reformed public schools. An emphasis on classics and verbal reasoning, culminating in the *Literae Humaniores* is accorded greater status than sciences and mathematics. These traditional 'subjects' are still valued in many grammar-type schools in the UK, in European Catholic schools, and in Greek schools which are influenced by Greek Orthodox humanism. The tradition is an essentially conservative one, associated with the acceptance of authority. Music, as an academic subject, fits well into this tradition, with opportunities to study historical and cultural contexts, to analyse music from scores, but not to participate in active music-making.

The naturalist tradition is equated with the ideas of Rousseau, Montessori, Froebel and Pestalozzi and the development of individualized, child-centred teaching methods. These can be found in a number of European countries both in 'alternative schools' and in vocational education systems. The nursery and early years of primary education in many European countries are based upon this ideal. In music, this involves allowing pupils to explore and experiment with musical sounds, to play games which involve singing and movement and generally to learn through making music.

These three models help to clarify, and in part to explain, the origins of systems, which currently prevail in the countries and regions of the European community. Many curriculums adhere overtly to one system or another, but the teaching and learning styles found in individual classrooms normally take account of a mixture of styles and beliefs about what constitutes worthwhile knowledge and how it should best be learned.

What does this mean for music education? The humanistic tradition in England, which was prevalent in grammar school education in the late nineteenth and twentieth centuries, no longer holds much sway for arts subjects like music in the English and Welsh curriculums. The place of music in an humanistic curriculum would be largely relegated to theoretical academic exercises involving musical analysis, and practical music-making would exist outside the school curriculum. The current focus in the English National Curriculum on practical music-making has more in common with the naturalistic, child-centred philosophies of Pestalozzi, Montessori and others, than with the encyclopaedic or humanistic traditions.

The encyclopaedic tradition, characterized by the Napoleonic French education system, still prevails in a number of European countries, including France, Italy and Portugal. In this, the rational disciplines of mathematics and logic are regarded as the most worthwhile, supreme forms of knowledge and the place of music and other arts is minimal. Most music education in this tradition is in fact 'musical education' and, in France and Italy, this is mostly offered outside the school curriculum. The Italian curriculum does not really include music education within the compulsory curriculum. Music education in Italy and France takes place mostly in summer schools, extracurricular music schools or through the intervention of *animateurs*. More seriously, the nature of musical education is frequently divorced from the prevailing musical culture.

> European teaching techniques characteristically involved the use of notation; the segregated instruction of instrumental and vocal techniques, of repertory, theory and history by specialists; wherever possible, teaching students in groups; the use of some music whose purpose is only to aid learning and practising. The teaching process was abstracted from the musical culture.
>
> (Nettl 1985: 72)

In European terms, the separation allows concentration on particular kinds of knowledge and learning and is deemed to be 'efficient'. The efficiency nearly always relates to the acquisition of particular executant skills rather than education through music. This separation has caused enormous confusion for teachers, who assume their task is to pass on skills in isolation, rather than to educate generally, using music as the vehicle.

The naturalist traditions of child-centred education are far more consonant with current ideals and traditions in education and make more sense to teachers attempting to deal with disaffected, urban pupils whose musical experience is often extensive, and influenced by popular culture, fashion and technology. By educating the pupil, account can be taken of previous musical experience and preferences. However, it is difficult for academic or practising musicians to identify and assess the key teaching and learning points which should be included in such a tradition. A naturalist approach takes account of many of the issues with which European teachers are grappling, such as how to use technology, how to manage pupils with short attention spans and how to deal with urban disaffection amongst pupils.

Worthwhile knowledge and Music curriculums

Music is a prescribed school curriculum subject in the United Kingdom, The Netherlands, some states of Germany and regions of Spain. England and Wales are unique in having a National Curriculum for Music, which defines what should be learned at which age phase, and requires every school pupil aged between 5 and 14 years to be assessed against criteria. The Netherlands have a published curriculum for Music, which states what should be learned and taught in primary and secondary schools. In The Netherlands, at secondary level there are Music curriculum guidelines, but Music is not compulsory in all secondary schools, and much of the teaching occurs in specialist music schools. In other European countries and states, the Music curriculum is negotiated locally and in some cases is left up to individual schools and teachers to decide. In countries and regions where Music is not a required part of the school curriculum, it may be offered as an additional activity outside normal school hours or be included during specific projects, or even provide a 'recreational' period in an otherwise academic, encyclopaedic curriculum.

In France, musicians can train to become *animateurs*, who are qualified to work in schools assisting teachers and setting up projects which involve music-making. These can be focused upon world musics, traditional music, composing, performing or a number of musical styles and genres. These 'projects' may be intercultural, in terms of musical styles, but are usually organized around a school or other institution, perhaps a youth group, and one particular *animateur*. Across Europe, a good deal of music education happens through intensive workshops and activities, not through the school curriculum. This can be advantageous if the *animateur* does not wish to be constrained by the curriculum and is able to use artistic licence to create a meaningful, musical experience for the participants.

Perhaps the most interesting microcosm of European Music education can be found in the curriculum of the European schools. Here, there are examples of music education being the synthesis of technical musicianship and artistic creation, as described by Kestenberg earlier.

In my research (Hoskyns 1997) into a European dimension in music education, this was the only school Music curriculum which had given serious thought to the issue of a European dimension in school music education. However, because of the particular foundation of the European schools, and their commitment to providing a European education for the children of people working for the Community, they have created a consensus for a Music curriculum, which can be accepted with modifications by all the European schools. There is no doubt that, as with the English National Curriculum, each school interprets the curriculum in its own way and local teaching methods, approaches and materials are used in each school. Some of the schools put a greater curriculum emphasis on the arts and music than others and this normally reflects the status of music as a curriculum subject in the particular location of the school. The Music curriculum culminates in a European Baccalaureate examination, which is specially tailored to meet the needs of the European schools and is examined by an international group, with adherence to the International Baccalaureate examinations board.

The rationale for this music curriculum places the curriculum model firmly in the naturalist/humanist category and actively rejects the kind of rational-encyclopaedic tradition proposed by McLean (1990) in his suggested model for a European curriculum. This is particularly surprising since the rationale for the overall curriculum is modelled so as to be 'comparable with the French Lycée or German Gymnasium in that lesson time is largely taken up with academic subjects' (DES 1990). These include ethics and philosophy, as well as one or two foreign languages and mother-tongue-learning. However, there may be reasons for such an apparently 'liberal' approach to the music curriculum. One is the commonly-held view that an academic curriculum needs moments of leisure and recuperation; music visual art and physical education have often been required to fill this slot in European education systems. Another reason is that the influence of

English, Dutch and Danish approaches to music teaching may have infiltrated the curriculum. Of course, the academic status which art music and PE carry in a 'leisure' curriculum is negligible, but this fits in with the fact that, until 1992, Music and Art were not examined as academic subjects in the European Baccalaureate. So these two subjects did not have sufficient status in the worthwhile knowledge stakes to be thought examinable. During the first half of the twentieth century, Music was not examined as an academic subject. Executant skills were observed in performance, but since studying performance took place outside the normal school day, there was no necessity to examine it.

In England and Wales, it can be seen that a consensus has been achieved as to the nature of worthwhile knowledge. Indeed, the influence of UK music educators on the European Schools' curriculum has been considerable. Where heads of Music in European schools are from the UK, they have promoted a more active curriculum, in which performing and composing are examinable as well as propositional knowledge about music. The Netherlands' curriculum too includes performing, and those responsible for designing it claim to have been influenced by UK music educators such as John Paynter.

In Catalonia, one of the largest and most influential Spanish regions, the school Music curriculum is attempting to make musical learning a more active experience for pupils. The reforms to the school system, which have taken place since the end of the Franco regime in Spain, have encouraged a more active approach to all parts of the school curriculum. The age of transfer to secondary school is now 12 years instead of 14, and this amongst other reforms has given an opportunity to revise and increase the number and nature of textbooks and school teaching materials which are available.

Other major strands in European community Music curriculums are to do with cultural traditions and folk heritage. In Ireland, Scotland, Greece, parts of Spain, Portugal, Finland and other states and regions, there is a significant emphasis in music education on the traditional and indigenous music of the country or region. This can mean pupils having specialist tuition on traditional instruments, or it may mean learning to sing traditional songs. In some parts of Europe it is a vital part of the transmission of the region's cultural heritage, especially where this is seen to be threatened for some reason. In Greece, particularly where it has borders with Albania and the former Yugoslavia, for example, traditional Greek music is a vital part of the Music curriculum.

It is significant that Kodály's renowned method and song collection were the result of a wish to recreate an identifiable Hungarian national music and song and to find ways to develop skill in sight-singing. According to Rainbow, he found an answer to his problem in England: 'Upon discovering the systematic method of training the inner ear which formed the basis of Curwen's teaching, Kodály determined to make it the basis of a system designed to meet the special needs of Hungarian schools' (1989: 327). It is interesting that his aim was both to develop a teaching method and to identify and preserve cultural heritage. In this instance, music is being used as a subversive influence to provide a teaching method and to maintain a particular cultural heritage. At the time, there was no accepted body of 'worthwhile knowledge' in Hungary which formed the basis for a Music curriculum.

European school music cultures

In essence, then, European states have tended to adopt a culture for music education within and beyond the school curriculum, which is not necessarily consonant with the local, regional or national musical cultures. This is largely because the prevailing educational culture, be it encyclopaedic or humanist, cannot easily accommodate a practical, artistic subject discipline. Of course, one might argue that school music should constitute a cultural area all of its own, but this would mean continuing the tradition of school music being divorced from contemporary musical cultures. If music education is to be relevant, then it cannot afford to create a culture which is separated from musical developments in the professional and contemporary musical world, if educators could actually agree what these are. Cultural isolation could seriously limit the development of new musical ideas. Where will new music come from and how will young people learn how to respond to musical stimuli if they are not taught in school? As the performing and entertainment industries become economically more significant, so the compulsory curriculum should train and educate pupils to recognize and participate in this market. A nineteenth-century curriculum model, valuing propositional knowledge about music, may not be the most appropriate for the twenty-first century.

As John Blacking so cogently tells us, 'the feelings which people express or receive through the medium of music, are drawn from a repertoire of collective sentiments as much as from personal experience' (1987: 75). If this is so, then music education should concentrate more upon recognizing and teaching a repertoire of collective sentiments. How we might agree about what these are, and should be, is difficult. It is also important to remember that the value and function of music education is different in each education system. There may be clearly held congruent ideals about what music education should do and could achieve, but there is very little agreement nationally or internationally as to how this might reasonably be done. Much of this confusion emanates from the fact that Music's place in any education varies and the value of music education is not always acknowledged in the education systems of Europe. The European Music Conference of the Council for Cultural Cooperation, convened in 1985, made a number of recommendations about how European music education might be achieved and one of the most important items was:

> That music teaching should be accompanied by humanist training in all aspects of culture.
>
> (DECS/CONF/Mus (85) 16: 4 II.5)

Here, they are clearly looking at ways of encouraging teachers and pupils to see music in a wider cultural context than that of 'school music' or institutional music for teaching purposes. They are also not suggesting that a humanist schooling style should be adopted, rather that, in order to understand music, students must recognize and understand the cultural context from which it emanates. However, this is unlikely to be taken very seriously, since every curriculum authority has the greatest difficulty in agreeing precisely on what in music is the most worthwhile knowledge. Different groups and factions will always want 'their' music to be of supreme importance, whether or not the worthwhile knowledge is actively or passively acquired.

As Abbs in his Opening Manifesto to *The Symbolic Order* says:

> any education in that art-form must include a working knowledge and under-standing of the field. It is not 'a return to tradition' so much as a return to the meaning of an arts discipline. To 'do' art is to activate the field. To talk of an initiation into the cosmos of art is, in truth, to talk of an initiation into the essence of our subject.
>
> (Abbs 1989: 10)

Music education in Europe exhibits a number of different features, styles and philosophies. To concentrate on school music is to engage in a study of schooling traditions, which will vary according to the country or state in which observations are made.

As an example, take this extract bemoaning the lack of status accorded the arts in French education:

> *la société française … des parents, mais aussi de nombreux enseignants, s'interrogent toujours sur l'utilité de l'éducation artistique et la considèrent comme une récréation. Les raisons de cette interrogation sont profondes: elles plongent leurs racines dans l'histoire des mentalités nationales. Fille du cartésianisme, l'école de France a fait des filières scientifiques, de l'apprentissage de la logique et de la raison.*

> (French society … parents, but also many teachers are always questioning the usefulness of education in the arts and consider it to be a form a recreation. The reasons for such questioning are deep-seated: they are rooted in the history of the national mentality. Inheriting Cartesian ideals, the French school system has created scientific pathways from apprenticeship, logic and reason.)
>
> (Sery 1995: 30)

However, in the 'French' mind, education is about teaching the next generation the important values which have produced the French culture. Therefore, philosophy and rational thought are considered to be the main subjects. Even in France, reforms are being embraced, as the politicians and teachers recognize that not everyone is best catered for by such an intellectual ideas-based curriculum.

Most Europeans enter formal schooling at age 6 or 7, whereas in the UK we start at 5. No other European State or country has a school leaving examination at 16 years of age (GCSE). For most European pupils, studying music beyond primary school is something which takes place in a specialist music school, where musical instruments are taught, ensembles are rehearsed and performances are prepared. For European pupils wishing to study music at a higher education institution such as a conservatoire or university music department, then they would need to demonstrate performing skill and probably to have attended special classes in music as part of their school leaving examination. Some of these classes are conducted in the conservatoires, not in schools.

Despite these differences, music is studied in all the countries of the European Union, but not always in the same way or as part of the entitlement curriculum in any particular age phase. In the early years, pupils are almost always exposed to musical games, rhymes and dances as part of their general education, but thereafter the inclusion of Music in the school curriculum is generally based upon whether it is considered to be part of the received canon of worthwhile knowledge.

To understand more about the traditions and values of European regions and states, it is instructive to note how and where music teachers are trained. In The Netherlands, Spain, Italy and some parts of Germany, specialist music teachers are often trained in conservatoires as part of an advanced training. Generalist teachers, at the primary or early years level, who teach Music as well as other subjects, are normally taught in teacher training institutions or universities, with the possibility of undertaking further specialist diplomas and training in Music once they are qualified. Another significant factor when studying the traditions in which music education occurs is which ministry is responsible for music education. In England and Wales, music education comes under the remit of the Department for Education and Employment. In France it is supervised by the Ministry of Culture, which is responsible for the *Cité de la Musique* in Paris, as well as the Centres which train musicians to work as *animateurs* in schools.

Summary

Music education in the countries, states and regions of Europe performs a number of different functions:

1   to train professional musicians, performers and composers;
2   to offer active musical and artistic events in which everyone can participate, and through doing, may learn about the nature of music;
3   to provide a 'body of knowledge' which may be analysed and studied both by the amateur music lover and the musicologist;
4   to provide a sense of identity and security and be used to promote particular emotions. These can be positive, negative, or neutral, but involve using music to manipulate feelings and emotions, as in advertising or promotional campaigns;
5   to provide a soothing background ('aural wallpaper' – this may be found in some language learning and therapeutic systems) where music provides support for other activities.

Depending upon both the school system and the curriculum tradition in which it is located, music education is used both to educate European citizens and to train professional musicians. However, the ways in which this occurs are very variable and varied across the European continent.

Plato, whose views on music education are important philosophically, if not literally, emphasizes the ways in which music can be an important cultural cement and purveyor of values: 'musical training is a more potent instrument than any other, because rhythm and harmony find their way into the inward places of the soul' (Plato *The Republic*, Book III: 88).This reminds us that music education continues to have a significant part to play in general education and schooling. However, in an era when all education systems and curriculums are being influenced by developments in technology, music has a truly significant part to play. In music we are able to use technology to communicate quickly, musically and audibly with those who are geographically distant. Already this has encouraged a blurring of boundaries and has excited artistic fusions in the professional musical world. In music education this provides both a challenge and an opportunity to offer music-making as an educative experience, not just in schools and other institutions, but to individual learners who in the past would not have had access to music education. Music education must become part of the global curriculum for lifelong learning, for who knows how long national and regional schools and their associated learning programmes and practices will remain the norm?

As a temporal art form, music-making will continue, and it has considerable educative value for all, wherever it is offered: in or out of school. Educators must continue to be involved in the making, teaching, understanding and broadcasting of music in order to prevent it becoming a product to be purchased, rather than a living art form, with a mountainous heritage and exciting educational possibilities.

References

Abbs, P. (ed.) (1989b) 'Introduction and chapter 1: aesthetic education: an opening manifesto', *The Symbolic Order: A contemporary reader on the arts debate*, London: The Falmer Press.

Blacking, J. (1987 and 1990 pb. edn) *A Commonsense View of all Music*, Cambridge: Cambridge University Press.

Commission of the European Communities (1994) *Maastricht: the Treaty on European Union*, Luxembourg: Office for Official Publications of the European Communities.

Council and Ministers of Education (1985) *Recommendation R (85)7 Music education*, Strasbourg: Council of Europe.

DES (1990) 900117S2.LH(3) *The European Schools and the European Baccalaureate.*

Grafton, A. and Jardine, L. (1986) *From Humanism to the Humanities. Education and the Liberal Arts in Fifteenth and Sixteenth Century Europe*, London: Duckworth.

Hoskyns, J. (1997) *Music Education and a European Dimension*, 'A la recherche de l'Europe perdue', unpublished D.Phil thesis, University of York.

Kestenberg, L. (1953) 'The present state of music education in the occidental world' in *Music in Education report from the International Conference*, 29 June – 9 July 1953, Paris: UNESCO, pp. 52–8.

McLean, M. (1990) *Britain and a Single Market Europe. Prospects for a Common School Curriculum*, Kogan Page in association with the Institute of Education, London: University of London.

Nettl, B. (1985) *The Western Impact on World Music Change, Adaptation and Survival*, New York and London: Schirmer Books.

Paynter, J.F. (1982) *Music in the Secondary School Curriculum*, Cambridge: Cambridge University Press.

Plato (1888 edn) *The Republic of Plato, 3rd Edn*, translated by Benjamin Jowett, Oxford: Clarendon Press.

Rainbow, B. (1989) *Music in Educational Thought and Practice. A survey from 800 BC*, Aberystwyth: Boethius Press.

Sery, M. (1995) 'Enquête – l'enfance des arts', pp. 28–48 in *Le Monde de l'Education*, No. 228 juillet-août.

5 Music psychology and the secondary music teacher

Alexandra Lamont

Introduction

Psychology represents a scientific approach to understanding 'how the mind works' in a broad range of human endeavours. Music psychology is a relatively new sub-field of psychology, which can be defined as 'the psychological study of human musical endeavour'. There are many points of overlap between music psychology and music education, but the links have not always been fully considered, and traditional disciplinary boundaries make it hard to appreciate the relevance of one field from the other. This chapter will show how researchers in music psychology and music education are often addressing similar questions, albeit from different points of view. Such questions might include the following:

- how do children 'develop' musically?
- are all children equally 'musical'?
- is musical development smooth or in stages?
- are there individual differences in musical development, and if so what causes them?
- is the acquisition of a symbolic understanding of music, for example through music notation, necessary or important for musical development?
- is musical development related to development in any other field, or is it completely self-contained?

A psychological approach to these questions would typically involve some kind of *experimental* study. This might be highly contrived, such as providing a group of students with background music while they work on paper-based tests, comparing their performance with a second group of students working in silence; or it could be more naturalistic, such as observing, recording and analysing children's spontaneous singing. As well as a range of different experimental techniques that can be applied to musical questions, psychology also provides a range of theoretical frameworks for understanding developmental questions like progression and expertise (see Berryman *et al.* 2001 for more detail). Just as there are many different 'flavours' of psychology, such as cognitive, social, developmental, biological and so on, there are many different types of music psychology that can be used to answer these kinds of question. This chapter will include a broad range of experimental techniques and theoretical views intended to help inform your understanding.

Early music psychology has been criticized for having an unclear and limited definition of the kinds of music it studies (e.g. Walker 1987). However, recently the field has expanded considerably to include many diverse areas of music and contexts of musical activity. Music psychology currently covers a broad range of research topics, ranging from the effects of passive exposure to music through to how the mind works in the complex activities of performing, improvising and composing music. It is also beginning to address cross-cultural and sub-cultural differences in these types of musical endeavour, and also to tackle whether music works in the same way for people with different experiences and backgrounds, such as those with and without formal musical training. Most importantly for the current purposes, music psychology is also providing some answers to the questions of musical development.

In an early and influential music psychology text, John Sloboda (1985) makes a useful distinction between enculturation and training, which you may recognize as similar to that in the National Curriculum between more passive and more active forms of musical behaviour. Sloboda defines *enculturation* as resulting from a shared set of primitive capacities, a shared set of experiences provided by culture, and the impact of a rapidly-changing general cognitive system (Sloboda 1985: 195–6). As such, he believes this kind of musical development is common amongst everyone in a given cultural context, and that it explains most of musical development up to the age of about 10 years. *Training*, on the other hand, is seen as a different kind of influence on musical development, involving specific and specialized experiences, self-conscious effort, and instructional methods (Sloboda 1985: 196).

The next sections will explore these two concepts – enculturation and training – in more detail to illustrate different kinds of music psychology research and to show how these can help inform work in the classroom.

Musical development for all – enculturation

The concept of enculturation implies that within a given context everybody will 'learn' the same things about music, in a passive way. This is sometimes also called acculturation, and it is based on the idea that we learn simply through experience. This kind of development is often very closely related to age, although it is not simply 'getting older' that causes it but rather the increased experiences we have as a consequence of the passing of time.

Returning to Sloboda's definition, let's take each element in turn. He firstly suggests that every infant is born with the same set of *primitive capacities*. Some of these capacities are physical, such as the existence of a functional auditory system and neural pathways leading to the brain. Others are perceptual, such as tendencies we might have to be able to perceive differences in sound qualities such as pitch, dynamics, time, timbre and space. Ingenious studies in the womb show that the auditory system is functional from about three months before birth (Lecanuet 1996) and that the foetus can respond to music, showing memory for previously-heard patterns (Shahidullah and Hepper 1994). Newborns have surprisingly sophisticated listening abilities. Research by Sandra Trehub and colleagues has shown that they can detect small differences in pitch, recognize similarities in rhythmic patterns, treat same-contour versions of melodies as different, and group together elements similar in pitch and timbre (for a summary, see Trehub, Schellenberg and Hill 1997). We can think of these abilities as kinds of predispositions in the perceptual system to be able to detect the important elements that are used in music, giving the baby an excellent head-start.

However, these primitive capacities in themselves don't result in any kind of musical understanding. This requires a second component – the *shared set of experiences provided by culture*. The most obvious of these experiences is the music that children actually hear. Although many people have suggested cross-cultural universals in music (e.g. Bernstein 1976), and some musical systems do share some common features, we can define and distinguish different musical cultures and sub-cultures in purely sound-based ways. One is the pitch system used by particular musical traditions. Children growing up in the West will experience music which is heavily based on the structure of western tonal music. Lullabies, nursery rhymes, pop songs, music on television and radio are all characterized by this system (as analysed by Dowling 1988). The role that music plays in different cultural contexts is also important here. For example, in industrialized societies music is omnipresent: on television and radio, in shops, on public transport, and even in doctors' surgeries and waiting rooms. This kind of music is far removed from the live performances concert-goers experience, or the inclusive active music-making activities of some non-western cultures. The contexts of musical experience can be very influential in shaping children's developing understanding of music (see Bronfenbrenner 1979).

Finally, Sloboda also includes the impact of a *rapidly changing cognitive system* in this general pattern of musical enculturation. This means that as children's mental or cognitive abilities develop, these will influence the ways they can understand music (as well as everything else they experience). Although there are aspects of understanding music that might be unique, there are also aspects of musical understanding which depend on and can be affected by the development of other cognitive or mental abilities. Remembering themes when listening to Allegri's *Miserere*, for instance, is likely to be related to the ability to remember other kinds of aurally-presented material such as the multiplication table or the words of a poem. The onset of symbolic skills such as writing and drawing may also have a general influence on children's understanding in a range of areas. Research has explored children's spontaneous and invented notations for music in the early school-age years. Davidson and Scripp (1988; 1989) found that children around 4 or 5 years of age focus on the global aspects of music, such as drawing a picture of a boat for *Row Your Boat*. As children get older, they are able to represent first one dimension of the music (pitch, rhythm, or words) and then more features simultaneously in their notations. Developments in the ability to use marks on the paper to stand for something musical are thus clearly related to the development of this ability in relation to language or to drawing.

In summary, these three elements – predispositions, culture, and cognition – are responsible for most of the musical development that takes place up to the age of about 10 years. You may be thinking that this does not really concern you as a secondary teacher, but the next section will show you how important it is to have some idea of the capacities that might be developed during these early years. I will also show that musical enculturation is likely to continue throughout the lifespan, and that it can help foster other kinds of musical understanding.

Research evidence for musical enculturation

I have just illustrated how each of the three components of musical enculturation can be studied independently. I am now going to describe some research that ties together different features of musical enculturation, to provide us with some broader music psychological frameworks of how children might understand music.

The first is based on research into spontaneous notations for music. Jeanne Bamberger (1982; 1991) has shown how the way children notate music can tell us something about the way they understand it. By asking children of different ages to write down a rhythm, Bamberger found the notations could be grouped into three different types. The first, which she terms 'action drawings', reflect an understanding of music which is purely based on action. These children, aged 4–5, drew a series of dots or squiggles on the page which represented a performance of the rhythm on paper, or drew around their hands to represent the clapping activity. Drawings from older children aged 6–12 represent more specific features of the rhythms, and can be divided into two categories. The first she calls 'figural', indicating an understanding of the shapes and gestures of a rhythmic pattern. Groups are emphasized rather than absolute durational values. The second is termed 'metric', and is found in children with more musical experience or those with formal training, showing an ability to represent the amounts and then the durational values of the rhythm.

Examples of these drawings are shown in Figure 5.1 below (they all represent the same rhythm). Can you work out which rhythm the children are drawing? Which drawings are easier to read, and why?[1]

This kind of research has also been carried out with adults and children with more musical training (Smith *et al.* 1994). Adults are more able to use different features of the rhythmic patterns at different points in time, whereas children with more musical training move between the two kinds of abstract drawings, figural and metric, during a single task. Having formal training seems to give children more flexibility in their understanding of music and the features of music they choose to emphasize when notating. However, Bamberger's earlier work does suggest a U-shaped pattern of development, with representations becoming somewhat stultified and over-formalized during the period when children encounter musical training, and only later moving to this more flexible stage. This shows that formal training may not be 'all good' in terms of developing musical understanding.

The next example of how we can study musical enculturation is drawn from my own work which studies the mental representations that children have for musical pitch (Lamont 1998a, 1998b).

First, here is a brief sidestep to explain the concept of *mental representation*. A

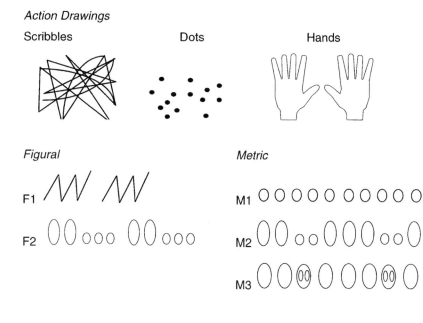

Figure 5.1 Bamberger's typology of rhythm drawings

Source: Adapted from Bamberger 1991: 46.

mental representation is a metaphorical model in the mind that is built up from experience with the world and that helps us understand new things we encounter. These are also sometimes called schemes (the word Piaget used), schemata, frames or scripts (Schank and Abelson 1977). A non-musical example is a script for eating in a restaurant. This consists of a sequence of events that typically occur when we go out for a meal, such as: wait to be shown to a table, look at a menu, order food, wait for food to be delivered, eat food, ask for the bill, pay, and leave. This mental representation has two main purposes. First, it saves us mental effort. Each time we go to a restaurant we don't need to work out from scratch what we need to do to get food; we simply follow the script. It is based on convention, so the waiter also has a script and everybody going to restaurants behaves in similar ways. Second, it helps us in new situations, such as going to a fast-food restaurant. This situation does not match the normal restaurant context (there are no waiters, and the decor is different), which indicates that different actions might be required. Waiting to be shown to a table will not be particularly fruitful in this situation! We can observe other people's actions, learning that whilst the same events are involved, their sequence is different: go to the counter, look at the menu, order food and pay, collect food, eat food, and leave. We then develop a new script for 'fast-food restaurants', and when encountering this kind of situation again we now have a script for dealing with it.

Returning to music psychology, children gradually build up mental representations for the different elements of music, and pitch is a particularly important one in a western context. Through listening to music, and without any conscious effort, children begin to understand which are the important notes in the tonal system. Nursery rhymes and lullabies actually help them do this, as they are stereotypical and tend to emphasize particular notes. Through hearing the same kinds of note relationships time and again, children begin to recognize the functions of the tonic and the dominant, for instance, as being more stable than the other scale notes. Their mental representations of pitch become more clearly defined the more music they hear in this particular system. When they start school, for example, children are able to recognize the difference between diatonic scale notes and non-diatonic notes, but by the time they enter secondary school they have a more sophisticated understanding of the functions of the various scale notes, which continues to develop the more experience they have.

We can study these mental representations by setting children musical 'problems' to solve. One technique is to play a particular musical sequence which should define a particular key, and follow this with all the possible chromatic notes (Krumhansl 1990). The children are asked to judge how well each one 'fits' with the previous sequence, and their ratings can show us how they understand note relations – in essence, what their mental representations 'look like'. I used a range of different musical sequences to define keys, some of which are more stable and conventional (such as a melodically-presented tonic major triad), whilst others are less stable and more bizarre (rapid randomly-ordered sequences of diatonic notes), and gave these problems to a large number of children aged between 5 and 16 in English schools. The children were asked about their family backgrounds, whether they had extra music lessons, and whether they played musical instruments. (All the children routinely played instruments as part of their classroom activities, yet they did not all tell me that they played.)

All children from the age of 5 gave higher ratings for diatonic notes compared with non-diatonic notes following all the context types. This shows that they have already developed a simple mental representation of 'more important' and 'less important' notes, based on their early experiences with music. During the primary school years, this representation becomes more detailed and shows an emphasis on the figural aspects of music, as defined by Bamberger's work above. In the secondary school period, children who say they play musical instruments, who we can think of as more motivated for music, develop to be able to represent music in a formal way (although this is not accompanied by explicit verbal abilities to reflect on their representations), whilst those who say they do not play musical instruments remain at the figural level of understanding. At this stage children are able to represent the full 'tonal hierarchy', showing highest preferences for the tonic, next the other tonic triad notes, and then the remaining diatonic scale notes. Finally, secondary school children with formal musical training reach a final explicit level of musical understanding for pitch, where they add the ability to reflect and consider alternatives to their abstract formal representations. This pattern of development is based on an interaction between age and experience – younger children with more musical experience can respond in similar ways to older children with less experience.

These studies show us how different children's representations of musical pitch can be, and how this seems to be closely related to the kinds of previous experiences they have had with music. In both examples, formal training has a dramatic effect on understanding, but there are also many different layers of understanding amongst those children without formal training. Something as simple as 'listening to music' can be seen to be a complex process for children, as they are in the process of building up their frameworks for knowing how to respond and what judgements to give.

Enculturation in the classroom

From a practical point of view, you might be wondering how this might be relevant to classroom practice. Conventional pedagogical wisdom states that passive experience is not the best way to learn. Whilst I do not dispute this, it is clear that 'passive' experiences do have a role to play in developing musical understanding. The music psychology research shows us how this might work, by illustrating how children respond to particular music at different points in development and how this is affected by their previous experiences. This provides a rationale for basing listening activities on the relevant features that children are able to understand.

Since the research shows us that children can continue to develop their mental representations for music in the secondary school years, these representations can be actively influenced by moulding the kinds of listening experiences that children have. This suggests that the range of music played in the classroom will actually affect pupils' understanding, and also that it may be advisable to begin with music that is not too far removed from the experiences they have had previously. Returning to the restaurant example above, it would be more difficult for a diner to learn the script for a drive-through fast-food restaurant without having previously experienced the more conventional fast-food restaurant. In the same way, music from cultures that share some of the features of western tonal music, such as North Indian music, will be easier to introduce to western pupils than music from a culture which uses an entirely different tuning system and structure of emphases, such as Javanese music.

This research also shows us how important it is not to underestimate the sophistication of pupils' listening skills. If babies are born with the ability to detect the difference between high and low sounds, then why should pupils in the classroom experience such difficulty in accurately describing music in this way? Music psychology research tells us that this cannot be a *perceptual* problem, and thus that the fault may lie with the task we give them. For example, Costa-Giomi and Descombes (1996) found that children's inability to describe pitch as high or low was firmly rooted in the mapping of a musical concept to a verbal one. As soon as the children were taught a separate set of words for *musical* high and low, they had no difficulty in describing these differences accurately (see also Mills, this volume).

Learning to describe something explicitly is quite a different task from being able to detect it implicitly. This section has reviewed some of the research into the implicit aspects of children's musical development. We can understand how children respond to and make judgements about collections of notes, for example, yet the children typically have no explicit awareness of how they reached those judgements. The challenge for music education is to draw out many of these implicit understandings and transform them into explicit knowledge, which is necessary in order to be able to assess such understanding. The next section now moves on to deal with the more conventionally explicit aspects of children's musical development – musical training.

Musical development for the few – training

Sloboda also proposes *training* as an alternative influence on musical development, involving specific and specialized experiences, self-conscious effort, and instructional methods (1985: 196). This kind of development is not necessarily related to age, since children may begin training at any point. In contrast to enculturation, it does not happen simply through experience, but rather is a deliberate activity that some people choose to engage in. Again I'll explore these issues in turn to show how they might be relevant.

The first component of musical training, according to Sloboda, is the notion that not everybody will experience training, and that it is therefore a *specialised activity*. The specific nature of music training means that it does not share many common features with training in other domains (such as sport or playing chess), although there may be some shared elements, like the amount of time devoted to the training or the degree of motivation required to continue with the training programme.

This brings us to the next factor of *self-conscious effort*. What is meant here is not that children have to be painfully aware of what they are doing at every moment, but that it requires effort on the part of the trainees and of which they are aware. The notion of *effort* has been studied in retrospective research into musical excellence by Sloboda and colleagues, showing that children who go on to become professional musicians have amassed on average 10,000 hours of musical practice by the age of 18, whereas children who engage in training but who do not 'make it' in the profession tend to have reached an average of 5,000 hours (Sloboda *et al.* 1996; Sloboda and Davidson 1996).

However, whilst this finding may have made the headlines, the research stresses several important factors which explain how children actually reach these levels of practice. These include motivation, developing from an initial emphasis on extrinsic motivation (external encouragement and reward) into intrinsic motivation (reward from the activity itself rather than external sources); parental and peer group support; gender biases for particular instruments; and the quality of the instrumental teachers. This brings us to the final component of Sloboda's definition – *instructional methods*. Research has focused on a number of ways that the teacher can influence the learning process (e.g. Davidson *et al.* 1998; Sloboda and Howe 1991; Jorgensen and Lehmann 1987), which will be discussed below.

Research evidence for musical training

The same questions can be posed for the development of musical expertise and musical training as we asked for general or normative musical development. Do children progress in the same way? Can all children benefit equally from music training? What should we expect from children of different ages and different levels of motivation? Again I will provide some answers by focusing on a few specific research studies in these areas.

One way of looking at musical training is as a kind of expertise. Psychological studies of expertise in other fields, such as chess, show that experts have a wider pool of resources to draw on which have been developed through extensive effort and practice, and that they often show more sophisticated strategies. A child chess expert has a better memory for chessboard layouts than an adult chess novice, but in terms of other non-chess-related kinds of memory the child will perform at a lower level than the adult (Chi 1978). The same kinds of differences are found with musically-trained children, who are much better at recalling a tonal melody than 'novice' adults (Oura and Hatano 1988). Adults with music training are often shown to outperform adults without training on a range of music perceptual tasks (Smith 1997).

How then might such expertise be developed? The expertise literature focuses mainly on decoding the nature of the skills and showing how individuals acquire these more efficient strategies. For music training, one very important strategy is that of practice, as shown by Sloboda's research. This has mainly been studied using retrospective methods, where individuals reflect back on experiences in childhood, to explore any features that successful or expert musicians may have had in common. Early starting ages seem to be advantageous for musical performers, particularly for pianists and violinists (Ericsson, Krampe and Tesch-Römer 1993). However, the importance and quality of practice is also emphasized. Andreas Lehmann (1997) discusses the features of this practice, distinguishing between 'sub-optimal' and 'deliberate' practice. Children who begin their training earlier, Lehmann shows us, and who are closely supervised (by parents or live-in teachers) typically reach more efficient deliberate practice strategies sooner and to higher levels than children who begin later or who do not have such supervision. Sloboda's studies also show that early teachers are often seen as 'warm' whilst later teachers are valued for their technical qualities, in the retrospective accounts of successful musicians.

The 'expertise' position assumes that music training is an isolated and separate area of skill. A different strand of research has adopted the alternative view that there may be possible transfer effects from music to other areas of children's development. Studies typically use an 'intervention' technique, where a group of children are randomly selected to experience a period of music training and a second group of children are given another kind of activity. Non-musical abilities are tested before training begins and at various stages during and after the training programme, and improvements in the music training group can be assumed to be due to the training itself rather than to any other factors.

Some of the results are contradictory, but music training has been shown to have one very specific non-musical effect. Children aged between 3 and 6 who experienced at least six months of piano lessons show an improvement in their spatial-temporal reasoning skills (e.g. Rauscher *et al.* 1997; Rauscher and Zupan 2000). (Spatial-temporal skills are used, for example, in following a map, involving relations in space that unfold over time, and have also been linked to certain kinds of mathematics abilities such as fractions and ratios; Graziano, Peterson and Shaw 1999). These findings have been used to suggest that early music training operates as a kind of brain exercise which helps strengthen connections in the spatial-temporal domain (Shaw 2000). The effectiveness of the piano compared with other kinds of musical training like singing (which do not produce these effects) is believed to relate to the spatial nature of the keyboard layout alongside the temporal nature of music. The findings are rather difficult to replicate (see Chabris 1999) and seem to be highly dependent on the way in which spatial-temporal skills are tested.

Research has also explored the long-term effects of music training on other abilities. Training has been found to help improve other skills that require temporal abilities, such as reading, particularly for children with dyslexia (Overy 2000). There is limited evidence for improvements in self-esteem (Costa-Giomi 1997) and in personal and social relationships (Zulauf 1993). Another kind of intervention work has explored children's attitudes towards gender stereotypes for particular musical instruments. Harrison and O'Neill (2000) tested three groups of 7–8-year-old children's gender-typed preferences for different musical instruments. One group then saw a concert with gender-consistent role models (a woman playing the flute or a man playing the drums), a second group saw gender-inconsistent role models, and a third group had no concert. Retesting the children's preferences for instruments after the concerts, the gender-inconsistent role models resulted in a change in preferences, with girls showing less preference for the piano after watching a man playing it and boys giving less preference to the guitar after they watched a woman playing it. Children in the gender-consistent and the 'control' groups did not change their preferences. These studies suggest that music can be a forum for exploring personal relationships and attitudes about social roles, and that these can actually be modified in some ways through the experiences that musical activities afford.

Training is most commonly associated with learning to play a musical instrument and performance skills. However, we also need to think about other kinds of generative skills that go to form perhaps the most important part of music – creating music. The most well-known research in this field is the developmental spiral model proposed by Swanwick and Tillman (1986), based on analysis of children's compositions at school. This model assumes a stage-like progression in children's compositional skills, with a progression from individual to societal within each of four distinct levels of sophistication. The four levels are *materials, expression, form* and *value*, corresponding (approximately) to ages 4–5, 7–8, 10–11 and 14 onwards. The two sub-stages of individual and social (referring to the Piagetian notions of assimilation and accommodation) within each of these levels produce eight modes of development (see also Mills, this volume). A developmental study with Brazilian children (Swanwick and Franca 1999) extends this model to apply to listening and performance skills as well as compositional abilities, finding that children's performance abilities in music often lag behind on the spiral. Returning to the social dimension of music-making, Miell and MacDonald (2000) have highlighted the importance of friendship-based collaborations in children's group work on composition, with pairs of friends engaging in deeper levels of interaction and producing more sophisticated compositions than non-friend pairs.

Musical training and the classroom

When we think of expert musicians, they often seem to be far removed from the kinds of musical activities carried out in the classroom. However, a great deal of the current National Curriculum is focused on developing some very specific musical skills in pupils. Some of these take the model of the expert as the intended end-point, but the activities of 'composing', 'performing', and 'improvising' at school often look very different from these expert types of behaviour. Music psychology research is particularly critical for the music teacher as it shows us the origins of this kind of activity and what it takes to reach those end-points. Clearly, not every child will go on to become an expert, and indeed many will not even opt to study Music beyond Key Stage 3. However, if pupils can be given a flavour of what it is to be a musician in this expert sense, then their learning will undoubtedly be strengthened, and a culture of musicianship in schools may be built up. At the very least, KS3 might be made a little more enjoyable!

The research on musical enculturation shows us that children can reach a sophisticated level of musical 'appreciation' without requiring formal training or any particularly specialized kind of music education, although clearly these will assist any child in reaching deeper levels of understanding. Aspects of the research on musical training can also be applied in a more focused way to classroom work. One important point is the emphasis on the specialized nature of musical training. Again this is not to dismiss the importance of working on cross-curricular themes, drawing links between the study of music history, for example, and general history, or sounds and science. But it is also important to recognize the individual and unique nature of music and the specialist skills it requires. (If this sounds a little like the current National Curriculum for England and Wales then you might be interested to know that, for the first time, two music psychologists were on the panel that drafted these documents.)

Another simple implication from this research is the issue of effort. Clearly, again, it is every teacher's goal to encourage (and cajole) their classes into putting effort into their work. It can be important in the context of composing and performing to recognize that in order to achieve a degree of mastery at these activities, pupils will need to devote time to them. They will not all be able to produce flawless performances of well-structured compositions off the cuff, and more opportunities for important practising time may be necessary, as well as encouraging pupils to learn from examples of famous and successful musicians (whether these are classical or not) who all had to strive to achieve their success.

On a related point, the music psychological literature helps to dispel some common myths about 'musical excellence' which it may be useful to re-emphasise in terms of the school classroom. An important myth relates to musical heredity. Instrumental teachers in particular often talk about musical talent or genius as if it were a fixed and innate ability which some children have and others do not. However, the research on musical training shows even more clearly that there is nothing mystical about musical ability in terms of performance. Although less research has been carried out on musical composition, it is apparent that this may be very similar. Again, whilst classes will differ in terms of ability, music psychology shows us that the vast majority of these differences will be due to differences in pupils' past experiences and attitudes, and these need not be treated as insurmountable.

Finally, whilst some studies have focused on children who choose to engage in music training, the intervention studies discussed above take a different approach by investigating the effects that music training can have on children who have not chosen to participate. These studies are particularly relevant for teachers of compulsory music classes who have to deal with some unwilling participants! Although the research evidence can be contradictory, it is interesting to see that formal music training, particularly on the keyboard, does seem to have some transfer effects in terms of other cognitive abilities even for children who are not motivated to participate. However, the studies of instrumental players indicate that individual motivation for a particular activity is far more critical than any transfer effects we might see, and thus developing motivation amongst pupils to engage with these compulsory programmes is a far more useful educational aim. Whilst music training may have extra-musical benefits, these are likely to be far less important than the specifically musical benefits that engaging in playing, improvising and composing music will bring to pupils in school.

Enculturation and training – a useful framework?

I have used the concepts of enculturation and training to divide up the field of music psychology research with an emphasis on development. It's time now to consider how these can relate together to be useful concepts when thinking about classroom practice.

The research shows us that enculturation does not stop at the age of 10, but can continue over the lifespan. This means it will be important to take account of and nurture this kind of musical development in the secondary school years. Pupils at every stage need to hear plenty of music, as well as being guided in how to listen to it. Their existing frameworks can be built on by moving to new and different musical styles and traditions in small steps.

Whilst musical training is often considered as the preserve of the select few, it is possible to engender elements of the processes of musical expertise even in those pupils who would not think of themselves as being particularly interested in music. Research shows us that this can have important consequences for pupils' understanding outside the domain of music, as well as strengthening their musical understanding and developing their technical and practical musical skills.

Finally, we often characterize children as 'musicians' and 'non-musicians' on the basis of whether they appear to demonstrate any kind of musical ability – most often based on whether they can play or compose, or less often on whether they show any interest in listening to music. Assessment procedures often serve to reinforce these distinctions. The SCAA documentation provides an excellent example of this in its characterizations of two different pupils' achievement in Music:

> Simon plays keyboard, piano, and a range of tuned percussion with confidence and control. He chooses from this wide range of instruments and is happy to experiment in order to get the exact sound he wants. He is a good ensemble player. He plays with confidence and fits his part with the other parts in a musically sensitive way ... Simon identifies conventions and utilises them in his own work ... He has a real understanding of how music works and is extremely interested in a vast range of music. Simon is able to hear and describe features of music at a sophisticated level. He recognises instruments and conventions, and analyses how textures are put together ... He has an excellent musical and expressive vocabulary, which enables him to analyse and comment clearly on changes in character and mood and make connections between music and its context.
>
> (SCAA 1996: 37)

> Teresa plays a range of classroom instruments, although she prefers the xylophone. She can perform with confidence, especially when she is given help by other members of the group and sufficient time to practise. However, her playing technique is basic. She tends to play relatively simple parts and does not make adjustments to reflect the effect or mood ... Whilst she has a musical vocabulary she often fails to recognise musical devices when listening to music ... She is able to make comparisons between stylistically similar music but her comments tend to stay at a simplistic level, referring to musical elements such as tempo and structure.
>
> (SCAA 1996: 23)

Extrapolating from the research in music psychology, we can begin to explain some of these differences. Simon, let's assume, has had piano lessons since he was 11 years old, with a visiting peripatetic music teacher, and he has learnt a wide variety of music, including Beethoven, Debussy and Gershwin. He would like to learn a brass instrument like the trombone or tuba and be in the school brass group with his friends. His parents often listen to classical music at home, and he has his own collection of classical and popular CDs. He likes music lessons at school as well as maths and science. Teresa, on the other hand, is an avid pop music fan. She loves chart music and often sings along to the music either on her own or with her friends at school. She doesn't play a musical instrument, and thinks the children who do are boring because they don't know anything about pop music and they don't wear trendy clothes. She finds music difficult at school but is good at English and history.

These two fictional case histories begin to help the teacher who has to teach these two pupils in the same class to understand how to encourage and develop their different ways of understanding music. Simon has an interest in classical music as well as the ability to read notation, and he has parental support for his music training. These qualities make him easier to teach, and his achievements at school music are clear from the quotations above. Simon deserves attention on two counts: first, whilst the teacher should obviously recognize his abilities, he should not be singled out as a 'musician' who does not need any more help in the class-room, and second, he should be encouraged to maintain his intuitive and sponta-neous enjoyment of music alongside the rule-based elements of musical understanding. Teresa, conversely, associates classical music with being boring. Her interest may be sparked by the inclusion of different forms of music-making, including pop as well as music of other cultures. She is struggling with the class-room activities of composing and performing and is not at present able to bring any emotional qualities to her music-making at school, although it would be easy to imagine her impassioned renditions of All Saints in her bedroom. Through her informal experience with music, Teresa does have considerably sophisticated ways of responding to and understanding music, and the research shows that these can be encouraged and developed through appropriate activities and contexts. She needs to be treated as a musician, perhaps of a different kind to Simon, but no less able to benefit from appropriate teaching and encouragement to reach her full musical potential.

Whilst there are vast differences in individual children's approaches to music, it is extremely rare to find a child who has no interest in music whatsoever – indeed, you might want to check for hearing difficulties in such cases. Music psychology can provide ways of understanding some of these differences alongside the pattern of norms that might be expected, and this chapter has shown how these can be useful in a practical setting.

Resources

A glance through the references for this chapter indicates that a high proportion of music psychology research is published in mainstream psychology journals. Whilst you are not discouraged from following these up, they are mostly aimed at a general psychology readership and may be less accessible. There are several journals specifically devoted to publishing research in music psychology that you may find more useful.

Psychology of Music is published by the Society for Research into Psychology of Music and Music Education (SRPMME) (two issues per year). This journal covers research in both psychology of music and music education, and most articles make some attempt to relate their findings to music education. Two other publications also focus specifically on music psychology research. *Music Perception* is a high-quality journal published by the University of California Press with four issues per year. It deals mainly with the perceptual and cognitive aspects of music psychology, with very little social or developmental work (although there are exceptions). *Psychomusicology*, published by the Center for Music Research at Florida University, appears less regularly but often contains interesting arti-cles, again focused mainly on the perception and cognition of music. You will also find some music psychology research published in mainstream music education journals such as *Music Education Research* or the *British Journal of Music Education*.

The SPRMME is a useful organization, holding biannual day conferences on themes of interest to music educators and sponsoring an email discussion list (PSYMUS) dealing with music psychology-related issues. You can find more information at http://www.srpmme.org.uk or by checking the current edition of *Psychology of Music*.

Note

1   The rhythm being drawn by Bamberger's children in Figure 5.1 is 'three, four, shut the door, five, six, pick up sticks'. People who are musically trained find the 'metric' drawings the easiest to read because they are the closest to standard musical notation. Most people without musical training, even adults, will tend to produce drawings more like the 'figural' versions. None of these drawings are better than the others — they simply prioritise and emphasise different aspects of the rhythm.

References

Bamberger, J. (1982) 'Revisiting children's drawings of simple rhythms: a function of reflection-in-action', in S. Strauss (ed.) *U-shaped Behavioral Growth*, New York: Academic Press.

—— (1991) *The Mind Behind the Musical Ear: How Children Develop Musical Intelligence*, Cambridge, MA: Harvard University Press.

Bernstein, L. (1976) *The Unanswered Question: Six Talks at Harvard*, London: Harvard University Press.

Berryman, J.C., Joiner, R., Smythe, P., Taylor Davies, A. and Lamont, A. (2001) *Developmental Psychology and You*, Leicester: BPS Books (2nd edn).

Bronfenbrenner, U. (1979) *The Ecology of Human Development*, Cambridge, MA: Harvard University Press.

Chabris, C. (1999) 'Prelude or Requiem for the "Mozart Effect"?' *Nature*, 400: 827–8.

Chi, M.T.H. (1978) 'Knowledge structures and memory development', in R.S. Siegler (ed.) *Children's Thinking: What Develops?*, Hillsdale, NJ: Lawrence Erlbaum.

Costa-Giomi, E. (1997) 'The McGill Piano Project: effects of piano instruction on children's cognitive abilities', *Proceedings of the Third Triennial ESCOM Conference*, Uppsala University, Sweden: 446–50.

Costa-Giomi, E. and Descombes, V. (1996) 'Pitch labels with single and multiple meanings: a study with french-speaking children', *Journal of Research in Music Education*, 44: 204–14.

Davidson, J.W., Sloboda, J.A., Moore, D.G. and Howe, M.J.A. (1998) 'Characteristics of music teachers and the progress of young instrumentalists', *Journal for Research in Music Education*, 46: 141–160.

Davidson, L. and Scripp, L. (1988), 'Young children's musical representations: windows on music cognition', in J.A. Sloboda (ed.) *Generative Processes in Music: The Psychology of Performance, Improvisation, and Composition*, Oxford: Clarendon Press.

—— (1989) Education and development in music from a cognitive perspective, in D.J. Hargreaves (ed.) *Children and the Arts*, Milton Keynes: Open University Press.

Dowling, W.J. (1988) 'Tonal structure and children's early learning of music', in J.A. Sloboda (ed.) *Generative Processes in Music: The Psychology of Performance, Improvisation and Composition*, Oxford: Clarendon Press.

Ericsson, K.A., Krampe, R.T. and Tesch-Römer, C. (1993) 'The role of deliberate practice in the acquisition of expert performance', *Psychological Review*, 100: 363–406.

Graziano, A.B., Peterson, M. and Shaw, G.L. (1999) 'Enhanced learning of proportional math through music training and spatial-temporal training', *Neurological Research*, 21: 139–52.

Harrison, A.C. and O'Neill, S.A. (2000) 'Children's gender-typed preferences for musical instruments: an intervention study', *Psychology of Music*, 28: 81–97.

Jorgensen, H. and Lehmann, A.C. (1997) *Does Practice Make Perfect? Current Theory and Research on Instrumental Music Practice*, Oslo: Norges Musikhogskule.

Krumhansl, C.L. (1990) *Cognitive Foundations of Musical Pitch*, Oxford: Oxford University Press.

Lamont, A. (1998a) 'Music, education, and the development of pitch perception: the role of context, age, and musical experience', *Psychology of Music*, 26: 7–25.

—— (1998b) *Cognitive Representations of Musical Pitch in Development*, unpublished PhD dissertation, University of Cambridge.

Lecanuet, J-P. (1996) 'Prenatal auditory experience', in I. Deliège and J. Sloboda (eds) *Musical Beginnings: Origins and Development of Musical Competence*, Oxford: Oxford University Press.

Lehmann, A. (1997) 'The acquisition of expertise in music: efficiency of deliberate practice as a moderating variable in accounting for sub-expert performance' in I. Deliège and J. Sloboda (eds) *Perception and Cognition of Music*, Hove: Psychology Press.

Miell, D. and MacDonald, R. (2000) 'Children's creative collaborations: the importance of friendship when working together on a musical composition', *Social Development*, 9(3): 348–69.

O'Neill, S.A. and Sloboda, J.A. (1997) 'The effects of failure on children's ability to perform a musical test', *Psychology of Music*, 25: 18–34.

Oura, Y. and Hatano, G. (1988) 'Memory for melodies among subjects differing in age and experience in music, *Psychology of Music*, 16: 91–109.

Overy, K. (2000) 'Dyslexia, temporal processing and music: the potential of music as an early learning aid for dyslexic children', *Psychology of Music*, 28(2): 218–29.

Rauscher, F.H. and Zupan, M. (2000) 'Classroom keyboard instruction improves kindergarten children's spatial-temporal performance: A field experiment', *Early Childhood Research Quarterly*, 15(2): 215–28.

Rauscher, F.H., Shaw, G.L., Levine, L.J., Wright, E.L., Dennis, W.R. and Newcomb, R.L. (1997) 'Music training causes long-term enhancement of preschool children's spatial-temporal reasoning', *Neurological Research*, 19: 2–8.

SCAA (1996) *Consistency in Teacher Assessment: Exemplification of Standards, Music: Key Stage 3*, London: School Curriculum and Assessment Authority Publications.

Schank, R.C. and Abelson, R.P. (1977) *Scripts, plans, goals and understanding*, Hillsdale, NJ: Lawrence Erlbaum.

Shahidullah, S. and Hepper, P.G. (1994) 'Frequency discrimination by the fetus', *Early Human Development*, 36: 13–26.

Shaw, G.L. (2000) *Keeping Mozart in Mind*, San Diego, CA: Academic Press.

Sloboda, J.A. (1985) *The Musical Mind: The Cognitive Psychology of Music*, Oxford: Clarendon Press.

Sloboda, J.A. and Davidson, J.W. (1996) 'The young performing musician' in I. Deliège and J. Sloboda (eds) *Musical Beginnings: Origins and Development of Musical Competence*, Oxford: Oxford University Press.

Sloboda, J.A. and Howe, M. (1991) 'Biographical precursors of musical excellence: an interview study', *Psychology of Music*, 19: 3–21.

Sloboda, J.A., Davidson, J.W., Howe, M.J.A. and Moore, D.G. (1996) 'The role of practice in the development of expert musical performance', *British Journal of Psychology*, 87: 287–309.

Smith, J.D. (1997) 'The place of musical novices in music science', *Music Perception*, 14: 227–62.

Smith, K.C., Cuddy, L.L. and Upitis, R. (1994) 'Figural and metric understanding of rhythm, *Psychology of Music*, 22: 117–35.

Swanwick, K. and Franca, C.C. (1999) 'Composing, performing and audience-listening as indicators of musical understanding', *British Journal of Music Education*, 16(1): 5–19.

Swanwick, K. and Tillman, J. (1986) 'The sequence of musical development: a study of children's composition', *British Journal of Music Education*, 6: 305–39.

Trehub, S.E., Schellenberg, E.G. and Hill, D. (1997) 'The origins of music perception and cognition: a developmental perspective', in I. Deliège and J. Sloboda (eds) *Perception and Cognition of Music*, Hove: Psychology Press.

Walker, R. (1987) 'Musical perspectives on psychological research and music education', *Psychology of Music*, 15: 167–86.

Zulauf, M. (1993) 'Three-year experiment in extended music teaching in Switzerland', *Bulletin of the Council for Research in Music Education*, 119: 111–21.

6 Musical development in the primary years

Janet Mills

Research in musical development

During the twentieth century, and particularly over the last thirty or so years, psychological research into children's musical qualities has mushroomed. Early research, such as that carried out by Carl Seashore at the turn of this century, was in the tradition of psychometric testing, and took place under carefully controlled conditions. It explored research questions concerned with musical perception. What is the highest note that can be perceived? What is the smallest pitch interval that can be recognized? Do the answers to these two questions depend on age? Measurement often required the use of sophisticated apparatus, and sometimes took place in laboratories.

Research into perception continues to this day and has a relevance to music education which is sometimes overlooked. But, alongside this, a tradition of exploring children's activity as musicians is developing. Here, the research questions are more directly related to composing, performing, listening and classrooms. How do children develop as composers? In what circumstances do children learn to sing in tune? And so on.

These two research traditions are not necessarily in opposition. The results of investigations in one tradition sometimes inform the questions asked in the other. Indeed, some researchers have worked in both areas at various points of their career. But because the questions asked are so different, and because the relevance of the research to music education is of a different nature, I consider the two areas separately.

Children as perceivers

Research in aural perception can be concerned with any of the parameters of sound, such as pitch, loudness or timbre. I shall focus on just one aspect of perception: pitch discrimination. This is the ability to assess that there is a difference in the pitch of two tones. Investigations of pitch discrimination often explore how close in pitch tones must be before they are judged to be the same. They may also explore whether the direction of the pitch movement can be assessed accurately. Thus an individual having his or her pitch discrimination assessed might be asked to listen to two tones and say whether the second one is the same, higher, or lower. One's ability in pitch discrimination depends on the frequency range used. Very high and very low intervals are harder to discriminate. The investigations referred to below use a frequency range in which children find discrimination particularly easy: their vocal range.

Children's pitch discrimination has been investigated by many researchers. The pattern that has emerged is as follows:

Children can discriminate very small intervals

In 1893, J. A. Gilbert (Shuter-Dyson and Gabriel 1981) found that children aged 7 could, on average, assess the direction of some intervals as small as two-thirds of a semitone. In the early 1960s, Arnold Bentley (1966) found they could assess one-third of a semitone. In the early 1980s, I found (Mills 1988a) that the average 7 year-old could assess an interval as small as one-sixth of a semitone, that is, a 1 per cent difference in frequency. Thus several researchers have agreed that normal 7 year-olds can discriminate very small intervals. Quite how small does not matter for the purposes of this argument. The discrepancies between the three sets of findings are probably attributable to the differing quality of the recording and replay equipment available at the time (Mills 1984); there is no reason to suppose that the children of the 1990s necessarily have pitch discrimination any finer than those of the 1890s.

Researchers of pitch discrimination have often reported the results of work with children aged at least 6 years. This is usually simply because younger children might have difficulty coping with the test situation, which often requires children to write their responses. There is no evidence that younger children do not perceive fine differences in pitch. Indeed, Bridger (1961) observed that some babies aged under five days notice pitch differences of about four semitones, and they may be able to perceive much smaller intervals. It is difficult to understand how children could acquire language, and particularly accent, without some pitch discrimination.

Children's discrimination improves with age

Bentley and Gilbert both wrote of marked improvement over the junior years and into the secondary years. I found that the average 11 year-old is able to assess the direction of an interval of about a 0.85 per cent difference in frequency. Thus the average 11-year-old ear competes with much scientific equipment for sensitivity.

In any age group, there is a considerable range of ability

This has been observed by many researchers. I found some children as young as 9 who could judge the direction of an interval as small as one-tenth of a semitone, that is, about a 0.6 per cent difference in frequency.

What is the use of these findings? Researchers (for example, Seashore 1938; Bentley 1966; Mills 1988a) used the range of ability, coupled with the observation that successful performers tend to have superior discrimination, as a basis for devising musical ability tests that include tests of pitch discrimination. The generally fine discrimination of children was, if anything, a nuisance. It meant that tests had to include very small intervals if they were to differentiate between children. And very small intervals are difficult to record accurately.

But some other implications of the three points I have drawn from the pitch discrimination research have more immediate relevance to class teachers.

Teaching the concept of pitch (up/down)

Pitch is one of the basic concepts of music. Understanding of pitch is one of the objectives set for 7 year-olds in *Music from 5 to 16* (DES 1985a). Yet many 7 year-olds do not understand it. We might suppose that a child who has yet to achieve this objective is unable to perceive the pitch differences we are presenting. Our reaction might be to present progressively larger pitch differences to children, in the hope of finding an interval wide enough for them to notice. But as the research shows that the average 7 year-old can discriminate differences much smaller than those usual in music, the child's problem may be labelling, not perception (see Crowther and Durkin 1982). 'Up' and 'down' are terms associated with spatial movement. Their application to a musical context may need explanation and illustration. Teachers often approach this through the association of musical movement with spatial movement. Children may be asked to sing up a scale as they walk up some steps. They may use a hand to draw the contour of the pitch of a melody that they are listening to or singing.

Many children learn the concept of pitch easily using these sorts of techniques. Where problems persist into the junior phase, a teacher may wish to test a child's pitch discrimination using a published test (for example, Mills 1988a). In any case, it would be unwise to assume that a child who does not sing in tune necessarily has any problem with discrimination (see page 65).

One question remains. If children have problems with the labelling of pitch movement, how do they manage to do pitch discrimination tests? The answer is, I think, linked with the recorded instructions that children are given as part of the test. These seem to be sufficient to enable children to apply the concept throughout the test, even if the children do not remember it, or become able to apply it on other more musical occasions. Certainly, some children who do not seem to understand the concept in a musical context display it during the test. Of course, there may be other children who would benefit from even more comprehensive instructions.

Coping with musically able children

The considerable variation in pitch discrimination in any age group means that some children have finer pitch discrimination than some teachers. This means that tuning tasks that are difficult for teachers are not necessarily difficult for children. A teacher is not necessarily the best arbiter of what is, or is not, in tune. This has some immediate implications. When children assert that two seemingly identical notes are different, we need to take them seriously. A child who complains that a guitar that her teacher has just tuned is out of tune may be justified. If such children are suppressed by statements such as 'it will do' or 'there's nothing the matter with it', they may not bother to listen so closely in future. Rather, their ability can be employed to the teacher's advantage: the children can assist the teacher with tuning.

There are all sorts of musical activities in which teachers can find that some children are more able than they are. This happens to everyone, not just those who have not had much formal musical experience. The most highly qualified music graduates still find children who play some instrument or other better than they do. We have to suppress a natural reaction to be threatened by this, and instead work out how to use some children's ability to promote the development of less fortunate children, and also ourselves.

Diagnosing children's musical problems

The masking of fine pitch discrimination by difficulty with verbal labelling shows the need to think carefully about the causes of children's musical problems. Does inability to echo a clapped rhythm indicate poor rhythmic memory, or some difficulty with motor co-ordination? Does failure to walk in time with a piece of music necessarily mean that a child cannot hear its regular pulse? Musical perception takes place inside the brain; we cannot tap directly into it. If we want to know whether someone is perceiving accurately or not, we have to ask them to sing, speak, write or move, for instance, and then measure how well they do that. Any problem may result from difficulty with the singing, speaking, writing or moving itself, rather than the perception.

Setting expectations for children

The significant variation in children's discrimination is a reminder of the need to guard against setting expectations of children so low that they become unable to show us what they can do. Recognition of the dangers of underestimating children is crucial to the effectiveness of curriculum planning.

The implications I have drawn from this research are personal. I have made use of the researchers' findings according to my particular circumstances as a music teacher. Teachers in different situations may see other implications as more significant. The point is that research questions that seem not to address concerns central to music education can still yield answers that are both relevant and useful. In particular, investigation of a characteristic that is at best only a component of musical activity can have implications relevant to music education.

That said, there are many research questions that can be answered more effectively through investigation of real music-making by children. We now turn to a selection of these.

Children as musicians

In this section, I focus on three studies. Each is based on children's ordinary musical activity in classrooms; in two the children are composing, and in the third they are performing. In each case, I draw out some implications of relevance to teaching and curriculum planning. The emphasis here is mine, not the research-ers'. The first study, an investigation of children's sequential development as composers, culminates in the proposition of a model of composing development which may also have wider applicability. The second, an investigation of children's development as song composers, serves also as a reminder of the danger of adher-ence to a simple model; development is inevitably multi-faceted, and not always apparently sequential. The third, an investigation of infants' developing vocal accuracy, points to the fact that a music curriculum intended for one group of chil-dren may be inappropriate for others.

Children's sequential development as composers

How do children develop as composers? If children were all to follow the same pattern in their development as composers, then life as a music teacher would be straightforward. Given that a child had produced a composition at some partic-ular position in this pattern, we would know where she or he was destined to move next; our job would be simply to lead the child there. As we all know, no aspect of child development – or even human development – is like that. Every model of learning is the result of some generalization, and few individuals follow any so-called normal patterns of development literally for more than the briefest period. There are many curriculum activities in which we accept this. Although we discern general patterns of development in children's writing or painting, we learn to respond to the expressive and technical aspects of work that seem to be out of sequence. We adapt reading and mathematics schemes to suit children's individual needs by adding a book here, or missing out a section there. The idea of a sequential model of children's musical development may be attractive, but we cannot expect it to answer all our questions about response to children's music-making.

In their article, 'The sequence of musical development: a study of children's composition' (Swanwick and Tillman 1986), Keith Swanwick and June Tillman describe a spiral model of development represented by the helix shown in Figure 6.1. The theoretical basis of the spiral arises from consideration of the psycholog-ical concepts of mastery, imitation, imaginative play and metacognition, and draws on the work of writers including Jean Piaget (1951), Helmut Moog (1976), Robert Bunting (1977) and Malcolm Ross (1984). The empirical evidence for the spiral arises from observation of several hundred compositions by forty-eight children taught, at various stages, by June Tillman.

The figures at the right-hand side of the helix correspond to the approximate ages at which Swanwick and Tillman believe children pass through the turns. Although only the first three turns are likely to be seen in primary school, I shall, for the sake of completeness, summarize all four. Using the explanation and exam-ples provided by Tillman (1988: 85–6), let us follow a fictional child, Julie, as she progresses, over ten years or so, from the sensory mode and a concern with materials, through to the systematic mode and a concern with value.

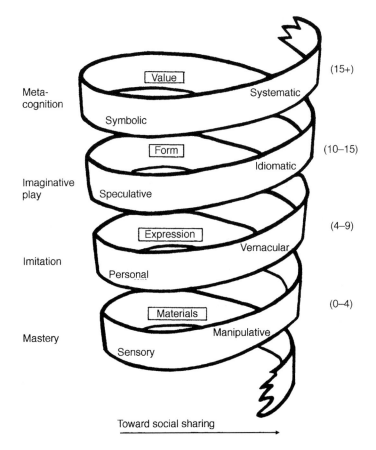

Figure 6.1 The Swanwick/Tillman model of musical development

Source: Swanwick, K. and Tillman, J. (1986) 'The sequence of musical development: a study of children's composition', *British Journal of Music Education*, 3(3): 331.

Turn 1: materials

Sensory mode

As Julie explores the tone colour of instruments in a seemingly random manner, she seems to be asking the question: 'What sound does it make?'. She is fascinated by the rattle of a tambourine and the rasping sound of the scraper.

Manipulative mode

Now, Julie seems to want to organize the sound she makes. Sometimes she beats out a steady pulse. Some of the patterns that she chooses – such as a glide up and down a xylophone – seem influenced by instrument shape.

Turn 2: expression

Julie's concern with materials continues. But two new modes develop.

Personal mode

Julie starts to show expressive character in her songs, and later in her instrumental compositions. The character is most clearly seen through changes in dynamics and speed. A song about the sun shining gets louder and faster until Julie 'almost shines herself'.

Vernacular mode

As Julie starts to use repeated melodies and rhythmic patterns, her compositions become shorter and less apparently exploratory. Her composition appears more derivative.

Turn 3: form

Again, two new modes develop.

Speculative

Julie starts to use contrast in her compositions. A repeated rhythm will suddenly change to give a feeling of surprise. Gradually, her use of contrast and surprise becomes more polished.

Idiomatic

Julie works within a particular musical idiom. This may be pop or jazz, or if she has taken piano lessons she may start to compose piano pieces in a style similar to those she has been learning.

Turn 4: value

Now two final modes are added.

Symbolic

Julie investigates a wider range of styles.

Systematic

Julie develops a personal and distinctive style which draws on her work in various idioms, and which she may adapt for particular pieces.

The frame of reference of the spiral is the compositions of a group of children. Yet it seems also to explain some other musical behaviour. Swanwick (1988) applies it to the account of a teenager at his first sitar recital. After some minutes of incomprehension, the teenager becomes impressed by the sounds themselves (Turn 1), then the shapes and colours they imply (Turn 2), before getting inside the structure to the extent that he becomes susceptible to surprise (Turn 3).

This is an experience that many of us have had as we start to listen to music of a type with which we are unfamiliar. To begin with, the music seems without shape, meaningless. We might wonder if the choice of notes and timing is arbitrary. Gradually, we find something that we can hold onto, even if we cannot explain what that is. Finally, we feel inside the idiom. We know what is arbitrary and what is not. We accept the idiom on its own terms.

We have to be careful not to generalize too far from this. A model that works well in one restricted situation, and seems to make sense in another, is not necessarily true of all musical activity. We do not know if it applies to the work of other teachers of composing, or to performing, or to all forms of listening. Neither do we know the extent to which it makes sense to superimpose composing, performing and listening spirals, for instance, and talk about a spiral of musical development.

Curriculum planning becomes less hassle-ridden when someone else has determined the aims of your curriculum. It can be tempting to cling to the spiral, to devise curriculums intended solely to promote helical progression and to assess children mainly – or possibly only – in terms of where, spirally speaking, they are. But the evidence for the validity of the spiral in all these contexts is, as yet, slender. And some potential areas of application would appear to require development as well as evidence. The use of a spiral model for assessment is fraught with difficulty. If it is musical to revisit lower turns, for instance to absorb new musical experiences, then nobody can be assessed simply in terms of how high up the spiral he or she is.

While we wait for further evidence, we may wish to think of the spiral as we try to make sense of children's music making. But this should be critical thinking; we should be testing the spiral, not using it as a frame of reference. We should also be open to other ways of thinking about children's composing, performing and listening. The responsibility for curriculum planning, teaching and assessment must continue to rest with us. Being the best model around is not enough. If we don spiral-shaped blinkers, we may miss something even better.

Children's development as song composers

Coral Davies's (1986) article, 'Say it till a song comes', offers an approach to thinking about a particular field of children's composing: song. Davies reflects on a collection of more than twenty songs composed by children aged 3–13. She seems not to be searching for a pattern of development so much as for a way of responding to the composition itself. Thus her approach is more reminiscent of that of Loane's (1984) work with secondary children than that of Swanwick and Tillman. Most of the children concerned were not learning to compose in any sustained way. Often, they produced their songs so that they could sing them in a play. Usually, they wrote the words first, and then repeated them rhythmically until a song emerged, repeating the song until it became stable. Davies's approach is descriptive rather than experimental, and the reader is left to come to her or his own conclusions. The main points I take away from her work are as follows.

The role of adaptation within composing

Many of Davies's composers base their songs on material they already know. This leads Davies to argue that a rich musical experience helps with composing. Some adaptation was explicit. For instance, a 3 year-old based her song on *The Big Ship Sails Through the Alley-Alley-O*. In other cases, the influence was better integrated. Adaptation seems to be taking place earlier than would be predicted from the Swanwick/Tillman spiral (vernacular mode). It is possible that children are more likely to adapt if they are not presented with an alternative model through being taught composing.

The differing needs of children as composers

Davies argues the impossibility of producing a single progressive music curriculum that will suit all children. Some children arrive at school already making up songs, whilst others need a rich diet of musical experience as raw material, and possibly also specific help.

Differing ways of assessing progress in composing

Progress may be evident in many ways, including:

> greater confidence in handling musical materials; an increase in melodic range, melodies which begin to open out rather than remain closed round the same few notes; a developing sense of shape and balance of phrases, or a more sustained, longer invention. It may be apparent in a more apt setting of words, use of more varied rhythm patterns, including syncopation, and a more imaginative turn of phrase in the words themselves.
>
> (Davies 1986: 288)

Davies's approach complements that of Swanwick and Tillman. She stresses the need for open-mindedness, thinking about composers and compositions on their own merits and avoidance of prescriptive teaching. She comments on what is different, on what breaks the mould, whilst they look for what is common. The two approaches were developed in isolation; neither was a response to the other. They illustrate the differing ways in which researchers choose to make sense of what they see around them.

Singing in tune

Roger Buckton's (1988) study took place in New Zealand, but has implications of relevance to contemporary education in the UK. It consists of a survey of the singing accuracy of forty-nine classes of children aged approximately 6: 1,135 children in all. It is difficult for a researcher to assess the individual singing accuracy of children without making them self-conscious, and consequently distressed and likely to underachieve. Buckton's approach was to devise a technique for measuring the children's singing accuracy in a situation close to a usual classroom setting. Individual children were assessed whilst singing, with their class and teacher, songs that they knew well. Personal microphones were distributed to ten children at a time. As everyone sang a song together, two microphones were switched on, with the result that two of the children were recorded individually using the two channels of a stereo tape recorder. At the end of a verse, a new pair of microphones was switched on. By the end of five verses, all ten children had been recorded. Further songs were chosen until all the children in the class had been recorded.

Buckton graded the children's singing on a seven-point scale, which ran from:

'7 – sung consistently with a high level of vocal accuracy',
through
'5 – occasionally vocally accurate, maintaining the general contour of the song, but singing incorrect intervals within that contour',
to
'2 – spoken, or unclear as to whether the child was speaking or singing'
and
'1 – invalid – no sound, indicating that the child was not singing, or a possible defect in recording'.

(Buckton 1988: 59)

Those children who were graded 1 (forty-six in all) were excluded from further analysis.

Analysis of the data shows, as usual, that the boys are less able singers than the girls. But, more interestingly, Buckton also analysed the interaction between ethnic background (as stated by the teacher) and singing grade. He found that the mean grade of Polynesian children exceeded that of European children, and that the difference in the mean singing grade of boys and girls was less marked amongst Polynesians. The results of comparing the mean singing grade of classes classified according to whether they were predominantly Polynesian, predominantly European, or mixed, were dramatic. When the forty-nine classes were arranged in descending order according to their mean singing grade – that is, starting with the class with the highest mean singing grade – the six predominantly Polynesian classes took first, second, third, fifth, ninth and seventeenth places. Only one of the thirty-two predominantly European classes appeared in the top nine.

Why is this? Were the Polynesian children receiving more systematic training in singing in tune in school? Quite the contrary. The more successful European classes *did* have systematic training. For instance, teachers provided children with opportunities to sing individually and kept records of their development. They took account of the need to find children's comfortable range, and develop confidence within this before working outwards. But Polynesian classes, though they sang a lot, did not have systematic training in singing in tune. Buckton came to the conclusion that his findings were the result of an interaction between cultural and educational factors. Singing is an integral part of Polynesian culture. Children sing with their families and in church from an early age. Fathers sing as much as mothers, so singing is probably less associated with females than it is in European culture. Children of European ethnic background, on the other hand, often arrive at school with little background in singing. Consequently, the educational needs of the two groups differ. The European children often need systematic help, whereas the Polynesian children just need practice.

What are the implications of Buckton's study for music education in the UK? It provides evidence that systematic singing tuition can help children learn to sing in tune earlier. But it also suggests that the system used needs to reflect the cultural and musical background of the children concerned. There is no way of teaching children to sing in tune, and methods imported from other situations may be of no help. We need to work out what children's problems are, and plan accordingly.

Generalizing from Buckton's investigation of singing, it would seem that matching the task to the child is as important in music as in any other subject. We need a mixed-ability approach to music teaching. It is inappropriate to take some externally devised music scheme, apply it to all children and hope for the best.

References

Bentley, A. (1966) *Musical Ability in Children and its Measurement,* London: Harrap.

—— (1968) *'Monotones' – a Comparison with 'Normal' Singers,* London: Novello.

Bridger, W.H. (1961) 'Sensory habituation and discrimination in the human neonate', *American Journal of Psychiatry,* 117: 991–6.

Buckton, R. (1988) 'Vocal accuracy of young children – a New Zealand survey' in A. Kemp (ed.) *Research in Music Education: A Festschrift for Arnold Bentley,* International Society for Music Education.

Bunting, R. (1977) 'The common language of music', *Music in the Secondary School Curriculum,* Working paper 6, Schools Council: York University.

Crowther, R. and Durkin, K. (1982) 'Research overview: language in music education', *Psychology of Music* 10 (1): 59–60.

Davies, C. (1986) 'Say it till a song comes (reflections on songs invented by children 3–13)', *British Journal of Music Education* 3(3): 279–93.

Department of Education and Science (1985) *Curriculum Matters 4: Music from 5 to 16,* London: HMSO.

Loane, B. (1984) 'Thinking about children's composition', *British Journal of Music Education* 1(3): 205–32.

Mills, J. (1984) 'The "Pitch" subtest of Bentley's "Measures of Musical Abilities": a test from the 1960s reconsidered in the 1980s', *Psychology of Music* 12(2): 94–105.

—— (1988) *Group Tests of Musical Abilities: Teacher's Guide and Recorded Test,* Windsor: NFER-Nelson.

Moog H. (1976) *The Musical Experience of the Pre-School Child* (translated by Claudia Clarke), London: Schott.

Piaget, J. (1951) *Play, Dreams and Imitation in Childhood,* London: Routledge & Kegan Paul.

Ross, M. (1984) *The Aesthetic Impulse,* Oxford: Pergamon Press.

Seashore, C. E. (1938) *The Psychology of Music*, London: McGraw-Hill.

Shuter-Dyson, R. and Gabriel, C. (1981) *The Psychology of Musical Ability*, London: Methuen.

Swanwick, K. (1988) *Music, Mind, and Education*, London: Routledge.

Swanwick, K. and Tillman, J. (1986) 'The sequence of musical development: a study of children's composition', *British Journal of Music Education* 3(3): 305–39.

Tillman, J. (1988) 'Music in the primary school and the National Curriculum' in W. Salaman and J. Mills (eds) *Challenging Assumptions: New Perspectives in the Education of Music Teachers*, Exeter: University of Exeter School of Education.

7 Planning for transfer and transition in music education

Helen Coll

> Nothing is more de-motivating for pupils than the situation where at each point of transfer the teacher decides it is easier to 'start again'.
>
> (Glover and Young 1999: 212)

Unfortunately, this is so often what happens when pupils move from primary to secondary school. The tendency for secondary music teachers to expect too little of their pupils and underestimate their prior knowledge has been documented in Ofsted annual reviews, beginning with the report on the first year of the National Curriculum in Music. Among its recommendations was one stating that:

> Secondary schools need to ... increase teachers' expectations of pupils new to the school ... build better links with contributory schools.
>
> (Ofsted 1993: 28)

The most recent available report recommends that:

> schools should ... recognise that pupils arrive at secondary school with experience of performing, composing and listening to music gained in primary school and in the community: develop a music curriculum that builds on pupils' prior learning and allows them the opportunity to achieve highly in music, however low or high their attainment in other subjects.
>
> (Ofsted 1999a)

It seems that little has changed in the six years between these reports. Clearly there are bound to be difficulties in all subjects when pupils move from one phase of education to another. For pupils it is a rite of passage and too seamless a transition would arguably detract from its significance. Pupils expect differences in curriculum content and teaching style and see these as appropriate to their new status, putting behind them the more secure, cosy atmosphere of primary school (see, for example, Measor and Woods 1984). Thus it is vital that curriculum content in Year 7 should leave behind any notion of childishness while, at the same time, work that is too difficult or inaccessible may damage the all-too-fragile confidence of Year 7 pupils.

Recent research commissioned by the DfEE (Galton *et al.* 1999) examines both transfer and transition, defining the former as the move from one school to another and the latter as the move between one year group and the next within a school. Transfer procedures have become better organized in the last twenty years with the result that fewer pupils now experience sustained anxiety about the move to a new school. However, curriculum continuity has not received so much attention and the apparent dip (which Galton *et al.* describe more precisely as a hiatus) in pupils' performance between the last term of Year 6 and the first term of Year 7 has caused considerable concern of late. There is also evidence that there is a similar 'dip' around Years 3 to 4 and Years 8 and 9 when pupils remain in the same school, suggesting that transition needs attention as well as transfer.

When moving to a new school, children's initial anxieties about coping with a new environment, different routines and new teachers and friends are apparently relatively short-lived, but the effect of the break in their learning can be more serious. The DfEE report surveys current practice and makes recommendations for addressing issues relating to both transition and transfer. They believe that:

> More radical approaches are needed which give attention to discontinuities in teaching approaches, which look at the gap between pupils' expectations of the next phase of schooling and the reality, and which help teachers develop strategies for helping pupils manage their own learning.
>
> (Galton *et al.* 1999)

They also recommend (for both transition and transfer) that schools need to take more account of pupils' preferred learning styles, paying particular attention to gender differences.

Continuity and the curriculum

The National Curriculum is itself intended to promote continuity between Key Stages. Indeed, one of the justifications for its introduction in 1988 was the need to address the situation whereby pupils could move from one part of the country to another with no guarantee of curriculum continuity. Curriculum 2000 includes a section on values, aims and purposes, and one of the four main purposes is identified as being 'To promote continuity and coherence'. It is claimed that:

> The National Curriculum contributes to a coherent national framework that promotes curriculum continuity and is sufficiently flexible to ensure progression in pupils' learning. It facilitates the transition of pupils between schools and phases of education.
>
> (DfEE/QCA 1999: 13)

It is interesting to look at texts written before the days of the National Curriculum to remind ourselves just how much things have changed. Derricott remarks that 'curricular continuity necessitates the presence of an agreed curriculum plan which is implemented in both the junior school or middle school and in the lower years of the secondary school to which children are transferred' (Derricott 1985: 16), and goes on to speculate about the location of responsibility for the design of such curriculums since local education authorities (LEAs) are seen as having responsibility for curriculums within their own areas. This responsibility has now been very firmly assumed by central government, and presumably many of the problems identified in earlier studies of curriculum continuity should have been solved. An article written in the early days of the National Curriculum claims that its existence is forcing primary, middle and secondary schools to look more closely at curriculum continuity (Tabor 1993: 10), and this is certainly a reasonable assumption.

It seems, however, that the existence of a National Curriculum has not solved the problem. Perhaps the hopes raised by a curriculum designed to foster continuity and progression, with statutory Programmes of Study and standardized assessment procedures, account for the recent publicity given to the Year 7 dip or hiatus. However, this is nothing new, and similar findings were in evidence nearly twenty years ago (Galton and Willcocks 1983).

In the days before the National Curriculum, it was often the case that little information was passed on between schools, and what was passed on was not always used. The attitude epitomized in a comment from a secondary head of faculty (quoted by Derricot) is unlikely to have encouraged primary schools to go to any great lengths to compile and transfer information: 'We like to give pupils a fresh start. We only look at the record cards, if there are any difficulties' (Derricott 1985: 25). Now, however, it is very different and in core subjects there are statutory requirements for the transfer of information and no shortage of advice on the promotion of continuity and the effective use of Key Stage 2 assessments at the point of transfer (SCAA 1996; SCAA 1997). The latter outlines the more detailed information now available on pupils' attainment in Year 6, and suggests ways of using it, emphasizing the importance of using assessment information so that 'appropriately challenging work' (SCAA 1997: 9) can be set, claiming that:

> in the past, teachers in Key Stage 3 have often lacked the information about pupils' attainment which they need to enable them to pitch work appropriately. As a result, many pupils have repeated work which they have done before or been given work which was not demanding enough.
>
> (ibid.: 10)

The above refers to the core subjects and it is noticeable that there is virtually no specific mention of foundation subjects in official publications such as these. Research into the role of LEAs in supporting continuity and progression (Mann 1997) gives examples of LEA initiatives. Among these are joint curriculum projects in specific subjects (core subjects, in the example given by Mann) and ones intended to develop cross-curricular links in Year 7 and thus build on the previous year's methodology. Comments from LEAs about the effect of the National Curriculum and its assessment arrangements include the view that the benefits include increased consistency of the KS2 curriculum and a clearer framework for the transfer of curriculum information. However, less positive views include a comment that the tendency to concentrate on SATs and pupil achievement can lessen the importance of curriculum continuity, and it was felt that open enrolment, which has led to a wider dispersal of pupils, has also impeded transfer liaison.

Continuity in music

Music is not mentioned in this survey and most of the responses relate to core subjects where data about pupil achievement is easily available. In subjects such as music there is often little or no information forthcoming from primary schools, and this undoubtedly fuels the 'fresh start' (which can all too easily turn into a 'start from scratch') approach of some secondary music teachers. One of the issues addressed in research undertaken in twelve middle and seven secondary schools in the Midlands was liaison between schools for music (Box 1997). In their replies to a questionnaire, respondents from all schools gave a positive response to a question about documentation being passed on to secondary schools. However, it transpired that this was no more than a list sent from the County Music Service of pupils receiving tuition. Only one teacher had passed on information about his pupils' achievements in the curriculum, and was understandably disheartened when he discovered that it had not been read. Discussion between teachers was another means of liaison identified in the questionnaire and responses indicated that these normally related to pupils' achievements in 'academic' subjects. The principal means of liaison as far as music was concerned was through musical events, for example the organization of joint concerts by a middle and secondary school. However, this too was very limited (ibid: 60–2).

This data gives a snapshot of one area, but Mills suggests that the national picture is similar, stating that:

> It is not always easy for secondary music teachers to gain a clear picture of the prior attainment in music of all pupils in Year 7. Some secondary schools have a large number of partner primary schools and almost all have large numbers of Year 7 pupils. The transfer records that secondary schools are sent by primary schools may contain little musical information other than reports to parents, which are not always copied to the music department, and lists of pupils taking lessons from peripatetic teachers.
>
> (Mills 1997: 21)

Is it therefore simply a question of primary schools providing information for secondary schools, and secondary schools making use of it? If so, this assumes that primary schools have the necessary information about what their pupils have achieved. But, as Glover and Young observe, there is a propensity for teachers to see primary school music 'more in terms of "what we do" than of what she or he learns'. They comment that:

> Some primary schools have excellent reputations for music which rest on a wide range of high-profile activities; yet they have no systems in place for monitoring the music learning and progress of each child as they pass through the school.
>
> (Glover and Young 1999: 213)

The reasons for this include the lack of any statutory requirement for formal assessment in music until the end of KS3; the intrinsic problems of assessment in some aspects of the arts (see Ross 1986; Spruce 1996; Swanwick 1997; Swanwick 1999) and the emphasis on assessment in the core subjects of the National Curriculum. The last has had the effect of downgrading music and other foundation subjects while at the same time reinforcing teachers' tendencies to see Music and the arts as a respite from more formally taught and constantly assessed subjects for both their pupils and themselves. Currently, 'high stakes' assessment procedures which emphasize formal, summative assessment and easily measurable outcomes predominate. The authors of 'All our Futures: Creativity, Culture and Education' (NACCCE Report 1999) claim that this has been at the expense of the more difficult task of assessing children's creative development which requires more emphasis on processes and a willingness to encourage children to experiment and take risks (ibid: 109–10). As they say, there is considerable literature and research on the assessment of creative capacities and achievements (in all subjects, not just the arts) and what is needed is guidance from QCA as part of its role in supporting curriculum development.

Although it seems likely that records of individual pupils' achievements in classroom music do not exist in many primary schools, information on curriculum content should be readily available, given the existence of a National Curriculum with its attendant Programmes of Study. However, this is more problematic in music than in most other subjects since there is a sense in which the Curriculum as laid out is virtually content free. The 1995 version consisted largely of activities rather than actual content (see Coll 1996); this left teachers with the welcome freedom to make professional judgements about content, within certain parameters, but also meant that even if all primary schools cover the Key Stages 1 and 2 curriculum (which of course they are legally obliged to do) there are a range of different ways in which the mandatory requirements may be interpreted by individual teachers.

In pre–2000 versions of the curriculum, Music, along with Art and PE, lacked the level descriptions in place for other subjects, which again reinforced the view that not only were these subjects of lesser significance but also that assessment in them was less important. However, in Curriculum 2000, level descriptions are in place for all subjects. Despite the drawbacks of hierarchical statements of attainment in subjects such as Music, many felt that it was important that Music was treated in the same way as other subjects in the hope that this would increase its standing. One view is that 'Perhaps they should be cautiously welcomed as a way of supporting more detailed planning of assessment' (Paterson 2000: 4). Another innovation which may prove to be highly significant is the publication by the DfEE/QCA of a scheme of work for Key Stages 1 and 2 in Music. The non-statutory nature of the scheme is emphasized:

> It must be stressed that the intention is for schools to supplement the given programme with their own units, developed by the teacher and supported through published materials. This scheme of work has been developed to demonstrate how the statutory requirements *could* be planned and taught across Key Stages 1 and 2.
>
> (QCA 2000a Teacher's Guide: 17)

Nevertheless, the official nature of the scheme and its relationship to the Programmes of Study in music may give the content a status lacked by commercially produced curriculum packs. The Key Stage 3 scheme draws attention to the need for secondary teachers to build on previous experiences and notes similarities and differences between the primary and secondary schemes, with the intention of facilitating continuity. If the primary schemes become, in effect, the curriculum in Music in primary schools, it will become much easier for secondary teachers to be clear about what their Year 7 pupils have done in music. And if the level descriptions are used to record what pupils have learned – and if the information is passed on, and if it is used in the receiving schools – then information will be available about both the curriculum and about individual pupils' attainment.

Continuity in other subjects

However, experience in other subjects suggests that this might be an over-optimistic view. Problems in ensuring continuity and progression have been identified in a number of subjects, including those which should have a stronger position in the curriculum than Music and the other foundation subjects. An article in the Times Educational Supplement describes findings from research into KS2–3 transition in Science:

> Secondary and primary teachers are generally ignorant of each other's schemes of work ... Secondary teachers are making little or no use of pupil information transferred from feeder schools, and are failing to build upon the work already done at primary level.
>
> (Thornton 1999)

One of the researchers summarized the current situation by claiming 'there is very little curriculum discussion going on between phases, and a lack of trust in the validity of assessments made by others. This seems to be about discontinuity between institutions' (Knott reported by Thornton 1999).

Recommendations about the promotion of continuity between KS2 and 3 in Ofsted annual reviews are not confined to Music. The research findings about Science discussed above are confirmed by inspection reports, and the summary includes a telling statement about the use of test data which suggests that the existence of such data, plus a statutory responsibility to pass it on to secondary schools, does not solve the problem:

Use of the Key Stage 2 test data to inform planning has improved but many schools find that this is not yet available when needed or is insufficiently discriminating.

(Ofsted 1999a)

Reviews of RE and Geography comment on the need for curriculum liaison between primary and secondary schools, noting that it is currently weak.

Of these three subjects, two at least should be in a stronger position than Music. Science is a core subject with statutory assessment, recording and reporting procedures and therefore data which must be passed to secondary schools, and Geography is a foundation subject which, unlike Music, has had level descriptions for some time. Maybe, then, bringing statutory requirements for Music more in line with those in other subjects will not lead to the anticipated improvements.

The sheer scale of gathering and passing on assessment data on all Year 6 pupils must not be overestimated. Secondary schools usually have large numbers of Year 7 pupils and commonly only one or two teachers in Music, and it would be difficult for more than the most basic information about each pupil to be absorbed and acted upon. It must also be remembered that the official curriculum is only one aspect of learning in Music and that if a full picture of individual pupils and their attainment is to be compiled, a variety of encounters with Music needs to be considered. Glover and Young list a range of musical activities including timetabled whole-class lessons, hymn practice for year groups or the whole school, singing and listening to music in assembly, classroom-based individual and group work, lunchtime or after-school activities, special musical events for the whole school and individual vocal or instrumental lessons (Glover and Young 1999: 108).

The effect of the emphasis on literacy and numeracy

All this is predicated upon an assumption that the KS1 and 2 curriculums in Music will actually be taught – in all schools and to all pupils. Doubting that this will happen may seem curious but there is evidence to suggest that it is not as straight-forward as might be imagined from the statutory nature of the National Curriculum. Undoubtedly, the position of foundation subjects was weakened during the two-year period (September 1988 to 2000) during which primary schools were not required to teach the full Programmes of Study in the six foundation subjects in order to ensure 'a sharper focus on literacy and numeracy' (QCA 1988: 4). The same document emphasizes the importance of the promotion of curriculum continuity (which could be considered to add insult to injury) and recommends that:

When primary schools make use of the increased flexibility in teaching the six subjects, it is important that secondary schools are made aware of the work they can expect children to have covered from the Key Stage 2 Programmes of Study.

(QCA 1998: 7)

It would be interesting to know whether this actually happened, but even if it did, secondary schools taking pupils from a number of primary schools which may have used this 'increased flexibility' in a variety of ways would find it difficult to make much sensible use of the information in their planning.

These new arrangements affected all six foundation subjects, and the 1999 review of inspection evidence in Geography includes comments on their effect on continuity:

> The reduction in the Key Stage 2 Geography curriculum in 1997/98 resulting from the literacy initiative is already beginning to affect Year 7 and reduce the breadth of geographical knowledge on entry to secondary school. This will require departments to look carefully at the content of geography courses to ensure that the range of skills can still be exercised and high expectations maintained.
>
> (Ofsted 1999a)

The review recommends that schools should:

> liais(e) more closely with primary schools from which pupils come to ascertain what their primary Geography teaching has covered given recent changes in emphasis in many primary schools to achieve higher standards of literacy;
>
> (Ofsted 1999a)

Officially the full National Curriculum in all subjects was reinstated with the implementation of Curriculum 2000 from September 2000. But the emphasis on literacy and numeracy in the curriculum and the importance of SATs remains, and it would be naive to believe that this will not continue to have an adverse effect on other subjects. The only subject for which a recommendation about curriculum time is made in Key Stages 1 and 2 is Physical Education ('two hours of physical activity a week … .should be an aspiration for all schools' – DfEE/QCA 1999: 16). The literacy hour and the numeracy strategy make their own demands, and many teachers continue to believe that there will not be sufficient available time to do justice to all the other subjects, despite National Curriculum requirements.

Music in primary schools

Currently, views differ on the effectiveness of teaching and learning in Music in primary schools. The official view is optimistic, and has been since the first publication of reviews of inspection evidence. We are told that inspection data indicates that Music is one of the best taught subjects in the primary curriculum (Ofsted 1999b). Music is apparently the third strongest subject (after English and Mathematics) as far as the level of teachers' subject knowledge is concerned. This runs counter to Wragg's research (1989) which placed Music bottom of the list of subjects in which teachers feel confident, although it could be that teachers' lack of confidence is misplaced, and there is not necessarily a correlation between teachers' confidence and their actual level of subject knowledge. Standards of achievement in Music rose sharply during the period covered by this review (1994–8), as did the standard of teaching, and the proportion of schools that provide very little music for some of their pupils has decreased (Ofsted 1999b). This is indeed good news, although it must be remembered that this review does not take into account the period covered by the 1998–2000 reduction in statutory requirements and we will have to wait for subsequent reviews to see what effect this has had.

It is hard to argue with data from Ofsted inspections, but it has to be said that this picture does not correspond with the perceptions of many music educators, although evidence is only anecdotal. Conversations with colleagues in school and in higher education – and with trainee teachers – reveal a very different picture. The belief that Music (among other subjects) has been, and continues to be, marginalized in the curriculum has been stated before; trainee teachers and their university tutors commonly report that they have very little opportunity to teach Music during teaching practice and that, although Music is timetabled, it is frequently cancelled so that more time can be devoted to other subjects. The perception is that the situation has worsened in the last few years. An experienced teacher trainer describes music provision as 'patchy' in terms of 'continuity of learning, and vulnerability to timetable pressure; breadth and depth of content; suitability of accommodation and quality of equipment and resources; the expertise and confidence of teachers' (Hennessy 2000: 183), and Glover's perception of the current position is that:

> Foundation subjects have become severely marginalised by recent initiatives in literacy and numeracy, often being relegated to tiny subject slots in the afternoons, or occurring periodically without the continuity of weekly work throughout the year. Under such conditions, music has inevitably suffered from a lack of focus, a lack of assessment and little attention to curriculum or staff development. With the best will in the world, it has been hard for subject leaders to sustain the progress that had been made since the introduction of the National Curriculum, and in many schools, for many children, ground has been lost.
>
> (Glover 2000: 3)

The role of secondary music teachers

While effective liaison between primary and secondary schools is bound to be affected by the state of Music in primary education, difficulties do not absolve secondary teachers from their responsibility to provide an appropriate curriculum for their pupils. The temptation to 'start from scratch' must be resisted along with the clearly unsustainable assumption that many 11-year-old pupils are likely to know nothing about music. If nothing else, they have lived in the world for 11 years and will have encountered music in the home and the community as well as in school. Whatever the truth about Music in primary schools, it is clear that many primary teachers – possibly because of their diffidence as 'non-specialists' when communicating with secondary specialists – give 'unduly modest accounts of the music curriculum in their school' (Mills 1997: 21). Some of the more extreme practices described by Mills in *Starting at Secondary School* (1996) seem almost designed to ensure that pupils lose interest.

In the absence of transfer information from feeder primary schools, one fairly common approach is to ask the pupils what they have done in Music in their previous school. This is problematical for various reasons, especially if it takes place in the first Music lesson in Year 7. Questions which seek information about pupils' skills and experience in music, when these are often acquired through individual or small-group instrumental or vocal lessons, are bound to be answered negatively by the majority of pupils since only a minority of pupils learn an instrument in this way. The experience of being asked these questions soon after entering secondary school may affect pupils' confidence and self esteem as musicians and make them believe that secondary school Music is not for them. In a subject where the gulf between children with certain types of experience in music and those without is notoriously wide, it seems odd to begin KS3 with procedures which may unwittingly reinforce this gulf.

Taking information on trust from pupils about their experience of Music in primary school is also problematical. It assumes a shared understanding of terminology (for instance the use of the word 'composing') and what is meant by 'Music lessons'. Does it mean ordinary lessons with their class teacher? Singing with a visiting specialist? Special events in the hall? Experiments with sound in science? Games with pitch and rhythm at odd times of the day? It is certainly unlikely that they would interpret it to cover everything listed by Glover and Young. Faced with a specialist teacher in purpose-built accommodation asking fairly intimidating questions, it is unlikely that most pupils would do justice to their previous musical experiences (Mills 1996: 9 and 1997: 19–20).

The variety of ways in which pupils in primary schools can encounter music can also be a barrier to secondary teachers seeking information from primary colleagues. Used as they are to a specialist, rigidly timetabled curriculum model, it can be hard for secondary teachers to understand the range of possibilities in primary schools. This not only applies to the variety of ways that music can be included in the pupils' curriculum (official and extended) but also to how its teaching is organized. There have been changes in recent years, and the current situation is very varied, with music in some primary schools taught by specialists (sometimes part time, or peripatetic) while in others it is the responsibility of every class teacher. Sometimes (but not always) there is a subject leader or co-ordinator who takes responsibility for curriculum support within the school. Sometimes these teachers are enthusiastic about their role and have considerable experience and appropriate training; in other instances it simply operates on the basis of 'Buggins' turn'. Sometimes there is LEA involvement. Sometimes practice within the same school varies for different years or Key Stages, often because of the skill and confidence of individual teachers or the other demands made on them. Discussions of the current situation include Harrison's account (1997) of the music co-ordinator's role in her own school, Ward's outline (2000) of the changing roles of generalists, specialists and curriculum leaders/co-ordinators, and accounts of some of the common ways of organizing the teaching of Music in Ofsted (1999b) and Clay *et al.* (1988: 61). The picture is varied and complex and trying to untangle and understand the different systems in use in different schools can be difficult for secondary teachers.

Despite these problems, it is imperative that secondary music teachers find ways of ensuring that their curriculum sets appropriate challenges for their pupils. The early weeks of Year 7 are vital since it is then that pupils decide which subjects and teachers they like and which they dislike. Music undoubtedly has low status in many schools for a variety of well-rehearsed reasons, some to do with the perceived importance of more 'academic' subjects, and some which may have more to do with the nature of music both in and out of school (Ross 1995 and Gammon 1996). However, Ofsted reports have consistently shown that, in general, secondary school pupils are enthusiastic about music. The 1997/8 review reports unsatisfactory responses in only one out of seventeen class lessons and, in Years 8 and 9, pupils' responses mirror the quality with which they are taught (Ofsted 1999a). There appear to be some contradictions between teachers' perceptions of the status of their subject (Cox 1999), pupils' views as reported by researchers (Ross 1998; Swanwick and Lawson 1999) and Ofsted findings. It is possible that these can be explained, in part at least, by differences in methodology. In research, pupils are often asked to compare Music with other subjects or to answer fairly open-ended questions about music in and out of school, whereas Ofsted inspection findings are based on direct observation. Pupils' own views on what it is socially and culturally acceptable to like and dislike may well be significant in any responses they make to specific research questions.

Music in Year 7

In Measor and Woods' pre-National Curriculum study (which discusses pupils' perceptions of different subjects and notes the way these perceptions affect their behaviour and attitude to work), a Year 7 pupil says, 'We're only doing triangles, we were using triangles at first school, we should be getting on to trombones and things' (Measor and Woods: 54). This rather extreme example exemplifies a dilemma faced by teachers when planning their first few lessons for Year 7 pupils – how to achieve an appropriate balance between familiarity and comfort, challenge and excitement. Many suggestions for promoting continuity in music involve the use of similar curriculum material at the end of Year 6 and the beginning of Year 7. An example is a project in Dudley where teachers and advisers have devised a package of materials that can be introduced in the last half term in Year 6 and then built upon in Year 7. There is evidence that where secondary teachers planned effectively for their use, pupils enjoyed the activities and were provided with appropriate challenge (Mills 1997: 23; Mills in Clay *et al.* 1998: 69). However, other teachers may want to set the scene for secondary school Music in a different way, by planning initial lessons that capitalize on and signal the differences between primary and secondary school Music (for instance by using music technology, or instruments unavailable to pupils in primary schools). There is certainly evidence that, in general, pupils welcome lessons that reinforce their feelings of moving on to a more adult environment. Derricott discusses the concept of 'planned discontinuity'. He describes this as 'a deliberate change in practice with the intention of stimulating growth and development … the disequilibrium caused by such an experience challenges children to accommodate to it and to develop new ways of learning' (Derricott 1985: 156–7). As he warns, though, it needs careful handling and is only appropriate in some areas.

Given the failure of the National Curriculum itself to provide sufficient continuity and progression, the current orthodoxy appears to be to devise explicit links in content to bridge phases. QCA schemes of work provide the ideal vehicle for this. In Mathematics, the QCA officer justified this strategy in part by claiming that 'Year 7 children found it comforting to do familiar topics in their first weeks of secondary school' (Churchman, reported by Cassidy 2000).

In Music, the final unit in the KS2 scheme is repeated (with some small differences) as Unit 1 in the KS3 scheme. In the latter, it is called 'Bridging the gap' and the intention is that teachers can use it 'to gain a sense of the attainment as pupils begin Year 7' (QCA 2000b: 9). The introduction to the unit makes this explicit:

> It provides an opportunity for pupils new to the school to develop and demonstrate music skills, knowledge and understanding achieved in Years 5 and 6 … it presents an opportunity to extend ideas further and share previous experiences. It will give an indication of the level of attainment of pupils in the class and highlight areas for future development.
>
> (QCA 2000b Unit 1)

Liaison between phases

Whichever approach teachers adopt to planning their initial lessons with Year 7, clearly the more they know about Music in their feeder primary schools the better. Often, liaison between the two phases focuses on extracurricular activities, with secondary school ensembles visiting primary schools, often largely as a marketing exercise. Sometimes secondary music teachers visit local primary schools to teach Music, usually with Year 6 pupils. Obviously this can be very valuable but there is a danger that primary teachers may be intimidated by secondary teachers' specialist skills and knowledge and the experience may reinforce any feelings of inadequacy, and even result in an increased reluctance to teach Music, rather than renewed enthusiasm for it. If these visits are to be productive, they must be planned carefully, in the context of the primary school's existing curriculum. The existence of the bridging unit in the QCA schemes of work for Music gives rise to various possibilities for collaboration. Visits by secondary teachers, not to teach or direct groups of pupils, but to observe primary pupils making music, are immensely valuable and may help to dispel some of the myths, but they need sensitive handling to overcome primary teachers' fears and feelings of being on trial and judged by experts. It is not always easy for secondary teachers to find time for activities such as these, although in theory there are opportunities once examination groups have left school in the summer term, and sometimes headteachers need convincing of their value. Allowing sufficient time for activities such as these to be productive is crucial. Although primary and secondary teachers may no longer have such parochial attitudes as those reported by Neal in his report of a Birmingham LEA initiative in 1975 (Derricott 1985), Steed and Sudworth note that 'it takes many hours of meetings before even committed colleagues feel secure enough to state what they really believe' (Derricott 1985: 37), and that only when this point of security is reached will real liaison begin to happen. A group of secondary headteachers working on a curriculum project stated that their real work began after approximately sixty hours of meetings (ibid.). The public and statutory nature of the curriculum itself might obviate the need for some of the initial discussions today, but the need for trust to be established still obtains, and hurried visits are unlikely to be productive.

There are many challenges to be faced by both primary and secondary teachers if effective continuity and progression are going to be achieved within and between phases. Only a limited amount can be achieved by individual teachers and it is essential that schools make continuity a priority, perhaps by implementing the recommendations of the recent DfEE research report (Galton *et al.* 1999). The concern expressed by the government about the hiatus in pupil attainment at transition and transfer points may help to make it a priority within schools. Meanwhile, individual teachers, both primary and secondary, need to do all they can to communicate and make meaningful links between their schools.

References

Box, E. (1997) 'An investigation of continuity between middle and secondary schools in music education', unpublished MA dissertation, Faculty of Education, University of Central England.

Cassidy, S. (2000) 'Maths "bridging" unit to ease path to secondary', *Times Educational Supplement*.

Clay, G., Hertrich, J., Jones, P., Mills, J. and Rose, J. (1998) *The Arts Inspected*, Oxford: Heinemann.

Coll, H. (1996) *Continuity between the Key Stages in the Music Curriculum*, Milton Keynes: The Open University.

Cox, G. (1999) 'Secondary school music teachers talking', *Music Education Research*, 1(1):37–45.

Derricott, R. (ed.) (1985) *Curriculum Continuity: Primary to Secondary*, Windsor: NFER-Nelson.

DfEE/QCA (1999) *The National Curriculum Handbook for Primary Teachers in England*, London: DfEE/QCA.

Galton, M. and Wilcocks, J. (eds) (1983) *Moving from the Primary Classroom*, London: Routledge & Kegan Paul.

Galton, M., Gray, J. and Ruddock, J. (1999) *The Impact of School Transitions and Transfers on Pupil Progress and Attainment*, DfEE Research Report 131, London: HMSO.

Gammon, V. (1996) 'What is wrong with school music? – a response to Malcolm Ross', *British Journal of Music Education*, 13(2):101–21.

Glover, J. and Young, S. (1999) *Primary Music Later Years*, London: Falmer Press.

Harrison, M. (1997) 'From specialist to generalist teaching', *Primary Music Today,* Issue 9, pp. 8–13.

Hennessy, S. (2000) 'Overcoming the red-feeling: the development of confidence to teach music in primary school amongst student teachers', *British Journal of Music Education,* 17(2):183–196.

Mann, P. (1997) *LEA Strategies for Effective Transition from KS2 to KS3,* Slough, Education Management Information Exchange, NFER.

Measor, L. and Woods, P. (1984) *Changing Schools,* Milton Keynes: Open University Press.

Mills, J. (1996) 'Starting at secondary school', *British Journal of Music Education,* 11(1):191–6.

—— (1997) 'First class?', *Music Teacher,* October 1997, pp. 19–23.

National Advisory Committee on Creative and Cultural Education (1999) *All our Futures: Creativity, Culture and Education,* London: DfEE.

Ofsted (1993) *Music Key Stages 1, 2 and 3 First Year, 1992–3* London: HMSO.

—— (1998) *Standards in the primary curriculum 1997–97* London: Ofsted.

—— (1999a) *Standards in the secondary curriculum 1997–98* London: Ofsted.

—— (1999b) *Primary Education 1994–8: a review of primary schools in England,* London: Ofsted.

QCA (1988) *Maintaining Breadth and Balance at Key Stages 1 and 2,* London: QCA.

—— (2000a) *A Scheme of Work for Key Stages 1 and 2 Music Teacher's guide,* London: QCA.

—— (2000b) *A Scheme of Work for Key Stage 3 Music Teacher's guide,* London: QCA.

Paterson, A. (2000) 'Schemes of Work for Music', *Primary Music Today,* issue 17, pp. 4–6.

Ross, M. (1986) *Assessment in Arts Education,* Oxford: Pergamon Press.

—— (1995) 'What's wrong with school music?', *British Journal of Music Education,* 12(3): 105–201.

—— (1998) 'Missing solemnis: reforming music in schools', *British Journal of Music Education,* 15(3): 255–62.

—— (1997) *Making Effective Use of Key Stage 2 Assessments,* London: SCAA.

Spruce, G. (1996) 'Assessment in the arts: issues of objectivity' in *Teaching Music,* G. Spruce (ed.) London: Routledge.

Swanwick, K. (1997) 'Assessing musical quality in the National Curriculum', *British Journal of Music Education,* 14(3):205–15.

—— (1999) *Teaching Music Musically,* London: Routledge.

Swanwick, K. and Lawson, D. (1999) '"Authentic" music and its effect on the attitudes and musical development of secondary schools pupils', *Music Education Research,* 1(1): 47–60.

Tabor, D. (1993) 'Smoothing their path: transition, continuity and pastoral liaison between primary and secondary school', *Pastoral Care,* March 1993, pp. 10–14.

Thornton, K. (1999) 'Secondary science "dumbed down"', *Times Educational Supplement.*

Ward, S. (2000) 'Primary music today: a decade of change', *Primary Music Today,* Issue 16, pp. 6–10.

Wragg, E.C., Bennett, S.N. and Carre, C.G. (1989) 'Primary teachers and the National Curriculum', University of Exeter: Research papers in Education.

8   Music with emotionally disturbed children

Yvonne Packer

The status of music in special education

> for children whose home background is not always as happy as might be desired, whose activities are necessarily limited, and whose friendships may not bring them complete fulfilment – pleasure in music-making with its accompanying sense of well-being and exultation can do much to compensate for their lack of other opportunities.
>
> (Dobbs 1966)

Compensatory education for the disadvantaged is, of necessity, one of the guiding principles in all special schools and those teachers who have experienced the effect of music on the lives of special needs children will surely appreciate the validity of Dobbs's statement and the potential power there is in music education to effect change and bring relief to damaged lives. Unfortunately, however, the situation at the present time is that if special schools are able to offer their children an adequate music education, they are exceptional.

The shortage of experienced Music teachers in special education is a problem highlighted in Daphne Kennard's report for the Disabled Living Foundation (1979) in which reference is made to the lack of music provision in schools and attention drawn to the inadequacy of teacher training in this field. Recording that there was in the mid-1970s no college of higher education offering training in Music and special education, Kennard expresses the hope that the training situation will not remain static in this pioneering field – but two decades later we seem to have moved hardly at all.

The expectation of those not actually working in special schools seems to be that teachers whose vocation is special needs work should first practise in mainstream schools for five years or so in order to equip themselves for transfer to special schools. I have rarely heard this view endorsed by special school teachers themselves and one wonders how much the principle is based on evidence that probationary teachers do benefit from being steered into the mainstream as a grounding for special education, or if it is rather an excuse disguising the fact that at the present time we seem unable to offer adequate training to those whose vocation is teaching Music to children with special needs.

In those special schools where one is fortunate enough to be able to observe some ongoing music education, one finds more often than not that the teachers themselves are suffering from feelings of professional isolation and that, whatever their level of competence, they experience the resultant feelings of underconfidence and inadequacy.

Rather than allaying these feelings of isolation, it would appear that each new report relating to music in schools intensifies the problem if for no other reason than the sin of omission. Take, for example, *Music from 5 to 16* (DES 1985) which supposedly refers to the needs of every child but makes no mention of the adaptations required to cater for special needs children, and demonstrates a total lack of awareness in the section relating to accommodation and equipment. A similar lack of awareness pervades the documentation on GCSE and the National Curriculum, almost suggesting that special education is an embarrassment which no one is quite sure how to tackle. Inevitably, teachers are left feeling isolated, resentful and in limbo with regard to professional guidance on subject teaching.

Compensatory/therapeutic education in EBD schools

If there is a problem of music provision throughout special education, it is intensified in that area of special education relating to the child with emotional and behavioural difficulties (EBD).

The concept of compensatory education becomes more crucial in this area for:

> in work with other types of handicap, the teacher educates the child who nevertheless remains handicapped: the teacher cannot, for example, cure blindness or deafness. Teachers of maladjusted children, however, have a different role: by educating their pupils well, they reduce the handicap. Indeed it is largely by their success in doing this that their efforts are judged.
>
> (DES 1965)

Yet it would appear to be the case that non-music specialists working with disabled children or those with mild/severe learning difficulties are more likely to risk trying out some kind of musical activities than are those teachers working with maladjusted children. (The word *risk* is used advisedly and I will expand on this later.) Music festivals for combined special schools tend to reflect the alienation of EBD schools, and even those National Conferences which have been devoted to Music in special education have so far overlooked the needs of maladjusted children.

The reason for this state of affairs may lie in the traditional attitude towards the education of the emotionally disturbed which used to be that these were sick children who had to be medically cured before their education could begin. In his *Pioneer Work with Maladjusted Children*, Bridgeland (1971) emphasizes the neglect of education in treatment, but over the years, the emphasis has changed and now most schools have replaced the old medical model with an educational/psychological approach with which to meet the children's needs. In *Educating Maladjusted Children*, Laslett (1977) expands on the value of therapeutic education, a term which sounds somewhat nebulous when discussing music in view of the increasing general awareness of music therapy; but in fact there are distinct differences between the two disciplines and it would seem that the teaching model is the most suited to the requirements of EBD schools. However, one must consider that such literature as does currently exist documenting the effect of music on disturbed children relates almost exclusively to music therapy. The work of Nordoff and Robbins and other leading music therapists has brought to our attention the value of music when used as a tool to effect clinical cure in patients, and the potential force of this tool should be borne in mind when considering the musical education of maladjusted children even though they are not medically sick.

One should also bear in mind the claims of transference relating to music education based on Kodály's principles as documented in Sandor's *Musical Education in Hungary* (1969), which suggests that music may stimulate the cortex and therefore result in improved performance intellectually, physically and in terms of social development. This would obviously be highly relevant in terms of the education of maladjusted children, though those who are sceptical of the Hungarian claims might prefer Dobbs's perception of transference, that being: 'on the success achieved in one activity and the confidence engendered by it, other successes, perhaps in the basic subjects, may be built'.

Dobbs's premise that this initial success may readily be achieved in music is borne out by my research in EBD schools and, to a lesser extent, so is the theory that the sense of well-being brought about by this success leads to improvement in other areas. When one considers that 'any study of the maladjusted child is essentially a study in failure' (Shedden 1984), the issue of providing success for the child becomes crucial, and one begins to realize the validity and enormity of the DES's assertion that teachers in EBD schools are working to reduce the handicapping condition of their pupils.

The lack of music in EBD schools

The enormity of the problem is also one of numbers as the increased demand for educational provision for maladjusted children reflects that it is one of the two fastest growth areas in special education. In 1945, there was only one tutorial class in London for disturbed children but by 1983 there were 226 units in the ILEA offering places for disruptive children.

Disturbed and disruptive are obviously not tautological terms, but there has since 1945 been a great deal of confusion regarding precisely what sort of child the label 'maladjusted' refers to. In 1955, the Underwood Committee highlighted the symptoms which were indicative of maladjustment: nervous behaviour, habit, psychotic and organic disorders, and educational and vocational difficulties. It is obviously a very mixed bag and though the emphasis is on *disturbed* behaviour, there is sufficient leeway amongst the categories to allow for *disruptive* behaviour to be included within the term maladjustment. As disruption and violence have been on the increase in schools, certainly since the raising of the school leaving age if not before, EBD schools now find themselves very often catering not only for genuinely disturbed children but also for those without emotional disorders but whose disruptive and deviant behaviour has made them difficult to contain in mainstream schools.

In their survey of the *Education of Disturbed Pupils* (1980), Wilson and Evans indicate that there are particular problems relating to the musical education of these children. Their difficulties concerning self-discipline, co-operation and concentration make composition, audition and performance extremely difficult to achieve, and though Wilson and Evans record that teachers value the importance of creative work, music teaching was only infrequently observed by them. Apart from the nature of the children, one of the principal reasons for this was seen to be the scarcity of suitable teachers 'who are skilled in the use of the medium – and who are skilled in the management of disturbed pupils. Such people are naturally extremely rare'.

Because of the nature of the work it would be rare to find a music specialist working full-time in an EBD school but the lack of Music in such schools is surely more of a reflection on the non-specialist teachers working in the field than the music specialists working elsewhere. Since most maladjusted schools conform to the primary model in the sense that class teachers are responsible for most of the subject teaching of their own children, one is led to ask why it is that teachers 'who happily tackle the teaching of mathematics, science, reading and other aspects of the school curriculum, shrink from organizing meaningful musical activities in their classrooms?' (Adams and Syers 1983). It is a question which I put to seventy-seven teachers in special schools. All those questioned were currently offering a range of subjects to their pupils and in many cases the teachers were each responsible for the complete classroom education of their group of children. The teachers were asked: 'Did your own higher education (teacher training/university course, etc.) equip you to offer some kind of music education to the children you are currently working with?' and despite the fact that they were all teaching a wide cross-section of subjects – academic, recreational and practical – only five of the seventy-seven teachers replied 'yes' to the question and only three of the five were involved in Music teaching at the time of answering.

Reporting on the *Music Consulting in Berkshire Primary Schools,* Smith (1987) speaks of the 'deep-seated insecurity and lack of confidence' non-specialists feel about embarking on musical activities with their children. One may imagine how greatly intensified these feelings become when the children involved are disturbed, for Wilson and Evans observed how vulnerable music-making was in respect of its 'disruptability', which brings us back to the element of risk involved in such an undertaking. An integral part of the children's disruptive behaviour (whether intentional or not) is a consistent and systematic attempt to de-skill the teacher and this obviously is particularly pertinent to the non-specialist teacher attempting to introduce music into the curriculum. It means that, as well as coping with the children's problems of poor self-control, lack of concentration, low motivation, retardation, etc., the teacher has to anticipate possible damage to him/herself both professionally and personally.

This issue was brought home to me during the course of an interview with a music therapist who had for many years been the headteacher of an EBD school.

Though teacher-trained in the creative arts, he had chosen not to teach Music in his school because in his opinion:

> to teach Music in this context one needs a cast-iron technique, clearly defined boundaries and sufficient maturity (or self-assurance) to cope with the children who seek to destroy it for you. You can't risk teaching something which is precious to you when you know that it will be ridiculed and denigrated.

He also felt that his pupils were very resistant to music education because of its 'exploratory nature which tends to frighten this type of child'.

This teacher believed that music education was threatening for the administrator principally because Music appeals to a subliminal level which other subjects do not; but in fact it would appear that many teachers share the feeling that they are similarly threatened whatever subject they teach. Rather than being a music-related issue, it would seem that it is more to do with the children's efforts to de-skill and demoralize the teacher. The fact that music has the capacity to appeal to the subliminal nature of the child does, however, suggest that it has the capacity to cause damage if handled badly. Nordoff and Robbins acknowledge that certain aspects of their music-making with children were 'powerfully intrusive. If these facts were disregarded there could be the danger of placing insupportable stresses on a child and hence engendering confusion and instability' (1971).

Bearing in mind these points, it perhaps becomes clear why there is so little music education happening in EBD schools, though in cases where teachers have observed it taking place, their negative comments tend to centre on such issues as the noise factor and the problems arising from end of term concerts, etc., rather than psychological damage sustained by staff and pupils. One should not, however, underestimate music's potential and it would obviously be wrong for the layperson to attempt amateur music therapy, but it would seem from my experience in EBD schools that there is a place for music education and that it can successfully be promoted by the non-specialist teacher. The musical activities I have seen used successfully with maladjusted children have largely been restricted to the type practised in junior or lower secondary classes, which would in itself seem to be desirable at a time when we are urged to bear in mind the integration (or very often in this case the re-integration) of special needs children. Since there is a marked relationship between maladjustment and academic failure, we need to ensure that EBD children are not further disadvantaged by our failure as teachers to provide them with such a restricted curriculum that they are unable to rejoin their mainstream classes largely because they have not followed the same course of work as their peers.

How may music be sustained in EBD schools?

Despite their reservations about music in EBD schools and the limited amount of practice they were able to observe, Wilson and Evans argue for the inclusion of Music and the other creative arts into the curriculum 'on the grounds that they may give pleasure, provide relief, facilitate communication or produce gratifying results'.

Unfortunately, there is, to date, very little written evidence endorsing their view, but one relevant article did appear in *Music Educators' Journal* (1972) in which Price, Rast and Winterfeldt outlined their music programme with emotionally disturbed children and indicated its success not only in terms of the classroom experience, but also in terms of developing the children's social skills which were then transferred from the music room into other areas of the school.

We return then to the theme of therapeutic education, but maybe this time we should approach it from a different angle. Overtones of music therapy are daunting to the Music teacher and non-specialist alike, but it would seem that the latter rejects the idea of teaching Music largely as a result of his/her inadequacy as a musician. The same teacher is, however, experienced in furthering the emotional, social and educational readjustment of his/her pupils, and it would therefore seem logical to assume that s/he would be able to utilize a new resource to the same effect if that resource were to be made 'user-friendly'.

The first priority must surely be to persuade non-specialists that teaching Music is not dependent on being able to play the piano, nor do they necessarily need to have experience of playing any other instrument. They should also be assured that teaching Music does not automatically mean that they move into the impresario business in which they are required to churn out performers. Rather than aiming at musical excellence, the non-specialist should seek to use musical activities in the same way as s/he uses other activities, first of all to engage the child, then to provide him/her with a satisfying experience and finally to cash in on this experience as a means of furthering the overall readjustment of the child. The last stage in this process will be the easiest for the EBD teacher (because that is what s/he is attempting to do all the time with the pupils) and the first stage probably the most difficult.

A guide to initial reading which gives an overview of music with special needs children is available from the Disabled Living Foundation. But the standard texts of Bentley, Salaman, Swanwick and Paynter are also relevant reading for, though they are specialist literature, we should aim to give maladjusted children as near normal an input as we are able. Non-specialists would be well-advised therefore to consider all that is available and extract from it what they can confidently utilize, though at the stage when non-specialists require advice on how to begin the actual teaching, guidelines in literature become more scarce. Though their work relates to primary schools, Jean Gilbert and Muriel Hart's suggested activities have starting points which are realistic for the non-specialist teacher in EBD schools and Storms's *Handbook of Music Games* is a useful resource. In addition, there is now available a compilation of musical activities which have been tried and tested in the EBD context (Packer 1987).

The material contained in this pamphlet is not unusual in itself but the suggestions made regarding the manner of presentation indicate the significant differences between mainstream and special music education. There is, for example, no suggestion of a step-by-step continuous programme but rather a seemingly random selection of diverse activities from which to select in order to catch the child's fleeting moment of interest. Many of the activities are presented as games and they are complete in themselves, designed to last no longer than twenty minutes, that being about the maximum time maladjusted children may be expected to engage in a single activity.

The overriding themes underlying the compilation are familiarity and instant success, components which may be desirable in mainstream education but are imperative in EBD schools. My own experience and that of colleagues has shown that to simultaneously ignore both of these ingredients is a recipe for disaster. This does not of course prohibit the introduction of new material, but it does mean that in order to ensure some degree of successful integration, the teacher has to resort to devious tactics. Sometimes, an acceptable level of familiarity may be established by using new music as a background sound for other activities, but otherwise a workable system is:

1   use familiar music when introducing a new activity to the child;
2   establish the new activity so that it becomes familiar to the child;
3   use the now familiar activity to introduce new music.

Though this appears to be a long-winded process, it is usually time- and labour-saving in the long run, for maladjusted children are notoriously resistant to change and, if they feel in any way threatened by material which is unfamiliar, there is little chance that the teacher will be able to engage them in listening to or appreciating new music.

The need to provide instant success is also common to other subject areas in EBD education but it is perhaps more readily achieved in music because there is little need for verbal communication or academic ability. Because they have in the past consistently failed academically and socially, maladjusted children do not have the normal capacities for effort, endurance, optimism, etc., and they will therefore give up at the smallest stumbling block. Rehearsal is a skill which consequently evades them, but it is possible to develop this skill so long as the children have experienced the sweet smell of instant success as a regular part of their musical education. The activities recommended therefore in this compilation, together with the suggested manner of presentation, combine to ensure (as far as is possible) that success is within the children's grasp.

Since Packer's *Musical Activities for Children with Behavioural Problems* is designed for the use of those who are not music specialists, the activities included represent a somewhat skewed sample, but it did provide much of the material for a day conference on music with maladjusted children. Held in July last year, the conference was the first of its kind to be held in this country and it brought together some of those currently involved with music education in EBD schools. The conference report (available from the Disabled Living Foundation) highlights the isolated and intermittent nature of this practice but also illustrates the success of that practice as observed by specialists and non-specialists alike. During the course of the day, reference was frequently made to the alleviation of anger and depression (the two most dominant emotions experienced by maladjusted children), and the recurring theme was the compensatory and therapeutic value of music. Apparent in every anecdote and recording which was presented were the high level of enjoyment which the children were deriving from their music-making and which, it was suggested, was a level of enjoyment rarely experienced in other areas of the curriculum.

The results of a questionnaire put to other teachers using music in EBD schools reflected similar findings. Those engaged in music education spoke of their children gaining self-esteem and self-confidence through music-making, developing awareness and appreciation of others to the extent that they could play together (constructive play rather than the usual playground fights), and they also observed that in music lessons, children who were normally very tense were able to find relaxation.

These observations were in keeping with the comments of teachers involved in my own research. One teacher summarized the effect of music education on her children thus: 'the children are insecure and damaged. Within the context of music they are confident, happy, relaxed and eager to share: a rare thing for our children!' Another observed that her class's response to singing and playing the instruments was

> spontaneous enjoyment which was for them quite rare. They could express themselves creatively and cooperatively in Music lessons which they were unable to do in Art, for example, as they found the latter more threatening and competitive. In Music they experienced immediate success so it acted as a great boost to their confidence.

Occasionally, class teachers' comments were something of a back-handed compliment: for example, 'I'm afraid you've got Duncan this afternoon but I should think he'll be okay. For some unknown reason he seems to enjoy his Music lessons: a bit odd really because usually nothing in the world pleases him!' and on other occasions, class teachers seemed to gain a new perspective on their children during the course of their music-making. One teacher was 'amazed' to see how one of her group, a normally extremely tense and anxious boy, joined in the Music lesson enthusiastically and uninhibitedly, and she said with regard to the performance of another little boy that she had seen him behave as a child for the first time ever.

Such comments suggested that it would be interesting to keep a record of the children's overall performance in Music lessons during the course of a term, and to compare this performance with the class teacher's perception of the child's performance in other subjects, but the problem presented was: how could the non-specialist teacher be expected to measure performance in Music? The solution was found in turning the focus of attention to the child's behaviour during the sessions, since this could be easily correlated between different subjects and could also be taken to be a fair indication of the level of the child's involvement with the activities being taught.

Class teachers were therefore asked (in advance of the start of the Music programme) to grade their children's average performance in the following areas. During lessons, does this child usually:

- co-operate with staff;
- co-operate with peers;
- express satisfaction (or any substantiated negative reaction) to the activity;
- share positive comments on related issues;
- volunteer information or initiate any other positive contribution;
- repeat or paraphrase information presented during the lesson?

Teachers were asked to grade the children's performance on a scale of 1–3 thus: (1) inappropriate/unacceptable; (2) inadequate/immature; (3) appropriate/acceptable, and to consider these terms in relation to the 'norm' for that child's chronological age.

None of the fifty-six children assessed was present for all the term's lessons but each child's individual total, averaged out over the term, showed that his/her performance during the Music lessons was consistently and markedly higher than the class teacher's original prediction had been. The chart showing Uri and Nigel's performance shows that occasionally they fall back to the teacher's estimation, and also it coincidentally indicates the high level of absenteeism associated with this type of school, for in the case of these two boys, they were only in school for four of the twelve lessons.

The first column shows the teacher's prediction before the Music programme was started, and the following columns show the class teacher's grading of the child's performance during each of the music lessons attended.

Uri	*Nigel*
2 3 3 2 3	1 3 3 2 3
1 1 3 3 3	1 2 3 3 3
2 2 3 3 3	2 3 3 3 3
2 3 3 3 3	2 3 3 3 2
2 3 3 3 3	2 2 3 2 2
2 3 3 3 3	2 3 3 2 2

Rosemary was present for six of the twelve lessons and her chart shows a significant difference between the class teacher's original prediction and his actual observation of her performance during the Music lessons.

Rosemary
1 3 3 3 2 3 3
1 3 3 3 2 3 3
1 3 3 3 3 3 3
1 3 3 3 3 3 3
1 3 3 3 3 3 3
1 3 3 3 3 3 3

One possible explanation for such an improved perception may be that during the course of these sessions two teachers were present, though one was cast as an observer rather than a teacher. There is, however, no evidence to suggest that improved staffing levels improve the performance of special needs pupils; in fact the research of McBrien and Weightman (1980) and Dalgleish and Matthews (1981) would seem to suggest the opposite, though their research does relate specifically to those with learning difficulties.

Another possible explanation is that the children would have naturally made this degree of progress during the course of a term and that it is therefore misguided to compare their ongoing performance with the teacher's original prediction (even though that prediction was in each case based on several years' acquaintance with the child). Though this theory was not borne out by the subjective view of the teachers themselves, we are currently involved in further research which may give a different view, but at this stage it would seem that the results are fairly similar.

One is obviously reluctant to make grandiose claims about the therapeutic value of music education, but one begins to suspect that Music can make a significant difference to the lives of some disturbed children and that it should therefore not be carelessly dismissed from the curriculum of EBD schools. It is, however, unreasonable to expect the non-music specialist to take the initiative and work in isolation to introduce music education for his/her pupils. The initiative must instead be taken by advisory music teachers and those in higher education to provide special school teachers with something along the lines of Reading University's Music Consultancy in Primary Schools (see Smith 1987). Such a model (providing that the majority of the training could be done *in situ*) would surely be sufficient to inspire confidence in teachers and provide them with a dynamic resource with which to effect the emotional and social readjustment of their pupils.

References

Adams, P. and Syers, A. (1984) *Music in the Primary School,* London: ILEA Music Centre.

Bridgeland, M. (1971) *Pioneer Work with Maladjusted Children,* St Albans: Staples Press.

Dalgleish, M. and Matthews, R. (1981) 'Some effects of the staffing levels and group size on the quality of daycare for severely mentally handicapped adults', *British Journal of Mental Subnormality* 27: 30–5.

DES (1965) *The Education of Maladjusted Children,* Education Pamphlet No. 47, London: HMSO.

—— (1985) *Music from 5 to 16,* Curriculum Matters 4, London: HMSO.

Dobbs, J.P.B. (1966) *The Slow Learner and Music,* London: Oxford University Press.

Gilbert, J. (1987) *Musical Starting Points with Young Children,* London: Ward Lock Educational.

Hart, M. (1974) *Music,* London: Heinemann Educational Books.

Kennard, D.J. (1979) *Access to Music for the Physically Handicapped Schoolchild and School Leaver,* London: Disabled Living Foundation.

Laslett, R. (1977) *Educating Maladjusted Children,* London: Crosby Lockwood Staples.

McBrien, J. and Weightman, J. (1980) 'The effect of room management procedures on the engagement of profoundly retarded children', *British Journal of Mental Subnormality* 26: 38–46.

Nordoff, P. and Robbins, C. (1971) *Therapy in Music for Handicapped Children*, London: Victor Gollancz.

Packer, Y.M. (1987) *Musical Activities for Children with Behavioural Problems*, London: Disabled Living Foundation.

Price, R., Rast, L. and Winterfeldt, C. (1972) 'Out of pandemonium music', *Music Educators' Journal* 58: 35–6.

Sandor, R. (ed.) (1969) *Musical Education in Hungary*, London: Boosey & Hawkes.

Smith, J. (1987) *Music Consultancy in Berkshire Primary Schools*, University of Reading, Berkshire: School of Music.

Shedden, J.A. (1984) 'Music and the Maladjusted Child', M.Ed. thesis, University of Newcastle upon Tyne.

Storms, G. (1981) *Handbook of Music Games*, London: Hutchinson.

Wilson, M. and Evans, M. (1980) *Education of Disturbed Pupils*, Schools Council Working Paper 65, London: Methuen Educational.

9 Assessment in the arts

Issues of objectivity

Gary Spruce

Introduction

In general terms, what are the characteristics that underpin an effective assessment model? Harlen *et al.* (1994) propose three roles for assessment: first that it should provide feedback about the on-going process of education (formative); second that it should communicate the level and nature of a pupil's experience (summative); and third that it should summarize for the purpose of selection. Harlen goes on to say that underpinning these roles are a number of key principles which should characterize the assessment model. These are that the assessment model should match the purpose for which it is intended, be integral to the teaching process, reflect the full range of the things that have been taught, be communicable to outside bodies, indicative of an institution's effectiveness and contribute to a national perspective.

Sally Brown (1994) advances a number of propositions about assessment which develop the ideas propounded by Harlen, giving them a qualitative context and relating them explicitly to teaching and learning. She argues that assessment should be broad-based and be seen to be 'fulfilling multiple purposes' – including fostering learning, improving teaching, providing valid information and enabling pupils and others to make choices; that there should be 'an increase in the range of qualities assessed and the context in which that assessment takes place'; that 'descriptive assessment' – a description of what the child has achieved – should replace a bland listing of marks and grades; that assessment should be devolved to 'schools, teachers, work-experience employers and young people themselves'; and finally, that there should be greater access to certification: 'certification should be available to a much greater proportion of the population of young people'. These, then, are the basic principles that must be at the heart of any assessment model.

Objectivity

Two particularly prevalent ways of thinking about assessment – one generic and one specific to the arts – can militate against the formulation of a successful assessment model. The first is that all assessment should be demonstrably objective and the second, at first sight mutually exclusive, is that the particular nature of the arts renders them unsuitable for any kind of external evaluation. Although neither position is entirely unsustainable, and elements of both perceptions may well contribute to an ideal assessment model for the arts, when applied in an inflexible and doctrinaire fashion, each has the potential to cause damage. This danger was acknowledged by HMI in their document *Music from 5–16* (1985).

> There has been a long-standing controversy about the feasibility and even the desirability of assessing progress in aesthetic subjects. Opponents of the idea cannot see any way of evaluating development which intimately involves human feelings and emotions; proponents contend that the effectiveness of all forms of educational provision should be subject to regular assessment. Ironically, certain aspects of musical progress have been more thoroughly assessed (via graded examinations) than almost any other area of the curriculum. Unfortunately, such examinations do not always identify such elusive qualities as musicianship and creativity, sometimes valuing technical accomplishment above musical understanding.
>
> (DES 1985: 18)

The significance attached to demonstrable objectivity in the formulation of assessment models is rooted in two diametrically opposed ways of perceiving the function of education and the nature of intelligence. The first derives from the highly stratified and essentially conservative nature of post-war English education, and the second from the comprehensivization of the nation's schools that took place during the ostensibly more liberal 1960s and early 1970s. It may be, as Gipps (1994) says, that: 'over the last twenty-five years, assessment has been undergoing a paradigm shift from psychometrics to a broader model of educational assessment, from a testing and examination culture to an assessment culture', but the requirement that assessment models should be as objective as possible has remained a common feature. Their validity has depended upon them being perceived as such.

In the context of the selective nature of post-war education, the importance of demonstrable objectivity in assessment is understandable. It proceeded from a perception of the purpose of education and the nature of intelligence which perfectly concorded with the prevailing philosophy. Intelligence was perceived as being inherited and fixed (much in the same way as is the colour of one's eyes) and could, through assessment, be demonstrated and quantified. Education was essentially a utilitarian process, the success of which was measured by summative assessment. The results of such assessment could then be norm-referenced and used as the basis for selection to type of school or as the means of access to higher education, job or career. Education and assessment were 'about sorting people into social roles for society' (Brown 1993: 227). It therefore follows that assessment was perceived as being primarily judgemental and its fairness had to be seen to be beyond reproach. This was achieved through the demonstrable objectivity of the assessment model.

The main criticism of demonstrable objectivity (and the key word here is *demonstrable*) is that, in the formulation of the assessment model, the need to demonstrate objectivity is frequently of such overriding concern that it is applied to the detriment of all other considerations. Such is the importance attached to demon-strability that the assessment model is designed not with the primary aim of exhib-iting a child's 'best performance' but rather to exhibit its objectivity. This is achieved by removing from the assessment model (where possible) all variables associated with subjective judgement. Consequently, the test model acquires a highly controlled context: timed tasks (almost always written) which assess the ability to memorize, retain and repeat bodies of prescribed information. Therefore, whereas it may have been an appropriate form of assessment for the stratified system of education that prevailed in England from the end of the Second World War through to the end of the 1980s, it was a singularly inappropriate one for a comprehensive system whose fundamental philosophical basis was a belief in the value of education for its own sake and the educability of all children. How then did the primacy of objectivity maintain its grip on the education system?

The answer, I believe, lies in the nature of the public service ethos of the 1960s and 1970s. Stewart Ranson (1992), in an analysis of the public service models of the period defines two types: the 'professional service management' model, and the 'cor-porate management' model. Both, although essentially liberal in design, perceived their function as delivering services to the community without involving the community in defining what those services should be. They believed in 'the essential atomism of society composed of private and self-sufficient individuals … thus the Welfare State identified with and served the needs of individual clients rather than enabling the development of whole communities' (Ranson 1992). In the early 1970s some progress was made towards involving the communities in defining their own needs. However, few authorities fully took on board the recommendations of the Bains Report (1972) that local government should not limit its perspective to the narrow provision of a series of services but should have 'within its purview the overall economic, cultural and physical well-being of that community'. In education, the omniscient style of local government became manifest through the 'professional domination' of the service provided: 'an educated public was to be delivered by specialists rather than lived and created by citizens with the support of professionals' (Ranson 1992). The rationale for such a system was that decisions made on behalf of the community were informed by professional, detached objectivity. Objectivity and hence neutrality were justifications for a monopoly of power over the deci-sion-making process. Therefore involvement in anything that could be construed as involving value judgements was, where possible, avoided.

Education became inextricably linked with this non-value laden – and hence frequently non-judgemental – philosophy. Assessment was applied in as objective a manner as possible and value judgements were eschewed. The impression to be given to the student was that a qualitative decision had been made through the mechanistic application of clear criteria. (This was the era of the multi-choice examination.) Thus it was that the continued adherence to the rigid application of objective criteria-based assessment and a resistance to the very notion of assessment, other than that which could be applied empirically, derived from the same philosophical stable.

The non-judgemental approach to education became particularly manifest in the arts. For, whereas objective assessment could easily be applied to Maths and the sciences it was possible to argue that the arts were purely concerned with feelings rather than with cognitive development, and therefore assessment was both inappropriate and impracticable. It proceeded, as David Best says, 'from the misguided assumption that emotional feelings in general and the kinds of feelings most centrally involved in the creation and appreciation of arts are purely subjective and therefore not open to objective evaluation' (Best 1992). This view received widespread support amongst arts teachers during the late 1970s and early 1980s. It was perceived as being what gave the arts their uniqueness and therefore a justification for their place on the curriculum.

However, as both Best (1992: 96) and Swanwick (1979: 149) point out, such an attitude is politically unwise and educationally unsound. For, unless arts educators can demonstrate that learning takes place within what *they* define as being the *raison d'être* of the arts – the realm of the creative imagination and the development of the artistic and aesthetic – the existence of the arts on the curriculum cannot be justified. The case for the arts is best articulated by demonstrating that they have a unique contribution to make to what is the main function of schools – teaching and learning. 'Unless artistic experience is answerable to cognition and reason, there can be no reason for including the arts in our educational institutions' (Best 1992: 29). It is only through assessment that we can confirm that this is so. What the arts require is an assessment model that has legitimacy in a whole-education context and also serves the specific needs of the curriculum area.

Arts versus science: a false dichotomy?

The assessment philosophy of post-war British education was therefore driven by the need to objectively evaluate. Consequently, as the sciences and humanities were more amenable to objective assessment than were the arts, their status increased accordingly.

Distinguishing the arts from the sciences along the lines of their relative objectivity is, however, a philosophy rooted in the nineteenth century. The Victorian desire to define existence in terms of verifiable facts – epitomized by the character of Gradgrind in Charles Dickens's novel *Hard Times:* 'Facts are all that are needed in Life' – inevitably marginalized the arts. The arts were perceived in terms of sensate experience and having little to do with cognition. They were seen either as pleasantly irrational or as deeply concerned with emotions – or most often as somewhere on the continuum between those two points. As Wittgenstein (1921) said, 'people nowadays think that scientists exist to instruct them whilst poets and musicians exist to give them pleasure. The idea that the latter have something to teach them, that does not occur to them'. The detachment of the arts from their social context was further increased by the changing perception of the nature of the artist in society:

> For the first time the musician was conceived of as an artist, a term that was beginning to take on a deeper meaning … Bach and Mozart never considered themselves as artists; they were very much functional and well-integrated members of their societies, achieving modest worldly success by virtue of their

abilities. Yet in the emerging Romantic art cult, the composer was thought of as a solitary individual, ruled by wayward passions, in fundamental opposition to a philistine society. The artist existed on a more exalted plane than the workaday world of his audience; he breathed a rarefied ether and consorted with those sublime Intelligences that had once been charged with turning the crystal spheres.

(James 1995: 194)

In such a way was accomplished the exclusion of arts and artists from the functioning of society. Science and art were considered to be separate and mutually exclusive. Society had lost its ancient belief in the 'serene order' of the universe, in which the arts and sciences were united in a quest to discover the key to eternal truths.

Yet, as Best and others have pointed out, there is an essentially false dichotomy here. Science has frequently required a creative impulse to effect the cognitive leap required for the greatest of its discoveries. Copernicus postulated the idea that the earth travels around the sun whilst it was left to Galileo, born twenty years after Copernicus's death, to mathematically verify the concept. Furthermore, objectivism is only contemporary – fit for the time – and is not in itself a demonstration of absolute and eternal proof. As the philosopher Karl Popper points out, we can never know for certain that a scientific statement is objectively true. What we have observed in the past, and observe now, cannot be guaranteed to occur in the future.

Furthermore, the idea that the arts are exclusively concerned with feelings and emotions and have no basis in cognitive experience is equally ill-founded. As the composer Schoenberg says: 'music is not merely another kind of amusement but a musical thinkers representation of musical ideas; and these ideas must respond to the laws of human logic'. Thomas Mann writes: 'her strictness, or whatever you like to call the moralism of her form, must stand for an excuse for the ravishments of her actual sounds' (Leverkuhn, *Dr Faustus* 1947). Thus, the arts *are* about cognitive development and the sciences *do* require creative input. The dichotomy is essentially false and we must therefore look to renew the links between the two disciplines.

New insights into the nature of human perception and intelligence, and developments in philosophy of the sciences and of the arts have begun to dissolve these dichotomies and to re-establish the relationships between artistic, scientific and other modes of understanding. The sciences have many characteristics that have come to be almost exclusively associated with the arts and vice versa. The processes of scientific enquiry draw deeply on the scientists' powers of creativity and personal judgement ... Equally work in the arts shares some of the recognized characteristics of the sciences. If the arts require creative imagination and aesthetic judgement, they also call on painstaking discipline in the acquisition and application of skills and intellectual rigour in the pursuit of formal and conceptual solutions. These affinities between different modes of understanding are significant both for the planning and practice of education.

(NCC 1990: par. 50)

The primacy of the sensate

Some arts educators have attempted to turn to their advantage the non-cognitive view of the arts by espousing the notion of the primacy of the sensate. This is essentially a retreat from the cognitive argument by justifying the existence of the curriculum area in other terms. The 'primacy of the sensate' argument therefore tends either to be dismissive of the role of cognitive development in arts education or seeks to reinterpret it in terms of sensate experience. It is an attitude which, whilst purporting to be radical and progressive is, as I indicated earlier, firmly rooted in the nineteenth century: 'The first concept is always the best and most natural. The intellect can err, the sentiment – never' (Schumann).

Ross and Mitchell (1993) articulate a persuasive case for the 'sensate' perspective, basing their argument on a distinction between two types of sensate experience: *sensate surface* and *sensate resonance*. Sensate surface includes 'every appeal to sensory apprehension offered by the work – everything we see touch or hear that constitutes the body of the piece', while sensate resonance is:

> the operation of those self-same structures to evoke a sense of order, feeling and imagination … If surface delights us, resonance is what moves us … we must hold to the primacy of perception of the sensate dimension. It is only and exactly upon the sensate dimension that aesthetic understanding operates. Every art work is constrained by its sensate parameters.
>
> (Ross and Mitchell 1993)

For Ross, arts education is about the enabling of personal expression. He considers the arts as being a subjective dream world, 'the realm of mood character, symbol metaphor'. Children's education is about enculturation as a means towards a developed personal expression.

> Feelings arise in a cultural context. They find expression and realization in ways and by means available in and acceptable (meaningful) to that culture. We appropriate the conventions available within our culture for the expression of personal feeling, for the transaction and communication of personal meaning. It is clearly of the utmost importance that children should be skilled in such forms, customs, conventions and practices as will permit and facilitate the legitimate expression of feeling … Children should be given the opportunity to appropriate the expressive forms they need from the full range now available in the modern world, both contemporary and traditional and to convert them into personal style or autograph.
>
> (Ross and Mitchell 1993)

From this perspective they propound an assessment ideal that is process-based and legitimate only in as much as it is negotiated through dialogue with the child. They argue that the essential purpose of assessment is to engage with the part of the child's creative process that results in the artefact, not to assess the artefact itself.

Ross and Mitchell believe that to do the latter would be to work against the 'non-judgemental environment [which is] of the essence'. However, the aim of any process – and particularly a creative process – is the production of an artefact, and it is arguably naive to attempt to remove this from the assessment equation. Furthermore, it seems to me that there are inherent dangers in giving absolute primacy to the child's inner world and/or in excluding external intervention. As Gardner says:

> if the creator is too removed from the domain, too much in his or her own world … there will not be any rules by which to operate, and those knowledgeable about the domain will be unable to relate to the work produced … In the absence of knowledgeable others, who can apprehend and judge what one has created, one's work is consigned to a kind of limbo.
>
> (Gardner 1995: 15)

Objectivity and criteria-related assessment

It is of critical importance that an assessment model should be seen to have legitimacy by all of those involved with it. A central precept of this legitimacy is the perception that the evaluation process is objective. This is most frequently achieved by formulating assessment models in terms of clearly defined criteria which are strictly applied in controlled contexts. However, there are dangers associated with criteria-led assessment, particularly in the way in which it connects with, and impacts upon, objectivity.

An attempt to achieve objectivity through laying down strict criteria can inhibit the educational experience by allowing into the subject area only that which can be objectively assessed: 'it is a generally held perception that formal assessment has hindered and distorted work in the secondary classroom through laying too much emphasis on what is easily examinable, regardless of its relevance as musical experience' (Aspin 1986). Thus there is a danger that the criteria might look not to the subject area and the children for their points of reference but to the assessment model itself. If this occurs, then the whole educational process becomes distorted: '[the] artistic endeavours of children are frequently assessed according to externally pre-determined sets of criteria and standards that "measure the measurable" often at the expense of those qualities arts education professes to develop' (Cartwright 1989: 283).

Furthermore, Margaret Brown (1991) has shown how strict criteria-related assessment can lead back to norm-referencing behind what Drever *et al.* (1983) (quoted in Brown) describe as 'a smoke screen of pseudo criteria'.

However, the main danger of an assessment model that is too rigidly criteria-related is that the process will become fragmented. This is particularly true of the assessment of musical performance, where there can be great temptation to separate music into its component parts of rhythm, pitch, etc., to assess these separately and then aggregate them for a summative mark. A number of exam. boards adopted such a model in the early years of GCSE. This was a typical example of the need to demonstrate objectivity taking precedence over higher educational – and in this case artistic – ideals. No doubt, adopting this system meant that every mark could be justified, but at the cost of missing the point of the musical exercise: the performance as a whole. As Suzanne Langer says:

> The first principle in music hearing, is not, as many people presume, the ability to distinguish the separate elements in a composition and recognize its devices, but to experience the primary illusion, to feel the consistent movement and recognize at once the commanding form which makes this piece *an inviolable whole.*

> (Langer 1953; emphasis added)

Furthermore, simply because an assessment model can demonstrate high objectivity, this does not in itself imply reliability. Janet Mills (1991) refers to a study carried out by Fiske (1977) which in fact demonstrated that holistic assessment resulted in a greater consensus of opinion than did assessment which was fragmented. Thus the theory that strictly applied criteria necessarily equal absolute objectivity was shown to be deeply flawed. Mills suggests two reasons why this might be so:

1   Overall performance is real. In other words, all the judges hear the same performance. If we are to assess a component of the performance, such as rhythm, on the other hand, we must partial out much of the other material. Our ability to do this, or our technique of doing this, will vary. Thus our perceptions of the rhythmic element of a performance may differ. Abstracting rhythm from melody is not a conceptually simple matter like filtering out impurities from a sample of rain water, or absorbing light rays within some defined frequency range: melody consists of a dynamic relationship between rhythm, pitch and a host of other variables. It is not clear what the expression 'the rhythm of a performance' means.
2   We are practised in the assessment of overall performance. Every time we listen to a TV jingle, a pop song, a Brahms symphony, or a passing ice-cream van, we have the opportunity to make judgements about what we hear. On the other hand, we are less frequently presented with examples of pure rhythm or intonation, or whatever this means, to assess.

> (Mills 1991)

Mills is writing here particularly about the summative assessment of musical performance. However, it seems to me that her point applies equally to formative evaluation. Her arguments are not designed to prevent the assessor from judging a performance holistically and then analysing the component parts in order to formatively feed back to the student. What must be avoided, however, is the adoption of an assessment model which loses sight of the whole through assessing the parts – not seeing the wood for the trees. As Goldman says:

Dissecting a work analytically may alienate the analyst from the work's expressive effects, especially from the expressive tone of the whole. This is not to dismiss the value of critical scrutiny or of its communication in educational settings; it is only to call into question the location of that value.

(Goldman 1990)

The important thing with criteria statements is, as Denis Lawton says, to avoid being so 'general that they become untestable' or so specific that 'they become trivial and atomistic'. However, as he somewhat gloomily concludes, 'this problem has not been solved' (Lawton 1994).

Constructing an assessment model

In addition to being perceived as having validity by all those involved with it, an assessment system should provide 'good quality information about pupils' performance without distorting good teaching practice and therefore learning' (Gipps 1994). Furthermore, it should be aware of the uniquely personal nature of creativity, recognizing that creativity is not only integral to the arts but is central to the entire educational process.

It seems to me that in constructing such an assessment model we are required to redefine our perception of the nature of intelligence and our concept of what constitutes objectivity. Having done this we can then proceed to devise a model which adopts a more holistic view of the assessment process and therefore a more appropriate one for the arts.

The perception that the arts are unconcerned with cognitive experience is based on the idea of intelligence as a unitary and fixed function. However, over the last decade there has developed the idea of the arts as constituting a distinct and unique 'way of knowing'. The arts as a way of knowing has become something of a clarion call for art educators. Essentially it is a means whereby the terms of reference of much of education can be redefined in favour of the establishment of a coherent arts curriculum. It has been interpreted in different ways by a number of arts educators – particularly Abbs (1985), Best (1992) and Ross and Mitchell (1993). However, I wish to consider it, perhaps somewhat tangentially, from the perspective of two particular publications: Howard Gardner's *Frames of Mind* (1984) and the Gulbenkian Report, *The Arts in Schools* (1982). Gardner, whose book is subtitled *The Theory of Multiple Intelligences*, argues for the existence of a number of intelligences: linguistic, musical, logical-mathematical, spatial, bodily-kinaesthetic and personal intelligence. Having defined this multiplicity of intelligences, he draws attention to the fact that only two are developed to any degree during formal schooling: the linguistic and the logical-mathematical. Gardner is therefore suggesting that much of a child's cognitive potential remains unexploited and particularly that which relates to the artistic and aesthetic. Perhaps then, as Peter Abbs suggests, the educational debate should centre around this failure rather than 'the present massive and barbaric retreat into "basics"' (Abbs 1985).

Gardner's particular way of thinking about intelligence obviously has great significance for assessment in arts education. If one accepts his theory of multiple intelligences, then it follows that there must be an equal multiplicity of ways of assessing cognitive development. It is no longer satisfactory to apply the psychometric model to learning, irrespective of its appropriateness to the learning model. This was clearly the view of the Gulbenkian Report, which said:

> Like others before us, we reject the view that the only valid kinds of knowledge are those that are open to deductive reasoning and empirical tests. The ways of getting knowledge are not limited to the intellectual, book learning or scientific kind. The aesthetic, the religious and the moral are quite as these others at conveying knowledge. In our view, public education has been too devoted to particular kinds of knowledge at the expense of others *which are of equal importance.*
>
> (Gulbenkian Report 1982: par. 24; emphasis added)

Furthermore, what follows naturally from this is a redefinition of what we mean by objectivity. The first misconception we must dispense with is the idea that objectivity and subjectivity are mutually exclusive and that in matters other than of concrete fact it is possible for an assessor to be totally objective:

> rather than treating subjectivity and objectivity as exclusive alternatives, we should think of them rather as two poles of a spectrum … At one end we might find entirely subjective remarks … such as 'I like strawberries'. This it is said makes no claims about the qualities of strawberries but merely reports how I, a subject, respond to them. At the other end of the spectrum there will be judgements which will be thought to be entirely objective: the judgement that triangles have three sides, perhaps. But for most of us, a large percentage of our judgements … will be more or less objective (or subjective). My judgement of *Othello* may be objective to the point that it avoids haste, prejudice, ignorance and the like, but my response may also be dependent on things which are part of my personal life history. The point I wish to make is that the fact that my judgement is for these latter reasons not entirely objective (since I cannot assume that we all have the same sort of psychology or cultural background) does not make it entirely subjective.
>
> (Lyas 1992: 377)

Gipps (1994) expands on the relationship between objectivity and the assessor, further arguing that absolute objectivity is simply not possible:

> The modernist view is that it is possible to be a disinterested observer while the post-modern view is that such detachment is not possible: we are social beings who construe the world according to our values and perceptions, our biographies are central to what we see and how we interpret it … reality is constructed by the observer and there are multiple constructions of reality.
>
> (Gipps 1994: 288)

Having therefore established that we need to redefine our perception of what intelligence is and having ceased worshipping at the temple of objectivity, we can proceed to develop an assessment model which is much less content-orientated and much more holistic in approach.

The nature of holistic assessment is that it should attempt to elicit 'best' rather than 'typical' performance and that it should be aware of factors external to the content of the test: specifically context and the relationship between assessor and assessed. As part of a definition of what characterizes good assessment, the late Desmond Nuttall in his classic paper 'The Validity of Assessments' draws attention to how assessment draws inferences from a sample of behaviour: 'every assessment is based on a sample of behaviour in which we are interested; we tend to generalize from the particular sample of behaviour we observe to the universe of that behaviour' (Nuttall 1987). Gipps, in an analysis of Nuttall's article, expands on these points, emphasizing that the quality and range of cognizance of the assessment model is of crucial importance to the delivery of an accurate sample of behaviour:

> Significantly what the paper brings into the definition of the universe of behaviour is the 'conditions and occasions' of assessment as well as the content (Nuttall p. 110). We know that the content, context mode of the assessment will affect pupil performance; we have to distinguish 'between competence (the basic ability to perform) and performance (the demonstration of the competence on a particular occasion or under particular circumstances)' (op. cit., p. 112). What marks out educational assessment from psychometrics is a different view of the learner, and a different relationship between pupil and assessor. At the heart of this lies an understanding that performance is affected by context including the relationship between pupil and assessor, the pupil's motivational state and the characteristics of the assessment task.
>
> (Gipps 1994: 286)

A successful relationship between pupil and teacher, which is so necessary to the successful functioning of holistic assessment, is founded upon a number of 'pupil awarenesses': first, that absolute objectivity is not possible and that what is being brought to bear is informed subjectivity; second, that the acquisition of informed subjectivity is one of the aims of arts education; and finally, that, although some assessment is, in the final analysis, judgemental, the process is essentially a collaborative seeking after 'best performance'.

Gipps considers that the key aspects in eliciting best performance are:

- a range of activities, offering a wide opportunity to perform;
- matched to classroom practice;
- extended interaction between pupil and teacher to explain the task;
- a normal classroom setting, which is therefore not unduly threatening;
- a range of response modes other than written.

The appropriateness of these aspects to arts education and their importance as the foundation stones of any arts-based assessment model are manifestly obvious. They have the virtue of being applicable to all areas of the curriculum whilst being particularly relevant to arts subjects, and they entirely dispense with the psychometric model of assessment which has so distorted arts education. The notion of holistic assessment therefore provides a philosophical basis for assessment which not only serves the arts well but also, of perhaps greater importance, is of equal applicability to other curriculum areas. To achieve a universal assessment model would be to bring together hitherto disparate curriculum areas in a unity of educational purpose.

In conclusion, I wish to consider once more the conflicting perspectives of those who believe in the necessity of assessment in the arts – either from a political and/or educational viewpoint – and those who are essentially opposed to it on philosophical and/or practical grounds. Possibly, there is no way of reconciling such divergent views. However, I believe Gardner comes closest to proposing an ideal accommodation. He rejects the idea of a non-judgemental approach whilst emphasizing the difficulties inherent in assessing in the arts. In doing so, he provides what I believe to be not only a framework for assessment, but also a philosophical framework for the teaching of the arts:

> The future creator must evolve into a certain type of person. He or she cannot be too ready to please, too influenced by the surrounds, too upset by critical feedback. Here is where shrewd parenting and teaching come in. It is equally damaging to tell the youngster that everything that she fashions is great, as it is to rip everything that she does to shreds. The educator of the future creator needs to walk a fine line – always encouraging the youngster to stretch, praising her where she succeeds, but equally important providing support and a non-condemnatory *interpretative* [my emphasis] framework when things do not go well … when the most demanding creative work is being tackled, it is important to have at one's side some other person who can provide sustenance … by later childhood, it is not inappropriate to introduce the standards of the domain and allow the student to see how judgements of quality are made. The field is not always correct; indeed the history of creativity is the history of judgements that were initially off the mark. But the point is one simply cannot do without some kind of evaluative feedback.
>
> (Gardner 1995)

References

Abbs, P. (1985) 'Art as a way of knowing: notes towards a more formal aesthetics', in A. Bloomfield (ed.) *Creative and Aesthetic Education*, Hull: The University of Hull.

Aspin, D. (1986) *Assessment and Progression in Music Education*, Music Advisers' National Association.

Best, D. (1992) *The Rationality of Feeling: Understanding the Arts in Education*, London: The Falmer Press.

Brown, M. (1991) 'Problematic issues in national assessment', *Cambridge Journal of Education* 21(2).

Brown, S. (1994) 'Assessment: a changing practice', in B. Moon and A. Shelton Mayes (eds) (1994) *Teaching and Learning in the Secondary School*, London: Routledge.

Cartwright, P. (1989) 'Assessment and examination in arts education', in M. Ross(ed.) *The Claims of Feeling*, London: The Falmer Press.

DES (1985) *Music from 5–16*, London: HMSO.

Drever, E. *et al.* (1983) 'A framework for decision – or "business as usual"?' *Scottish Educational Review* 15(2).

Fiske, H. E. (1977) 'Relationship of selected factors in trumpet performance adjudication reliability', *Journal of Research in Music Education* 25(4).

Gardner, H. (1984) *Frames of Mind: The Theory of Multiple Intelligences*, London: Heinemann.

—— (1995) 'Creating creativity', *Times Educational Supplement*, 6 January 1995.

Gipps, C. (1994) 'Developments in educational assessment: what makes a good test?' *Assessment in Education*, 1(3).

Goldman, A. H. (1990) 'The education of taste', *British Journal of Aesthetics*, 30(2).

Gulbenkian Report (1982) *The Arts in Schools*, London: Calouste Gulbenkian.

Harlen, W., Gipps, C., Broadfoot, P. and Nuttall, D. (1994) 'Assessment and the improvement of education', in B. Moon and A. Shelton Mayes (eds) (1994) *Teaching and Learning in the Secondary School*, London: Routledge.

HMSO (1972) *Bains Report*, London: HMSO.

James, J. (1995) *The Music of the Spheres*, London: Little, Brown & Co.

Langer, S. (1953) *Feeling and Form: A Theory of Art Developed from Philosophy in a New Key*, London: Routledge & Kegan Paul.

Lawton, D. (1994) 'The National Curriculum and its assessment', *Forum* 6(4).

Lyas, C. (1992) 'The evaluation of art', in O. Hanfling (ed.) *Philosophical Aesthetics: An Introduction*, Milton Keynes: Open University Press.

Mills, J. (1991) 'Assessing musical performance musically', *Educational Studies*, 17(2).

National Curriculum Council (NCC), Arts in Schools Project (1990) *The Arts 5–16*, London: Oliver & Boyd.

Nuttall, D. (1987) 'The validity of assessments', *European Journal of Psychology of Education* 2(2).

Ranson, S. (1992) 'Towards the learning society', *Education Management and Administration* 20(2).

Ross, M. and Mitchell, S. (1993) 'Assessing achievement in the arts', *British Journal of Aesthetics* 33(2).

Swanwick, K. (1979) *A Basis for Music Education*, London: NFER.

10 In search of a child's musical imagination

Robert Walker

Overture

In searching for a child's musical imagination, some questions spring to mind as being important preliminaries. If we identify musical imagination in adults, can we draw some conclusions that would be applicable to children? Furthermore, can we expect the same type of behaviour as manifests musical imagination in adults to occur in children? Do we expect children to do the same things as adults? What kind of behaviour contains evidence of musical imagination as far as both children and adults are concerned?

Some would be tempted to agree that a child of pre-school age who could play an unaccompanied violin sonata by J.S. Bach displayed more musical imagination than one who could merely bang tin cans and play-bricks together, accompanied by shouts and screams, or even a reasonably well-sung song. Yet if we can recognize children's musical imagination only in behaviour we call musical in the adult sense, then there are certain implications. First, and perhaps most important, is the odd position this gives music in a child's range of behaviours. We might accept 'child-ish' drawings on their merit as important sources of information about children's mentality and visual representation in the way Rudolf Arnheim has done, but 'childish' musical actions would be rejected as such. And it would mean that as far as musical behaviour is concerned, we expect children to be like little adults; that is, we can take them seriously only when they play or compose adult music like a Bach violin sonata. Applied to visual art, it would mean looking for children who could paint a *Blue Boy* or *The Adoration of the Magi*, and so on. Such a view would mean that very few children are capable of either displaying or even possessing musical imagination. One feels intuitively that something must be wrong with this view of music and children.

Theme 1

Gardner (1983) regards what he calls musical intelligence as one of man's finite number of intelligences, along with spatial, logical-mathematical, and others. Interestingly, he explains the term by reference to the behaviour of unassailably musical adults. In claiming that no other intelligence 'emerges earlier than musical talent' (1983: 99), he cites examples of precocious behaviour in children as the manifestation of musical intelligence, at least in western culture or, more precisely, recent western culture.

But, as if aware of the problem inherent in the precocity argument, he goes on to explain that the music of other cultures contains different acoustic emphases than that of the western traditions. This is quite a crucial point, which needs exploring further.

Some African tribal music contains enormously complex or tediously repetitive (to the western ear) rhythms played on sticks and drums and voices chanting pitches that western music does not utilize. Some North American Indian music uses different vocal timbres and minute frequency changes near the threshold of auditory functioning in humans, which have never been employed in recent western traditions, except in the work of some of today's avant-garde musicians. Many singers in other cultures across the world can produce more than one note simultaneously, a practice never used in the west, and in some South Pacific islands there is a flute that is played with the nose. Some cultures revere the sound of the rattle above all else as possessing special powers, particularly when it is shaken by the most powerful persons in their society. Thus the rattling together of bits of metal, slivers of bone or shell, or dried seeds is thought by many to contain deep spiritual significance. Similarly, in some societies dried skins from the backs of humans, seasoned with the urine of descendants, are thought to make drums of frightening power and which have the ability to communicate with spirits of the dead (Sachs 1942).

Considering music in such a world context, it can be argued that for some cultures, at least, a child banging tin cans and play-bricks may well be regarded as displaying musical imagination in a more comprehensible manner than a child playing a violin. But there is another point: the type of technique required to make some of the musical sounds of cultures outside the western tradition of high art is of a different order than that needed to play a Bach violin sonata. So the role of specialized training and access to it assume some importance. Little technical training appears necessary to make some of the sounds heard in various non-western cultures, compared with the rigour and scope of that needed to play the violin, and certainly little training appears necessary for success in the pop-rock scene – a form of musical communication that seems to transcend cultural barriers in a way no other musical behaviour may be capable of doing, Therefore, apart from any lingering nineteenth-century notions of western cultural superiority, there seems little to suggest that mere skill acquisition through rigorous training can contribute much to the development of musical imagination. Irrespective of the possibility that pre-school children who can play Bach sonatas are 'freaks', *ipso facto*, it must follow that precocity cannot be the only behavioural attribute in which musical imagination is manifest. If that were so, musical imagination would be found only in such freaks. It is, of course, quite conceivable that some freaks, like any other subgrouping, may display musical imagination, but it is surely unaccept-able that only musical freaks can.

In fact, it is possible to illustrate this point through reference to child prodigies and musicians in history. One of the most celebrated of all time was Wolfgang

Amadeus Mozart. At least this is how history has brought him down to us. Those in the eighteenth century might have seen things differently! There were literally hundreds of child prodigies at the time, of whom Mozart was but one, even though he was highly regarded. In England, for example, there was William Crotch of Norwich, who in 1778, at the age of three, was giving recitals in London and Cambridge. The 1954 edition of Grove's *Dictionary of Music* states that 'Crotch's precocity is almost unparalleled in music; even Mozart and Mendelssohn hardly equalled him in this respect'. He was also precocious in drawing and painting and was the subject of an enquiry by the Royal Society at the age of five.

If anyone can be said to display musical imagination, it must be Mozart, whose compositions and legendary fame at improvising and making fun of others' musical mannerisms earned him, respectively, posthumous and contemporaneous reputations. He even made fun of the young Beethoven, much to the latter's annoyance, imitating his excessively loud playing and furious sounds. The same cannot be said of William Crotch, who has been all but forgotten as a prodigy and is not known at all as a composer, except in the organ lofts of some English cathedrals. If we contrast this with a most unprecocious French composer, Hector Berlioz, whose music is discussed under headings like 'Berlioz and the Romantic imagination', we are surely able to draw some conclusions!

Berlioz could almost be said to have been the antithesis of a precociously talented youngster. He could not play any instrument really well, and he showed a certain lack of aptitude at his musical studies. One of the professors (Cherubini) at the Paris Conservatoire actually had him thrown out. Berlioz attempted to study music somewhat illegally, while a student of medicine, and his angry father cut off his allowance on hearing of his musical activities. Yet few now would disagree that the mature Berlioz displayed outstanding musical imagination in his compositions.

From this we can say with some assurance that precocious behaviour in music is by no means a *sine qua non* for manifestations of musical imagination. We might even say that it should be possible to identify musical imagination in non-precocious children. Berlioz was certainly not the only imaginative musician to lack a precocious beginning.

Theme 2

It is no easy task to identify musical imagination in adults, even within an artistic tradition like western high art. For example, would we consider a composer whose music was described by his contemporaries as 'obscene' or 'obscure, idle balderdash' as imaginative? These were just some of the opinions expressed about Berlioz's symphonies (Strunk 1950). If we read the terms 'madness' and 'musical contortions' about someone's music, would we be likely to say the composer displayed musical imagination? A prominent nineteenth-century German music critic wrote such things about Tchaikovsky's music for orchestra, and Liszt's piano music was described as 'the invitation to stamping and hissing' (Sitwell 1967).

Development and variations

Today, in contrast, no one would have any compunction agreeing that all three composers displayed what can be called musical imagination, and not just in comparison with any mediocrity that surrounded them. We say things like Berlioz's music plumbs the depths of individual sensibility by pitting itself against the collective insensitivity in unique ways, and that Liszt and Tchaikovsky provide musical transportations into realms of consciousness not achieved or even attempted previously. We might also add that their imitators in this century have earned millions by providing diluted resemblances of such musical imagination for the movies and television.

Judging by these contemporary opinions of the three composers, we can say that they represented disturbing departures from acceptable norms of musical expectation to some people in the nineteenth century, even though to their supporters they exemplified the epitome of musical and romantic imagination. It is significant that the names of those many musicians who tended to conform to societal expectations do not appear in retrospect as exemplars of musical imagination in the commentaries of those who write about such things. We do not see chapter headings such as 'Cherubini and the Romantic imagination'. One supposes this has nothing to do with the fact that it was this gentleman who was responsible for getting Berlioz thrown out of the Paris Conservatoire library, not only as a nuisance but as an 'untalented wastrel'.

There certainly seems to be something worth following up in the observation that those who conform to expected norms in music do not earn reputations for being imaginative in the way that those who create their own independent expressions do. Many could learn to write music like Cherubini, and still do in some music academies, but few, if any, could learn to write like Berlioz, Tchaikovsky or Liszt. It is this presence in music of a disparity between the mediocre and the unique and brilliant that has fired people's imaginations for two or three centuries in western European musical culture. Mozart delighted or infuriated his contemporaries with his brilliant powers of mimicry as he exposed unimaginativeness, mannerism and transparency in others, while producing music incapable of such imitation himself. The very fact that his music was so unassailable in this way is testimony to its perfect synthesis with his entire being, his whole consciousness and his single-mindedness. He could not have written music for someone else's tastes if he tried. In fact, he did try without success.

At the age of fourteen, he visited Bologna and met the eminent teacher Padre Martini. It was suggested that he sit the examination for the Diploma in Music, Bologna's highest academic honour. The task involved writing three parts above a given antiphon melody 'in istile osservats' – strict counterpoint. Mozart failed miserably (Einstein 1945). He was unable to write in any style save his own, and Martini had to show him the correct answers. The archives of the Accademia Filarmonica and the Liceo Musicale at Bologna retain the manuscripts of this event (Einstein 1945: 147).

These examples do not mean that anarchy and a total lack of any continuity and uniformity characterize musical imagination, but they do suggest that we are not able to draw any conclusions about identifying musical imagination simply by looking for norms. We could almost make a case for looking for deviations from norms as a first prerequisite to discovering musical imagination. We certainly cannot derive any clear relationship between actions that may contain evidence of musical imagination and laws of musical art distilled from musical practices at a given time or place. We can no more recognize a Mozart until he is dead than we can an Elvis Presley or a John Lennon until the sales figures tell us. It is against this background of an apparent uniqueness and a non-conformity with established norms that I want to suggest alternative ways of viewing musical imagination as it might appear in children.

Episode and fugue

Generally speaking, not many people associate music with children making their own compositions, in the way they associate visual art with children drawing and painting, or myth and literature with children telling their own stories. To claim that music is different, or is regarded differently, may seem like a lame excuse for being unable to explain why all children are not regarded as capable of composing a piece of music in the way they are of drawing a picture. Nevertheless, it is a fact that adults in western culture generally either regard musical activity as something that has to be taught or consider that, to make up his or her own music, a child would have to be a genius.

Look around any school and there will be evidence of children's activities in drawing, painting and writing stories, but virtually none of their musical inventions. So the first thing to establish is that, apart from trying to identify how imagination manifests itself in children's music-making, there is the problem of actually finding and observing the musical equivalent to children drawing and telling their own stories. Children are not encouraged to make up their own music; instead, they are made to play someone else's, who always happens to be an adult.

This is not to suggest that there is universal regard for children's inventions in visual art and storytelling, but none for music. To many, all such activities appear to be a category of 'things children do' until they grow up, rather like listening to pop-rock, wearing jeans, getting dirty frequently, or throwing stones at birds or into ponds. Despite the work of many researchers into children's behaviour, there is still a lack of general understanding of what is seen by some people as disorganized, un-adult creative play that should perhaps be tolerated, at least until children learn something of greater value. This is a far cry from regarding children's behaviour in producing 'scribbly' drawings or cacophonous sounds as a category that might be different from mere worthless children's play. Yet it is probably not an exaggeration to claim that far more attention has been paid by researchers to children's drawings and storytelling than to their exploration and expression using sound, despite the work of Harvard's Project Zero team between 1977 and 1987. There is no large corpus of research into children's musical behaviour among psychologists, in spite of the growing numbers who are now entering the field of music psychology. Those who do attempt to fill this gap have the difficulty of dealing with an historically biased population among both musical practitioners and observers. This bias is largely because of the nature of musical art: it is a performance activity in which a composer cannot be heard without performers, many of whom have spent years perfecting historical techniques. Musical taste and preference consequently tend to oscillate between classical rigidities founded upon notions of quality derived from Plato and Aristotle, and a bewildered acceptance of anything, in the face of the overwhelming influence of pop-rock music. The feeling of safety in attributing musical imagination to the precocious 4 year-old who can play Bach is a product of ancient Greek views of music buried deep in western belief systems.

In *The Republic*, Plato warns that we must:

> identify those rhythms appropriate to illiberality and insolence or madness or other evils so that we can use the opposite ... good speech, then good accord and good grace and good rhythm wait upon a good disposition ... music has power to affect his spirit, his soul, disposition, and abilities in all things.
>
> (Strunk 1950: 7–11)

And Aristotle, in *The Politics*, explains that 'rhythms and melodies contain representations of anger, mildness, courage, temperance and all their opposites and other moral qualities' (Strunk 1950: 18).

Upon such foundations there developed a belief in a relationship between character, personality, or moral worth, and types of musical sound. In such a belief system, music actually represented these various qualities. Thus it was possible for American jazz to be outlawed in the 1920s and 1930s. Similarly, there was the outrage that greeted the rise of rock and roll in the 1950s, when one governor in the United States issued a warrant for the arrest of Elvis Presley on the grounds of corrupting the morals of minors. The eminent cellist Pablo Casals summed up the feeling of many when he described rock and roll as 'poison put to sound'.

The obverse of such attitudes is exemplified in the sanctification of 'great' composers, such as Beethoven, who was almost deified by some because of his noble music and a belief in an inextricable link between his personal behaviour and his music. We still do not like our musicians to be as revolutionary or antisocial as our visual artists, in whom we tolerate such behaviour. The musician is expected to be dressed in a dinner suit; the visual artist can wear jeans and sloppy sweaters.

This has remained in our education systems as a legacy from history. And so it is perhaps not so much a desire to see every child play a violin sonata by Bach that motivates such views, as a lingering belief in the connection between the music one plays and type of person he or she is. We still tend to believe in a relationship between a noble or saintly exterior, as someone plays a 'great' piece of music, and his or her inner being. It is the same legacy that makes us prize logical thought, in the fashion of the ancient Greeks, above all other types of mental activity. This in turn causes us to pay more attention to a child's music-making that most nearly resembles an adult's rationalizations about music than to his or her expressive use of sound not conforming to such notions.

Many obviously unique talents have suffered throughout recent history from such attitudes. They prompted some of William Blake's contemporaries to regard his paintings and poetry as the daubings and rantings of a madman; similarly, some people were convinced Beethoven had lost his wits, when they heard his later quartets and piano sonatas. It is not just the battle between the rational and intuitive that is referred to here, but rather a modern legacy of this ancient debate. Children's activities in music today are regarded by some people in much the same way that music of the Romanticists was regarded by the empiricists and rationalists of the nineteenth century. In fact, many attempts at explaining artistic activity of any kind in a logical framework have produced a number of theories and formulae.

Joshua Reynolds, for example, was convinced that blue was a cold colour and could never be used as the centre of a successful painting. Thomas Gainsborough's response was to paint the now celebrated *Blue Boy* (Saw 1972). Birkhoff (1933), inspired by ancient Greek notions of balance, proportion and harmony, produced the formula $M = O/C$, where M is the aesthetic measure, O the degree of order, and C the degree of complexity. There are obvious difficulties in assigning a number to concepts like order or complexity in a painting or a piece of music, yet later researchers have modified the equation to $M = O \times C$ (Eysenck 1968; Smets 1973). Such ideas can be traced back to Euclid, from whom the notion of the 'Golden Section' was developed. This is expressed as a ratio of approximately 62:38 between opposing elements.

It is difficult to see how such applications of mathematical methodology can yield anything of significance as far as artists are concerned. Certainly, there has been no such measure applied to real art, and it is doubtful that any will be attempted. Art cannot be measured in such a way, and such methods seem of little value in identifying imagination at work.

Of more use, it is suggested, are questions about the content of actual art works. For example, does musical imagination lie in the fury of a last movement of a Beethoven piano sonata, or the almost static harmonies and rhythmic motionlessness of Erik Satie's *Gymnopedies* or *Sarabandes,* or the elegant sonata structures of Mendelssohn, or the wit and clarity of Mozart, or the musical happenings of John Cage? Can it lie in the mixture of blues, country and hillbilly that is Elvis Presley's style or the throaty patriotic sounds of Bruce Springsteen? Or does it in fact lie in the very diversity of musical practices all these represent? Illogicality, arbitrariness, contradiction and the unexpected seem far more helpful clues to seeking out imagination in the music of western culture than logical explanations or mathematical formulae. But this is the problem of aesthetics: it is more a matter of looking at what artists do than of applying some external measure.

Sonata

In describing music from a more multi-cultural standpoint, Wachsmann (1971) explains it as a 'special kind of time, and the creation of musical time is a universal pre-occupation of man'. The notion of the creation of musical time, one's own personal musical time, seems far more applicable to what actually happens in music than does anything mathematical. It also seems far more appropriate in trying to understand what children may do with sound when they create their own 'musical time' than does looking for evidence of incipient greatness or adult behaviour.

Children can do with sound what they do with two-dimensional space in drawing and painting or with words in creating their stories. But to a child, the texture of a sound is more important than an adult concept like pitch or melody, and the duration of a sound is more significant than the concept of rhythm. Sergeant (1983) demonstrates that the basic unit of pitch in western music, the octave (a frequency ratio of 2:1), is a concept, not a percept. He explains that young children tend to identify similarities between tones by listening for similarities of sound rather than for a more logical octave generalization. In other research (Walker 1978, 1981, 1985) there is evidence that visual matchings for sound textures, duration and loudness yield more consistency in young children than do those of pitch differentiation.

This would seem to point in the direction of children having greater involvement with elements of musical textures, durations and loudness than with concepts like pitch, derived from high art, in the early stages of their activities in music. It also suggests that musical imagination in children should be sought in observing their use of the basic parameters of musical sound (loudness, timbre, duration and pitch) in creating their own 'musical time'. In such observations, one should bear in mind the relationships between the great artists of the past and the norms of expectancy from which they diverged, each in their own unique manner as they created their own musical time.

Looked at in this way, some of the extant studies of children's musical explorations provide some relevant insights. John Paynter (1971) describes an experiment in which he observed a number of 5 and 6 year-olds in an open-ended task. The children were given freedom to explore a variety of tuned and untuned percussion instruments over a period of several weeks. Paynter reports that after an initial exploration in apparently random and somewhat chaotic manner, the children began to settle down to purposeful activities. These are described in the children's own words. A little girl explained that she was looking out of the window and watching the rain falling off the roof of the bicycle sheds into a puddle, so that she could play the rain on her chime bar. A pair of children described how they were 'playing' a conversation between themselves on their instruments. Other children were composing stories or describing events in music.

In another set of observations, Bamberger (1982) describes how a fourth-grade class invented their own drawings for the rhythm of a class composition. The class took about ten minutes to produce the drawings, which were categorized into two types by Bamberger: figural and metric. A second experiment included more children and a greater age range. Although the two types of drawing were to some degree confirmed, there were some interesting deviations, particularly among younger children aged around 4 years. Bamberger describes them as 'the children's invention for externalizing their "knowledge in action" – that is what they know how to do but had not before tried to put down in some external, static way' (1982: 193–4).

Bamberger hypothesizes in some detail about the motivations for the various drawings, using Piaget's models of children's behaviour. These include imitation of the movements needed to produce the rhythm acoustically. The interest for this writer lies in the clear indication that the children could perceive movements in musical time that contained varied loudness due to rhythmic accents, as well as repetition, and could externalize the mental images that resulted. The rhythm used was a simple four-beat pattern with an accent on the first beat. Many children tended to write a larger shape for each first beat, with correspondingly smaller ones for the remaining three. Thus there was evidence of a proclivity to use figural representations of loudness rather than metric representations of rhythm. Bamberger comments that musicians will tend to see rhythms in purely metric terms, having forgotten their own earlier figural interpretations because of their musical training. In Bamberger's view, these conflicts between figural and metric domains 'remain tacit barriers, especially to effective teaching' (1982: 225).

Other studies (Walker 1978, 1981) indicate that children will readily provide drawings that faithfully represent, in visual metaphors, auditory movement in the basic parameters of sound: frequency, wave shape, amplitude and duration. A consistency of visual representation was reported in all age groups from 5 year-olds to adult, though age was clearly a factor in maintaining the consistency of representation of frequency by vertical placement, wave-shape by visual pattern or texture, amplitude by size and duration by horizontal length. The same consistency was observed in congenitally blind subjects (Walker 1985) and across different cultures (Walker 1986).

This seems to imply that children respond to the sensuous parameters of sound rather than to adult musical concepts, and that musical sounds are perceived by children as auditory expressions. In fact, there is some indication in these studies that children are attracted to the sensuous properties of sound and by their potential for personal expressive use. It is to this latter aspect that I finally want to turn, for this, it is maintained, constitutes a basic ingredient of musicality.

It is a fairly reliable assertion that if children are asked to invent some music – which may be just 'a piece' or might describe their friends or their parents – they will use the sounds available rather than search for some Mozartian melody or Bach-like counterpoint. In one such session observed by the writer, a 6 year-old described her friend by a loud, long continuous slapping on a variety of instruments. When asked why, she replied that her friend was always talking, and never stopped even in her sleep. Another girl described her mother as alternately like a glockenspiel played softly on a variety of notes and a loud banging on a drum. This related to her perception of her mother as often calm and loving, but sometimes angry.

In using stories as a basis for making music with children, the same proclivity to use what was available, but with as much variety in sound as possible, was noticed. For example, the story of Beowulf fighting the monster Grendel elicited an interesting range of sounds. Young children depicted the walk of the monster Grendel by a combination of cymbal, drum and woodblocks to indicate its weirdness, unnaturalness and terror. An older group, including some well-educated and accomplished musicians, produced a five-beat ostinato pattern with accents shifting at random to any of the five beats in a measure, and a combination of cello, double bass, piano, drum, trumpet and clarinet playing a fugue-like structure above this.

These and many other examples serve to illustrate a dichotomy in musical education. It lies between what Bamberger calls the figural and the metric in rhythm – what is referred to earlier in this chapter as the adult conception of music based upon Greek notions of refinement and the perception of the auditory parameters of sound that comprises musical expression – and what Langer calls expressive form as opposed to the abstraction of a concept for discursive thought (1969: 139).

Coda

In case this might seem like an argument in favour of educational strategies in music that are based on progressions from concrete to abstract experiences, it is important to emphasize the nature of musical communication. It is not like verbal language. The letters c-a-t have a specific symbolic and syntactic function of communication in language. In contrast, a musical element such as the chord of C major has no symbolic function and no syntactic constraints of the kind the noun *cat* has. Moreover, the word *cat* can be translated exactly into other languages whose speakers will instantly recognize the small, four-legged domestic pet it symbolizes. There is no equivalent to a C major chord in any other music save the tradition of the west. Moreover, it is just not possible to translate musical elements from one culture to another by means of identifying their symbolic function and meaning. In western music, slow, sad music is played at funerals and gay, happy music at weddings. In Dervish music, fast, happy-sounding music is played at funerals as well as at weddings. There is no matching of musical variety with occasion. They never had a Plato to categorize musical sounds and attribute specific representational qualities to them.

The point is that the kind of abstract and concrete experiences referred to by writers on educational development, while clearly relating to language or mathematical activity, have no relevance to music. When a child hears a tune in C major that modulates to the dominant and back, the meaning he or she derives has nothing to do with C major or the dominant. It has to do with the sound being what Langer calls 'expressive form'. How different it is with language or mathematics! The child does not abstract meaning from the expressive form of the sound of words in a story, for example, but from the fixed meaning of words. He or she may note the tone of voice and manner of delivery, but it is the ideas symbolized in the words that contain the meaning. Entirely the opposite is true of music. There are no ideas as such expressed in the symbolism of tones, chords or rhythms. They express only themselves, in the opinion of many musicians and writers about music. But it must be added that there was, historically, some support for a capacity of music to express a certain level of generality of meaning. This was found particularly in the nineteenth-century tradition of Romantic music following the writings of Schopenhauer. The arguments are long and tedious on both sides. Suffice it to say that few composers actually believe that what they write in music has any significance outside of the sounds and structures of music (see Strunk 1950; Langer 1969), in the way that words do.

So for this reason, despite the nineteenth-century belief in music having some

representational powers, it seems reasonable to say that current educational practices, based as they seem to be on notions of language acquisition, not only are
inappropriate to an activity like music, but are possibly inimical to the true nature
of musical expression and perception as it occurs in cultural tradition. The very
lack of children's musical compositions in schools is testimony to the misconceptions about music referred to here, and to the timorous attitudes toward children's
activities with sound, particularly those that do not result in recognizable rhythms
or melodies.

References

Bamberger, J. (1982) 'Revisiting children's drawings of simple rhythms: a function for
reflection-in-action', in S. Strauss (ed.) *U-shaped Behavioural Growth*, New York:
Academic Press.

Birkhoff, G. (1933) Cited in D.E. Berlyne (1974) *Studies in the New Experimental Aesthetics*,
New York: Wiley.

Einstein, A. (194,5) *Mozart*, London: Oxford University Press.

Eysenck, H.J. (1968) Cited in D.E. Berlyne (1974) *Studies in the New Experimental Aesthetics*,
New York: Wiley.

Gardner, H. (1983) *Frames of Mind*, New York: Basic Books.

Langer, S.K. (1969) *Philosophy in a New Key*, Cambridge, MA: Harvard University Press.

Paynter, J. (1971) 'Creative music in the classroom', unpublished PhD. dissertation,
University of York, England.

Sachs, Curt (1942) *The History of Musical Instruments*, London: Dent.

Saw, R.L. (1972) *Aesthetics: An Introduction*, London: Macmillan.

Sergeant, D. (1983) 'The octave – percept or concept?' *Psychology of Music* 2(l): 3–18.

Sitwell, S. (1967) *Liszt*, New York: Dover.

Smets, D. (1973) Cited in D.E. Berlyne (1974) *Studies in the New Experimental Aesthetics*,
New York: Wiley.

Strunk, O. (1950) *Source Readings in Music History*, New York: W.W. Norton.

Wachsmann, K.P. (1971), 'Universal perspectives in music', *Ethnomusicology*, 15(3)
September, Middletown, CT: Wesleyan University Press.

Walker, R. (1978) 'Perception and music notation', *Psychology of Music* 6.

—— (1981) 'The presence of internalized images for musical sounds and their relevance to
music education', *Council for Research in Music Education USA Bulletin* 66/67.

—— (1985) 'Mental imagery and musical concept formation', *Council for Research in Music
Education*, special issue of papers read to the Tenth International Research Seminar on
Music Education.

—— (1986) 'Some differences between pitch perception and basic auditory functioning in
children of different cultural and musical backgrounds', paper invited to the Eleventh
International Research Seminar on Music Education, Frankfurt, West Germany, July
1986, Council for Research in Music Education.

Section 3

Musical contexts

11 ICT and the music curriculum

Paul Wright

.

Music and ICT

In this chapter we will see how ICT can:

- improve the teaching and learning of music;
- enrich the music curriculum by extending the range of resources available;
- change the way we think about and practise music and therefore what we teach.

Below are three approaches to the use of music technology in schools. The first demonstrates one way in which ICT can help teachers to teach more effectively, the second shows how ICT expands the range of people and resources that pupils can access, and the third is an example of how the nature of what we understand as music and musical learning can be transformed through the use of technology.

1   *Teaching more efficiently*: A mixed class of 13–14 year-olds began a unit on reggae by listening to *Africa must be Free by 1983* and *Africa Dub*. They were encouraged through discussion to describe differences between the two recordings, identifying discrete layers of material and the use of digital sound processing. *Africa Dub* had been recorded on two tracks of the school's portastudio, and pupils were set the task of recording two other tracks using skeletal instrumental parts provided, adding sound processing, and 'toasting' their own verses live over their dub. Dividing into groups, a round of tasks included writing their own verses, rehearsing the parts, investigating the development of dubs and re-mixes in black music using a multimedia CD-ROM, and making a final recording with the portastudio.

2   *Expanding the possibilities of what can be taught and learned*: A class of 11 year-olds, in a large city with many boroughs, has opted to take part in 'A Millennium Composition for a City', funded by the local Arts Board and to involve a nationally renowned composer. Pupils visit the project web site to gain information, and from where a composing programme called Metasynth is downloadable for the teacher, together with a brief manual and pupil worksheets. Pupils are able to access Metasynth by drawing and painting with

a mouse, or tracker ball in the case of one pupil with special needs. The worksheet guides pupils to an understanding of how their drawings are turned into sound by the software. They can also record local environmental sounds into the program. Each school has a structured role in providing materials via the web site for a piece to be assembled by the professional composer and premiered on local radio in January 2000. Pupils can access information about the composer, email him for advice, or look at the web site for answers to 'frequently asked questions', progress reports and images by other schools. Each school's contribution is located on a web site map of the city and can be downloaded as sounds and images.

3   *Transforming music itself and changing what we teach*: A class of 12 year-olds is set the task of composing and performing a piece of electroacoustic music using a CD-ROM that provides software for creative work. They divide into a carousel of groups whose activities include:

- collecting sounds using a portable minidisk recorder;
- listening to a piece of electroacoustic music, *Deuce* by Evelyn Ficarra, which uses the actual sound and rhythm of a bouncing ping-pong ball as source material;
- making a list of images from a picture by M.C. Escher that suggest sounds;
- tackling a worksheet accompanying a recording of *Catalyst* by Rachel McInturk, including her description of how she developed the material of the piece.

All groups have an opportunity to make a short piece of electroacoustic music out of the sounds they have collected using multitracking and sound processing software.

The role of technology in music

Music and technology have always operated in tandem. The development and spread of 'music machines' in the sixteenth century did more than force conservative composers to make their music 'apt for voices and viols': it inspired a new generation to explore the compositional possibilities of the new technology, leading in time to the sophisticated repertoire of the modern symphony orchestra. Bach's *Forty Eight Preludes and Fugues* was an adventurous exploitation of what were then experimental keyboards, which departed from 'nature' by dividing the octave into twelve equal parts. Hence its other, possibly ironical, title – *The Well Tempered* (or tuned) *Clavier*. Similarly, the same quest gave us the new sonorities and textures so characteristic of Chopin's engagement with the developing technical refinements of the piano.

In the twentieth century, the development of 'crooning' is a by-product of 'close miked' vocal amplification and the Beatles' album *Sergeant Pepper* is an example of new sound layering possibilities opened up by the multitrack recorder.

Arguably the most profound change in the musical culture of the twentieth century has been the development of sound recording. Indeed, the fact that all the music we hear from loudspeakers has undergone sound crafting through a recording studio has become such an everyday experience that we have virtually ceased to notice it.

Moreover, recording, storing and replaying musical material has become of interest not only to the studio engineer, but – through the introduction of digital technology – to composers themselves, who can now intervene crucially in the process to change the musical material in a variety of ways before replaying. At one extreme, recorded note information can be printed out as score and parts, while at the other, radical transformations of the sounds themselves have created completely new musical languages and genres, from electroacoustic music through rock, pop and jazz to worldwide dance cultures such as techno, house and jungle. Indeed, there is hardly a musical form or culture on the planet which has not been touched by the process.

But, despite these advantages and attractions, is it possible for the soul of music to be lost in an excess of technological enterprise? Of course, the answer is, yes, it can be. To avoid this it is vital that we concentrate at all times on what the technology enables musically and not on the technology itself.

Planning for the use of ICT in the teaching of Music

Planning musical objectives

In this section we will look in some detail at exactly what it is that ICT enables us to do musically. We begin by examining the way digital technology handles familiar elements of sound:

- timbre
- dynamics
- pitch
- rhythm/duration (temporal profile)
- spatial.

Finally, in order to set objectives for compositional work, we shall look at some of the ways ICT enables these sounds to be combined to build musical structures.

Timbre

Objectives/concepts/Programme of Study: *Sounds modified using reverberation or other effects to creating timbres that are rich, wide, thin, or moving, that is, changing across time.*
Western music has not, traditionally, been very concerned with timbre. Musicians are trained to produce a single 'perfect' sound with a limited range of tone colour, whereas musicians in other cultures make a very sophisticated use of this element.

Technology allows us to regain control of timbre and take it to places we never imagined. Even using simple tone controls – treble/bass – on a tape recorder can have dramatic effect, especially when changed during the course of a sound. This technique is much used in contemporary dance music: trance, 'drum 'n' bass', and so forth. Careful mixing allows us to cross certain sounds to make new hybrids. This is often done in recording a bass guitar; the direct line from the instrument is plugged directly into the one channel on a mixing desk while the simultaneous 'live' sound from a microphone picking up the guitar's amplifier is fed to another. Both channels are then mixed together to create a unique timbre. More radical uses of this process allow us to move seamlessly from one sound to another: a bassoon turns into a motor, a voice into a bird, whispering into water. An electroacoustic piece by Trevor Wishart, *Vox 5*, makes stunning music from the idea of sounds transforming into each other: in one celebrated instance, a human voice is transformed into a swarm of bees. With such a range of possibilities we need some useful categories for timbre:

- *Dense* – rich or noisy; tam-tams and gongs are timbrally dense and complex, also side-drum with snare, cabassa and maracas.
- *Wide* – a sound that has extremes of frequency, but not necessarily dense. Wide timbre: orchestral effects such as the famous three flutes and a bass trombone from Berlioz's *Requiem*.
- *Thin* – a narrow range of frequencies in the spectrum, but can be high, medium or low in pitch: bass guitars, french horns, bass drum, triangle.
- *Moving* – sounds that move between categories: thin, wide, or dense: saxophones have a wider timbral range than most western instruments; the didgeridoo relies on a mobile timbre to create different sounds, as it only has one pitch.

Dynamics

Objectives/concepts/Programme of Study: *Progression from shaping simple dynamics to molding the envelope of a sound.*
Technology gives you a very precise control of dynamics. Knobs and sliders obviously control volume, but computer programs for sound editing or multimedia will allow you to change dynamics very suddenly and take the values of loud and quiet to extremes. The minute dynamic changes lasting only a few milliseconds at the start of a trumpet or violin sound are an important part of our recognition of their timbre, resulting, of course, from the way the instrument is played: blown or bowed. This dynamic shaping is known as the *envelope* of the sound and the ability to change or recreate the envelope is found in synthesizers and samplers. It is also possible to play one sound with the envelope of another. A dramatic illustration of this would be to create a trumpet-like sound that had the plucked attack of a violin played pizzicato. Obviously, you can go much further than that: modifying samples by this method can forge entirely new sounds.

Pitch

Objectives/concepts/Programme of Study: *Progression from simple melodies, patterns of notes, to drones, modes, nodes and irregular tunings.*
Technology allows us to have a minutely-detailed control over pitch. You can have pitches higher than a piccolo and lower than a double bass on the same 'instrument', and they can move in steps that are just perceivable, or in huge leaps. We can create nodes (a pitch area without a clear single pitch such as cymbals produce) in any register, or create 'hierarchies' of pitch: new tonalities, modes, ragas, or irregular tunings.

Temporal profile (pulse and duration)

Objectives/concepts/Programme of Study: *Progressive use of delay to create time-based structures from regular beat to faster/ slower + irregular metre, or polyrhythms.*
Technology allows us much greater control over time than hitherto. Using the tempo controls on computer sequencing packages – measured in beats per minute (BPM) – we can create the smoothest of accelerations, from something so slow it hardly moves, to something so fast that we cease to hear individual attacks. We can have multiple tempi working together to create patterns which would be impossible to sustain otherwise, or create the gentlest of flows, smoother and longer than breath or voice could sustain. The use of simple delay processes, in reggae for example, can create a layer of slightly dragged triplets over a simple beat, while the echo effect was used extensively in the 1950s and 1960s to thicken the sound of guitars and voices.

Spatial profile

Objectives/concepts/Programme of Study: *Progress from a sense of place, developed by treating sounds with 'reverberation', to an understanding of 'stereo image', and the movement of sounds in space as a structural feature in a composition.*
The spatial aspect of music has been somewhat neglected since the sixteenth century but is assuming greater importance now that sound can be made to appear from almost anywhere in relation to a listener by using a multi-rig of loudspeakers. The location of loudspeakers in respect to a listener gives scope for developing the spatial dimension in recorded music. A pair of suitably sited loudspeakers or good quality headphones can suggest the location and movement of sounds, not only from left to right, but also from front to back. This phenomenon is known as *stereo image*. An extension of this is where multi-loudspeaker rigs for electroacoustic music or multimedia installations bring opportunities for sounds to originate above, in front of or behind a listener, and move freely around the space.

The placement and mixing of microphones in a documentary recording (for example, a CD recording of a concert) exploits this effect to add realism, but many electroacoustic composers and popular musicians now use this technique to craft imaginary spaces and dazzle the senses with extraordinary sound movements.

Indeed, the spatial dimension has now become a structural feature of much music. Within that framework there are significant creative possibilities, such as the familiar studio 'treatment' of drum tracks, where the snare appears to be in one space, the ride cymbal in another, and the kick-drum somewhere else.

Composing with ICT

Because of the way digital technology handles sound, almost any sound, not just those instrumental or vocal sounds which are traditionally regarded as 'musical', can be a starting point for composition. In order, therefore, to set clear objectives for composing with ICT we need to:

- broaden our definition of musical sound;
- consider the function of sound material within a composition.

Sound types

- *Mimetic* – sounds or behaves like something else or alludes to something else: voices imitating trumpets in a gospel choir piece, for example, or honky tonk bar-room piano evoked in Copland's *Billy the Kid*.
- *Abstract* – not like anything else: refers only to the sound itself. This includes the standard use of instruments and voices.
- *Electronic* – obviously, electronically synthesized. There are many examples in pop music: synthesizer bands in the1980s; some drum machine sounds, and bands like 'Kraftwork'.
- *Concrete* – derived from real sound, but not necessarily recognizable; includes samples of real sounds; 'atmosphere' created at the beginning or end of pop music tracks, e.g. birds or sea; bands such as 'Test Department', that use electric grinders, metal sheets and sledgehammers (*Tactics of Evolution* by Test Department KK1 66D).

How sounds function within a composition

- *Event* – something special. In popular music this might be a 'stab' (a sampled orchestral chord), a 'power chord' (a loud sustained guitar chord) or a short sampled sound: for example, a voice interjection like a 'shout' in an otherwise instrumental number.
- *Gesture* – longer than an event and maybe made up of a series of events to make a 'shape': for example, a drum break such as the clichéd run of four semiquavers on each tom followed by a cymbal crash.
- *Texture* – this can be static or moving. 'Rhythm guitar' parts are functionally textural, as are 'pad sounds' ('filling-in' parts on keyboards) and most 'ambient' music.
- *Process* – something evolving, growing bigger or smaller; a strong feature of

electroacoustic music. (I find it helpful here to talk to pupils about 'energy flow' in peaks and troughs.)

- *Trigger* – a sound which sets other sounds in motion.
- *Stop* – a sound that causes other sounds to stop: for example, a cymbal crash or guitar 'chop'.
- *Open* – a soft trigger that gently sets other sounds in motion.
- *Close* – a soft stop: a sound that suggests other sounds should stop or rest: for example, a cymbal roll crescendo/diminuendo.

The function of a sound depends, to a great extent, on its context. An *event* might be only a tiny sound in the context of something quiet, but in a very busy or loud piece would need to be much stronger. *Textures* and *processes* range from gentle breezes to raging storms. Only your ears will tell you whether a sound is acting successfully as a *trigger* or *stop*, *open* or *close*. Samplers can capture a number of *events* which, when played, become *gestures*. Sound processors can, for example, turn an *event* into a swooping *gesture* moving up or down through a combination of the pitch shift and echo facilities.

When it comes to 'developing' such sounds, technology offers new sound vocabulary. Whilst we can multiply durations or beats on conventional instruments in order to stretch out music, with a sampler for example, we can really stretch a sound, so that a single drum beat becomes a long note. And of course, in the opposite direction, sound editing tools can cut a sound with dramatic effect: a long sound, for example a gong lasting 20 seconds, can be cut to 2 seconds. Going still further, a technique called *brassage* lengthens a sound by chopping it into tiny segments which repeat and overlap many times giving a shuffling or grainy quality to a sound.

There are many examples of music where reversing the order of notes is used as a structural device: for example the retrograde of a fugue subject or note row. But with technology we can reverse the sound itself: the decaying sound of a gong becomes a crescendo; sharp percussive sounds become soft and lisping – the sound of a reversed cymbal, where the sound begins softly and builds dramatically to a sudden cut off, is well known in popular music.

Multitrack recorders, which allow material to be recorded together or separately onto discrete tracks which can then be edited and played back, enable us to create anything from a duo to a group of a thousand of any sound we possess. Computer editing features, such as cutting and pasting, repetition, re-ordering and refining, create opportunities for building new structures or taking familiar ones to new places. A piece may be a single trajectory of continuous development without sections or sudden contrasts, it might be a dialogue between two groups of material, or be narrative, either in the sense of telling a story, or representing a series of extra-musical ideas. One might use chance or mathematical formulas to make decisions about materials or structure, or use simple patterns like the ubiquitous A-B-A. Repetitions might drive the piece, as in the systems of minimalist composers like Reich, Glass, Nyman, La Monte Young, and techno styles such as drum 'n' bass.

A final category – *collaboration* – is very important. There are few composers who have not collaborated to some degree in making music for dance, film or some other medium. As multimedia software becomes more and more available, the shift towards including composing for film, video or animation as a core musical activity – like song writing – is inevitable. In activities involving multimedia, we need to ensure that music has equal partnership with the other disciplines involved. This means that music should not play a subordinate role, for example acting merely as an afterthought to a pre-ordained visual medium. Objectives should, therefore, include a common way of working between art forms. The above descriptions of how sound functions within a composition, although designed to encompass the possibilities opened up by new technology, can also provide a framework for the composition of music in a variety of styles and for collaboration with other disciplines, especially performance arts. For example:

- collecting, appraising and choosing raw materials;
- developing, lengthening or performing chosen materials into longer gestures;
- putting gestures together to make structures;
- building with structures to make finished work.

These are processes which have broad meanings within a number of art forms: in performance arts like video (or dance made into video), or non-time-based arts like photography or design.

Resources

Electronic keyboards

Electronic keyboards are so widely used in music teaching today that I will only touch upon general matters. Some teachers count on them almost exclusively as their tool for the delivery of the music curriculum. Others, with two teaching rooms, have one wired for electronic keyboards and the other for conventional 'acoustic' activities. A middle way, which integrates all the resources, is to be preferred. This is the position taken by Alan Smith in *Keyboards in Context* (BECTA 1997). He identifies two strands in keyboard practice: the development of playing skills and an introduction to some of the sophisticated features found on more expensive models. He develops both strands through improvising/composing, performing and listening activities, alongside other resources such as the voice; and a listening programme that covers a wide range of twentieth-century music from Debussy, Stravinsky, Messiaen, Cage, Stockhausen, Vaughan Williams, Britten, Mike Oldfield, and the Beatles. He also builds work around oriental scales, the whole-tone scale, and a 'scale of limited transposition' found in Messiaen's *Les Enfants de Dieu*. This is a bold and exciting context for keyboard work, which does much to balance the tired sounds and inadequate simulation of acoustic instruments, and the over-mechanical rhythm and chord presets associated with them. Indeed, as a general rule, music technology is at its weakest when trying to imitate acoustic instruments, for, however good sampling gets, the timbral and pitch nuances produced by distinguished live players will always elude capture. No matter: new technology has a wealth of 'instruments' and genres of its own.

Indiscriminate use of keyboards may therefore:

- emphasize keyboard skills as a prerequisite for musical participation without creating a realistic context for all pupils to acquire them;
- inhibit other ways pupils can gain access to performing and composing music which do not require traditional instrumental skills and give as great, or greater, musical rewards.

Sound processors

Sound processors or 'effects units', or sometimes just 'FX', are an excellent resource for the classroom. Some models allow you to plug a microphone directly into them connected in turn to one (or two) self-powered (active) high-quality speaker(s), or hi-fi amplifier and speakers (see below). Sound processors capture small portions of sound and immediately change or 'process' them in astonishing ways. They have dozens of different 'programs', of which the following four are the most useful:

1 *Reverberation* – lengthens sounds. Mimics the effect of sound bouncing off the surfaces of a space, from small halls to cathedrals to imaginary spaces so large that known materials could not build them.
2 *Echo* – repeats sounds entire with a space between. When set to repeat the sound (musical phrase/gesture) only once it is usually called delay.
3 *Pitch shift* – splits the sound it 'hears' into one, two or three different pitches. It can be set to any notes of the chromatic scale or anything between, including glissando. This 'effect' can also transform unpitched timbres, e.g. everyday sounds, in surprising ways.
4 *Pitch shift* plus *echo* – sounds move up or down by a programmable amount as they repeat. Again it works 'magic' on everyday sounds.

At least two sound-processing set-ups are desirable for full classes, where there is a group carousel of varied activities. The classroom computer(s) may then be available for CD-ROM/internet support. Classroom compositions and performances should be recorded to mini-disk format.

Multitrack recorders

Also known as 'portastudios', these devices have many classroom applications. Portastudios let you layer musical material on discrete 'tracks'. These can then be 'mixed down' to stereo with the possibility of creative features found in profession-ally-made recordings. These include adding effects, taking layers in and out, modifying the timbre of sounds with treble/bass tone controls, building your own stereo image, and adding effects or sound processing.

Traditionally cassette-based, many newer models are digital, or use mini-disk format. Portastudios are sensitive units capable of producing work of quality and creativity in any genre. They are less suited to whole-classroom activities than to work with small sub-groups. Apt to be 'fiddly', the user needs a checklist of settings for knobs and switches which can be accidentally moved, leading to non-operation.

MIDI sequencing software

Musical Instrument Digital Interface (MIDI) was developed collaboratively by the music industry in the mid-1980s when computer memory was bulky and expensive. Instead of handling sound itself – as computer-based recording systems now do – it provided a universal code for sending details of the manual, i.e. physical, operation of an instrument. On an electronic keyboard, for example, this would be values for which note you pressed, how hard you pressed it, how long you pressed it for, and so forth: not dissimilar from the old piano rolls which recorded 'performance information' by punching holes of varying sizes/spaces in a piece of paper.

With suitable software, MIDI information can be stored in a computer and displayed on a screen either graphically or in standard musical notation and sent back to the instrument to trigger the sounds with the original performance data. While the information is stored in the computer, it can be edited in a way analogous to a word processor: cutting, pasting, and so forth. You can also edit performance details like tempo, articulation, phrasing, dynamics, and voicing. Pupils can play into the computer slowly – to suit their technique – and adjust the tempo for playback, or enter the information line by line for simultaneous 'performance' later. Performance data can also be input from a number of other MIDI modified instruments: electric guitar, a wind controller – similar to a clarinet in technique – drum pads, and so forth. It is important to understand that these instruments – or MIDI controllers, as they are known – have no sounds of their own, they merely trigger voices set via MIDI in a sound module or synthesizer. This means that a MIDI controller is not restricted to playing sounds traditionally associated with that instrument; a MIDI guitar could play organ or drum sounds, or trigger samples of voices or environmental sounds.

Sequencing is a very useful educational tool but has some drawbacks. Firstly, when it was introduced it mapped contemporary performance features so snugly that it has a tendency to shape all popular-style music made with it in a time warp of the late 1980s. Secondly, although it allows pupils with little or no instrumental skill to enter notes and create compositions and performances, it is a very time-consuming task to add or adjust all the data that make a truly spontaneous and expressive performance. Thirdly, it can provide a musical score of performances, but it does so in a very literal way and correcting it requires a very good knowledge of musical theory.

Samplers

Samplers capture sounds and then allow the user to replay them at will from a MIDI controller such as a keyboard. A whole culture has grown up around these versatile musical instruments. Currently, two types are emerging which reflect different musical usage.

The 'traditional' type is designed mainly to meet the needs of popular musicians wanting to capture and craft a sound away from the performance situation, secure it to disk, and add it to the list of available timbres for their next 'gig'. These units give very high-quality sound and offer comprehensive editing features. Captured sounds can be exactly trimmed to length, looped to play continuously when you hold down a note-key on the controller, reversed, time-stretched and more. The system can require as many as seventeen button presses to record a sound, although templates can be made.

Other models are made for the DJ-Mixer who wants to capture a sound 'on the fly' and play it immediately with some real time changes, such as opening a filter in order to modify the timbre of the sounds. The latter fit the bustle of the classroom, but versatility, precision and quality may have to be sacrificed.

Hard disk recording

At last it is possible to record sound directly into a computer at reasonable cost. Newer versions of MIDI software have been developed with 'audio' recording capability. Cubase becomes Cubase Audio, or the cheaper but good Virtual Studio Technology (VST); Logic becomes Logic Audio. Both handle live sound and MIDI, the user integrating the two at will: for example, recording a voice into audio tracks synchronized with instruments controlled by MIDI. A superb professional audio recording package called ProTools is easier to use than Logic or VST, but unfortunately only available for the Power Mac. However, it is worth considering buying an iMac just to run this program, particularly as an early version of ProTools is available free of charge from the manufacturers. All these packages allow for independent sound-processing software which 'plugs in' to integrate with the editing process or use live. There are also 'virtual' samplers as 'plug-ins'.

The graphics show sound in wave forms, and simulate known equipment like mixers, enabling pupils to move on easily from experience of, for example, a portastudio.

Although hard disk recording is an excellent educational resource, it requires accessories. Because real sound uses enormous amounts of memory, you need to work from an external hard drive attached to your computer, and ideally, another drive with retractable media, like a Zip or Jaz disk, to store pupils' work. You also need – unless you are running a Mac – a sound card fitted to your computer, but multimedia PCs now being purchased by local authorities and schools will have this capability. However, the facility of digital recording and editing is a superior musical tool, which you should consider seriously.

Microphones

Microphones for educational use should deliver good sound quality, be robust in design, and suited by type for the purpose in hand. Unidirectional mikes ignore sound coming from anywhere except in front of them, and so work well in a classroom for small group work. If you want to record the whole class, or live performances of individual groups, then it is worth having a pair of 'ambient' or boundary mikes, which consist of flat plates. You can attach them to the wall of the classroom and have them permanently plugged into a recording facility for spontaneous use. A microphone boom stand is essential if you are to avoid 'handling' noise, or if you want to set up the microphone really near a sound source.

Experience suggests that *dynamic* mikes – which do not require batteries or other power source – are probably best for the classroom. Condenser mikes – which do need power – are generally of better quality, but are more vulnerable. The sensitivity of the latter also militates against a clean recording in a bustling classroom. If you can afford it, get a dynamic, a condenser and a pair of boundary mikes as a working set.

Loudspeakers and headphones

Loudspeakers, though sometimes problematic, promote working in groups where technology is integrated alongside live acoustic sound. To say that loudspeakers are the only things that make any sound in an ICT system and should therefore be the best you can afford may sound rather obvious, but is sometimes overlooked. The quality of headphones, if used, is equally important. Some teachers ban headphones altogether because they militate against integrated work. Others use them almost exclusively where the classroom strategy is to encourage individuals or pairs to work in uninterrupted isolation, for example with keyboard labs. To have a few really good pairs, judiciously used, is the preferred option.

Loudspeakers can be active – with an inbuilt amplifier, or passive – connected to a separate amplifier, as in a home hi-fi system. It is useful to have some pairs of each. Although active speakers can be used separately, mixing down from a portastudio or 'virtual' mixer must be to a pair of speakers (or headphones) if pupils are to gain an experience of crafting a stereo image.

Headphones will be chosen to fit snugly if outside sound needs to be suppressed. The use of powered headphone splitters, which allow users to set individual volumes, is desirable, or, alternatively, purchase headphones with individual volume adjustment.

Mini-disk recorders

These combine good quality, hiss-free, digital recording, with ease of use and portability. Disks will hold 74 minutes of stereo recording and are re-writable. The microphone input on some models has a 'limiter' which prevents pupils over-recording sounds by sensing when the dynamic level of a signal is about to go over the boundary into distortion, and pulling it back. Numbering tracks is a one-button operation, 'on the fly' if you wish. No more frantic searching for a track on a self-compiled cassette tape! No more waiting for tapes to wind on, or back. Digital goes straight there!

CD-ROMS

A CD-ROM is a format which, when placed in a computer CD-ROM drive, allows access to text, pictures, animation and video. Some CD-ROMS have software that allows pupils to change or edit musical material by changing its tempo, repeating sections or adjusting the balance of parts.

In a carousel of classroom groups, CD-ROMS which focus on information, recordings and supplementary activities which support the session objectives are a superb resource.

There are a few CD-ROMs which allow the user to change parameters of existing pieces of music creatively: alternative mix-downs, for example. In the future, CD-ROM technology may be expected to provide a more comprehensive software resource, both more focused on pupil creativity, and delivered more cheaply than the industry software packages mentioned above.

Points to consider when purchasing a CD-ROM are whether the sound is accessed from high-quality CD recordings; whether the information is conveyed in a logical manner with a rich mixture of sounds, pictures and text; whether the subject matter is pitched at the right level for its users; whether there are opportunities for pupils to improve their skills, for example in aural perception, as well as to gain knowledge and understanding of the subject matter.

Resources for special needs

Music technology also has a particularly important role to play in offering increased access for pupils with physical or learning disabilities. It increases access to musical participation by providing switches and other interactive devices for those who cannot readily use conventional musical instruments and it offers a way of handing over the raw materials of music to pupils for them to make their own.

The following hardware is of particular significance for pupils with physical and learning disabilities:

- microphones: when connected to active speakers, they isolate and enlarge individual sounds;
- transducers: these are inexpensive items which work a little like microphones and can turn unexpected objects into amazing musical instruments;
- sound processors: connected between microphones or transducers and active speakers; they enlarge and transform sounds in an astounding way;
- samplers: connected between microphones and active speakers, they capture pupils' own sounds which pupils can then trigger with a variety of MIDI controllers – switches, pads, an ultrasonic beam, and, of course, keyboards;

- ultrasonic beam generators, such as Soundbeam or MIDI Gesture, change physical movement into MIDI signals to trigger samplers and the preset sounds of electronic keyboards;
- Portastudios/hard disks record pupils' sounds and music in layers, and can add processing if desired.

Safety

Safety issues are of particular concern where many pieces of equipment are plugged into the mains, with wires trailing in the classroom. However, there are some fundamental measures to take that minimize the risk of serious injury to pupils or staff. Always use a power breaker on the socket that conveys the mains current to your system. Some schools already have these fitted as part of the wiring, but they can be purchased from any DIY store for under £20. Tuck mains leads away from pupils as far as possible and use cable ties to secure them in a convenient bundle.

It is reassuring to know that the following cables do not carry mains electricity and therefore pose no risk of electrocution: speaker cables, microphone, headphone, and MIDI cables; in fact, any cables carrying music information between devices.

Teaching: implementing Music ICT in the classroom

Integrating ICT into the classroom

ICT is not a substitute for teachers or conventional instruments. Nor should it be used as the only vehicle of musical learning. Most importantly, it should integrate with other activities and resources as well as giving pupils access to contemporary sounds and genres. ICT can be integrated into classroom music teaching and learning to:

- provide a workbench for transforming sound in improvisation, composition and performance;
- be part of a carousel of related activities;
- engage small groups for a prolonged activity;
- offer unique support for modelling compositional ideas;
- extend pupils' knowledge and experience of music in different styles, times and places;
- create an opportunity for the exchange of performances, compositions and ideas around the world.

Planning schemes of work

Table 1 demonstrates ways in which ICT may be used to explore sounds for their musical possibilities; to develop and refine musical ideas; and to widen knowledge and understanding of musical processes and styles.

Table 11.1 Planning schemes of work

Exploring sounds for their musical possibilities	Developing and refining musical ideas	Widening knowledge and understanding of musical processes and styles	Appropriate equipment
Live exploration of sounds and creation of new sounds by applying treatments: reverberation, echo, pitch-shift, etc.	Perform compositions with live sound transformation. Enhance compositions with sound treatments.	Widen understanding of time-based attributes of musical sound; increase knowledge of sound processing used in specific genres.	Sound or 'effects' processors, microphones, transducers and loudspeakers.
Explore differing attributes of sounds and note patterns played live from a variety of instruments – some allowing for limited movement or control.	Organize sounds by exploring tempo, dynamics, articulation; build compositions by layering, structuring and refining musical material.	Develop an understanding of how musical structures are modelled in a computer for later performance by live players.	MIDI controllers: keyboard, drum pad, ultrasonic beam; switches; MIDI sequencing equipment.
Capture sounds to use: for composing; modifying the timbres of sounds; spatial movement of sounds and creating a stereo image.	Layer and structure musical material; refine compositions; provide pre-made material to use in conjunction with live performance.	Reflect on own and others' compositions and performances. Increase understanding of the working of musical structures.	Recording equipment: analogue or digital i.e. multitrack recording devices including panning and EQ.
Create melodic and harmonic material; change timbres.	Perform music individually and in groups.	Consider aspects of musical style.	Electronic keyboards: including preset accompaniments.
Capture and transform own sounds or those of others.	Develop compositions. Modify the compositions of others.	Investigate musical topics, access high quality performances.	CD-ROM
Download sounds for use in compositions.	Compose and perform with others worldwide.	Access music information worldwide, contacting artists or academic authorities.	The internet

Planning lessons

We have already noted that it is what the technology enables musically that is important for the development of the curriculum, not the technology itself. To illustrate this, we will be looking at the planning of a series of lessons to show how the technology supports the musical objectives.

The Lessons

A class of 11 year-olds is exploring the expressive possibilities of the voice in three lessons through simple exercises involving vowels, consonants and so forth, which are then used in conjunction with a sound processor.

In lesson one, pupils will have their first experience of the musical possibilities of reverberation and echo, but this is expressed in terms of the spatial, the temporal and the timbral outcomes of sound processing as a means of musical expression.

Aim

To begin to explore the importance of space, time and timbre in musical expression.

Learning objectives

Pupils will:

- use the voice to make and control expressively a range of new sounds from sibilants, vowels and consonants;
- experience, and describe or draw, the sound transformations of reverberation and echo achieved by a sound processor;
- use these resources to make a simple composition from the words and ideas suggested by a given poem.

Role of ICT

The activities involving ICT are set out as musical processes and skills to be achieved. 'Pupils will learn to use a sampler' or 'pupils will find out how a sound processor works' are inappropriate aims in Music, but might fit into another syllabus, for example, Science or Technology. Of course, pupils *do* need to know 'how to', but these skills should be achieved by attaching such activities to musical outcomes.

Progression

Progression from lesson to lesson is achieved through an agenda of musical 'processes' *enabled* by technology. In this lesson, pupils work with *reverberation* and *echo*.

In the second lesson, they revise reverberation and echo and are introduced to a new process: *pitch shift*. In the third lesson, pitch shift is introduced and combined with processes introduced in previous lessons:, echo, reverb, pitch shift, and so forth.

Lesson tasks and extension activities

Here are some 'extension' activities to the above which give a succinct overview of how this translates into lesson tasks:

EXTENDING SESSION ONE: REVERBERATION AND ECHO

Ask the class, or a group, to make a list of greetings in as many languages and local dialects as they can. Use these to make up a voice composition using the techniques they have learned. Saying goodbye, with echo, for example, extends the sound into a musical gesture. By now they should have a vocabulary of similar musical ideas from using a sound processor. They should write down their ideas and make a sketch plan of their piece, including ideas about processing, so that they can make the most of their time with the equipment. How many ways of saying hello and goodbye are there? In what situation might somebody say goodbye joyfully, and hello drearily? Could you make a short musical fragment out of the idea of two people who spoke different languages mistaking each others greetings? Could this lead on to ideas of conflict or reconciliation as starting points for a composition?

EXTENDING SESSION TWO: REVERB, ECHO AND PITCH SHIFT

Either in small groups or as a whole class, perform and record songs they have learnt at some other time. Add suitable 'processing' by connecting the sound processor to the tape recorder. You can try out a number of processes with single verses until you find one that you like. Then record the whole song.

Set a long reverb – 5–7 seconds – and compose a short piece for voices and/or instruments that works in that space. This might be a piece in older (baroque) style on a keyboard. What do you discover about music for large spaces? Listen to some music designed for a large space, for example *Miserere* by Allegri, which also includes some plainchant. Why does this work so well in a cathedral? Why does the priest leading the service in a cathedral often 'intone' the words of the prayers?

EXTENDING SESSION THREE: ALL THE RESOURCES OF THE THESE THREE LESSONS, INCLUDING A NEW PROCESS: COMBINED PITCH SHIFT AND ECHO

Here we show how you can put this third session into a task description for your pupils. You will need to adapt this to your particular situation. This task suggests collaboration with drama to make a piece of radio.

Think about sounds in other large spaces such as railway stations. Make up an announcement for a railway station with a particular reverberation time. Use a watch with a second hand to work out to the nearest second how to make the announcement work in the 'acoustic' you have chosen. You could now try this with the with the sound processor, dividing tasks between members of your group: one person to speak, one to direct, one to operate the tape recorder, and a 'studio manager' to place the microphone and work the sound processor, set at the right reverberation to check your design model. Write an account of what you did and how successful it was.

Now make up a short piece for radio which uses what you have learned. Base it on short scraps of conversation (including, perhaps, some of the greetings from Extending Lesson One) and other sounds you might hear at a station. Keep the same reverberation, but vary the pace, as well as the sounds you feed into the processor to create different moods. Maybe there will be a dramatic moment where the reverberation creates a mood of fear, for example. You could add short musical gestures to help the mood and structure if you wish. Use the full resources of sound processing that you have learned: close/distant miking, pitch shift, pitch shift plus echo, gradual mix of source (dry) and treated (wet) sound. So that you can include many more 'effects' for the processor than you can record live, record some moments that you have carefully crafted and play them into the final performance on cue.

Think about the shape of your piece: a beginning, a middle and an end. Draw a performance score that shows the energy flow of your piece, the pace of change, and climax(es). Don't forget to include a surprise somewhere in the structure of your piece. Work out performance needs: plan cueing sections including simple hand gestures, nods with eye contact, and 'when I do that, you do this' moments. Settle for simple, practical ideas and rehearse so that you can perform your piece with passion to the rest of the class.

Organizing the classroom

In this section we will be looking at how ICT can be presented in the classroom and consider a number of ways of setting up equipment for teaching and learning.

Set-up one

[Microphone, microphone boom stand, sound processor, active loudspeaker.]

If you are introducing the treatment of sounds with reverberation or echo, it is important to give all the pupils the opportunity to experience their sound being modified by a sound processor. Their very first encounter will almost certainly produce excitement and laughter. Getting them to say their own name with reverberation or echo is usually a safe start, but then move them on to experimenting with sounds from other languages, and 'sss' or 'p' sounds. This introduction can be done by taking the microphone around the room using a long lead, or setting the microphone up on a boom stand at about two metres high, but pointing downwards, so that by moving in a circle – either as a small group or a whole class – each pupil can perform their sound as they pass underneath the suspended mike.

Ideas should be kept as simple and straightforward as possible, with plenty of discussion of what is happening to individual sounds. Do not be tempted to experiment wildly at this stage, because magical effects can be created by the imaginative use of just one form of transformation.

Set-up two

[Microphone, microphone boom stand, portastudio, sound processor two loudspeakers.]

Again, introduce the portastudio as a musical instrument for recording and playing sounds in layers. Set up the portastudio with the faders away from the class so that the players/performers are facing the class. It is a good idea to give each pupil a worksheet which has a labelled diagrammatic portastudio.

One idea is a topic called 'The Newspaper Orchestra'.

The Newspaper Orchestra

- Divide the class into four groups: A, B, C, D.
- Each group finds their own sentence in distributed newspaper cuttings.
- Group A repeats sentences in a normal voice; B in a slow growly voice, like a tape recording at slow speed; C in a high voice, like tape recording at fast speed; D repeats only the consonants of their sentences, making them very explosive.
- Develop this, if you want, with a conductor(s) controlling dynamics, start/stop, and a graphic score, to make quite a sophisticated piece.
- Each group records 45 seconds of contrasting vocal sounds onto discrete tracks 1–4 of the portastudio.

As well as having volunteer 'engineers' to place the microphone and work the portastudio, this is a good opportunity to inculcate a recording drill without which no recording will be of good enough quality for use in composing.

Setting level:

- start with the fader down (on the microphone channel);
- place the microphone in the chosen position, and test the level by raising the fader;

- if the sound is too soft and the fader goes all the way up, capture it, turn down the 'gain' (this is usually at the top of the channel it affects, but consult the manual);
- if the sound is too loud and the fader hardly goes up at all (level meter heavily into the red sector), turn up the gain;
- a reasonable level has been achieved if the fader is about three-quarters up when the level meter just touches the red sector (beneath the red sector for any digital recording).

RECORDING

- work out a signalling system between the engineer and the performer so they know when to get ready and stop;
- bring down the fader;
- signal for silence and press play/record to start the tape;
- bring up the fader;
- signal the performers to start;
- signal silence from performers when they finish;
- bring down the fader;
- press stop to end the recording.

If you reverse the last two operations you will get an unpleasant electronic click from the switch, recorded on the tape after the music.

You can now replay the four tracks together with volunteers moving faders to achieve different 'mixes'. This can include structural changes to the piece by taking out a channel(s) for a while. Other creative changes can be introduced, such as using 'pan' (the spatial controller for each channel) to set a stereo image; or EQ (treble/bass tone controls) to mould timbres 'on the fly' (very popular device in contemporary technology). Different teams can take charge of these 'performances' with plenty of class discussion about musical outcomes.

You can practise 'mixing down' by creating your own four-track tape, using pre-made MIDI files. These files have sequenced tracks of popular music standards which you can play on instruments connected in a sequencer set-up. Connect four separate synthesizers (or four separate instrumental outputs on one, if it has them) to the four tracks of portastudio and mix down.

Of course, you do not need to teach all the above in one introductory session. It can be stepped through a number of sessions, attached to musical outcomes each time. It is always good to put a limit on technical processes but not on musical imagination.

Set-up three

[Sampler triggered from a MIDI keyboard, CD player with non-copyright samples disc, or mini-disk with pre-recorded sounds, perhaps downloaded from the internet, two loudspeakers.]

A stunning way to introduce sampling is to set up the sampler to play a different sample for up to six 'key ranges' on the keyboard. Key ranges are a chosen spread of notes – typically a fifth – set to play the same sample. For example, if the sound sampled is played back exactly by E on the keyboard, notes below that – say down to C – will be slower, and change timbre as a tape recorder would. (Notes played above E – say up to G – will have the opposite characteristics. Sampled rhythmic fragments such as drum beats can, therefore, be speeded up or slowed down by triggering from different notes within the key range. You can even play several versions of the same sample simultaneously at different speeds (i.e. pitches) – exactly what techno musicians do to achieve 'break beats': sudden, usually dramatic, changes in drum tempo during the course of a phrase.

You can buy CDs of commercially made (non-copyright) techno samples: drum beats for 'breaking', bass riff, organ chords, shouts (male and female), analogue synth sweeps, and so forth. As not all samples need a fifth range – vocal shouts can be triggered from one note, for example – an electronic keyboard that's long enough can accommodate as many as six players at once. Indeed, there are opportunities here for differentiation by task with varying demands being made of different groups or individuals. Once each team has got going with their improvisation you can bring their piece to an end with a master fade down on volume. Once again, rotating teams of 'engineers' can train to take over the technical processes from you.

Set-up four

[Sampler, computer-running MIDI software, loudspeakers, etc.]

A dramatic way to demonstrate the power of MIDI is to retain set-up three in techno mode but send/return MIDI signals from keyboard to the sampler *via the computer*. When MIDI is set to record, the pupils' keyboard manipulations will be stored in the computer. When set to play, the computer will replace the keyboard and trigger the samples exactly as the pupils played them. The result will be displayed graphically, or in standard musical notation (subject to our previous caution about the literal way MIDI handles notation). This can then be edited further to make more pieces or refine any aspect of performance – other than timbre. (Of course it could be deliberately set to play *different* samples, with intriguing results, something that a GCSE Music pupil might take forward, though perhaps a little risky for whole-class work.)

MIDI set-ups can also be used to provide auto-accompaniments to class performing or improvising. A program like Band in a Box is able to give quite sophisticated rhythm and bass accompaniments in a range of popular genres. Of course they have the disadvantage of being very metronomic, as keyboard auto-accompaniments are, but that can be a starting point for class discussion and reflection, especially by making a comparison with a professional performance, where, for example, the drummer might lay down the snare track a little ahead of the beat to give driving energy to the performance.

Set-up five

[Computer, hard disk recording from CD-ROM or commercial software package.]

This set-up can be introduced as a computer equivalent to the portastudio. However, it is a pity to see it solely in such terms. It is much more worthwhile to demonstrate the compositional advantages it has over the portastudio. For this, you would need to record some short tracks of material, perhaps recorded at an earlier session of the Newspaper Orchestra. These would be displayed on the screen as wave forms running from right to left, vertically layered. Such programs give you a 'cut and paste' facility, this time with real sound, not just 'performance information' as with a MIDI sequencing set-up.

Chopping up tracks into smaller pieces and then re-ordering them is an interesting contemporary compositional technique. A professional piece to play alongside this introduction is *Mambo à la Braque* by the Javier Alvarez. Alvarez has made a 3-minute composition by recording many examples of Mambos from professional CDs, then cutting and pasting the material to make a very exciting piece. The teacher can relate this compositional process to the contemporary artist, Braque, who makes pictures by cutting up everyday materials and juxtaposing them in a collage.

Once again, teams can work with very technically-constrained tasks, before the whole class produces a performable 'class piece' in a few minutes.

Where next?

The internet: the world in the classroom, the classroom in the world

The internet provides an opportunity for a communications revolution which could further transform music in the classroom by dynamic use of the internet. Two schools in America, one in Kentucky and another in Tennessee, decided to do a music research project together on folk songs in their two states using email and the world wide web. The target class in each school emailed the other with questions for an opening brainstorm session to fix the aims of the project: what makes a good folk song; what are the names; what are the subjects; what are the instruments used; who are the singers? Answers exchanged by email moved the project on to establish a research method: use all information sources available; primary sources, i.e. any folk singers they could find; secondary sources, i.e. family members, books, CDs, school library, world wide web. Classes divided into working groups of two or three pupils, paired with similar groups in the other school.

Worksheets gave ideas for good starting web sites and guidance, such as that information found during the project should not only be written word examples but musical examples that could be sung or listened to. Part of the research was to decide if Tennessee and Kentucky folk songs were similar or different. Using a wall map to pinpoint the known locations of folk songs, it also became possible to see that many songs crossed state boundaries and followed natural geography instead.

The culmination was the compilation of their own joint web site containing all the findings plus pictures of themselves, local views and sound bites, and short performances of their own newly-minted folk songs.

Pupils can design their own web site either in the music lesson, or in collaboration with the schools' art departments. The actual mechanics of putting a web site together are not difficult or costly. There are a number of software programs which translate a design into HTML – the programming language of the web pages. But learning HTML is not that difficult, especially with the aid of books for beginners, which are widely available. Alternatively, you could hand over all the actual programming and web site maintenance to the person in the school responsible for web pages.

Where the internet scores over CD-ROMs is that the information stored on the latter is fixed like a book, but the internet is always changing and provides direct access to the latest information, authorities and performers.

Research and the practice of teachers and arts *animateurs* confirm beyond doubt that the creative applications of new technology can unlock musical creativity in children and young people, even those with the most severe physical and learning difficulties. And the work of contemporary composers and performers across all genres shows that music with technology, far from breeding a generation of solitary computer enthusiasts, is providing new opportunities and new venues for live, tactile, inclusive group music-making in previously undreamed-of ways.

We know as teachers that when we introduce the music of a Birtwistle or a Turnage, the idiom is strange and unfamiliar; but not so the new vocabularies of electroacoustic music – experimental or popular – which are already in the ears of the young. What makes the future in the classroom so exciting is that we are at last finding the right tools to give our pupils the raw materials of music and empowering teaching methods to let them fashion for themselves the future music that they need.

Further reading

British Communications and Technology Agency (BECTA) (1997) *The Music IT Pack*, Coventry: BECTA (1998a and b).

Brown, R. (1977) *Dance Music Programming Secrets*, New York: Prentice Hall.

Buick, L. and Lennard, V. (1995) *Music Technology Reference Book*, Tonbridge, Kent: PC Publishing.

Millward, S.(1998) *Fast Guide to Cubase VST*, Tonbridge, Kent: PC Publishing.

Petersen, G. and Oppenheimer, S. (1993) *Technology Term*, Minnesota: Hal Leonard Publishing Cooperation.

Waters, S. (1994) *Living Without Boundaries*, Bath: Bath College of Higher Education Press.

Wright, P. (1998) *Sound Processing and Recording*, BECTA.

12 The place of composing in the Music curriculum

Ted Bunting

> The human activity some of us call music and which can roughly be defined as *expressively organising undesignated sounds*
>
> (Swanwick 1996: 17)

Composing in the National Curriculum

The Schools Council Inquiry 1 (1968) reported that many secondary pupils found school music to be not only one of the most 'useless' but also one of the most 'boring' curriculum subjects, (Plummeridge 1991: 136). Until this point, few had openly questioned the validity of a curriculum based on the imparting of inert facts about music, usually delivered through the music appreciation lesson, and with little or no active musical experience. But following this damning judgement, there ensued what amounted to a revolution in classroom Music teaching, in which music educators re-evaluated views about the nature of music and what might constitute musical learning. The aim was to develop the basis for a curriculum that would lead to children *knowing* music, rather than *knowing about* music. What emerged was the general acceptance that performing, composing, and listening were the essentially musical activities that would enable this. These came to form the basis for the National Criteria for the GCSE examination (DES 1985), introducing composing for the first time in an examination at this level, and, ultimately, the National Curriculum. Shepherd and Vulliamy (1994) give an intriguing account of the debates and politicking that surrounded the birth of the first National Curriculum for Music. They describe how 'composing' was chosen instead of 'composition' to emphasize the active approach that was envisaged, and how a new word, 'appraising', was introduced to highlight the fact that listening/appraising was an active process and not a continuation of the old appreciation lessons.

The present National Curriculum's statement that 'teaching should ensure that listening, and applying knowledge and understanding, are developed through the inter-related skills of performing, composing and appraising' (DfEE, 1999: 172), whilst not beyond debate, provides a basis on which to construct an active Music curriculum. It enables performing, composing and appraising to be integrated in Programmes of Study.

- bringing music to life through performing;
- studying its effect, seeing how others have achieved results, and considering how pupils' own musical activity can be developed through appraising; and
- taking hold of the sonic raw materials and constructing music in composing.

Initially it was the new term 'appraising' that was felt to be in need of explanation, and Flynn and Pratt's (1995) report on the work of the Research into Applied Musical Perception (RAMP) Unit was, and remains, very helpful in developing teachers' understanding of appraising, and its vital role in music education. At the time, music teachers felt comfortable with performing and composing in the narrow way in which they defined it, and little attention was paid to these aspects of the curriculum. However, a number of studies (Spencer 1993, Ross 1995, Gammon 1996) would suggest that this sense of comfort was unfounded and that we need to investigate composing in the school curriculum in a similarly rigorous way.

What is composing?

Simply put, composing is 'making up' music, but once we move beyond that simple definition, things cease to be so straightforward.

Cultural considerations

Walker (1987) describes how concepts of music are inextricably linked to the culture that produces them. What it sounds like; what constitutes the accepted theoretical knowledge that underpins it (such as the diatonic scale system and metrical rhythms in western music); what are considered to be musical activities; and who engages in those activities, are all dependent on their cultural milieu. Walker argues that in western society only the revered few are accepted as composers, a view supported by Sir Harrison Birtwistle's comment that 'music was something that composers in the past did; it was a mysterious thing and slightly holy in a way, something that you don't tamper with' (from Ross 1998: 255). Such an attitude results in children being encouraged to paint and draw, the graphical equivalent of composing in music, with considerable value being attached to their efforts, whereas this is generally not true of their efforts to compose music. There is no prevailing cultural attitude suggesting that painting and drawing are things that should be left to the great masters, or that sees their picture as being so inferior in comparison to the work of established graphic artists, that it is not actually a picture at all. But, I would suggest, children's musical compositions frequently are viewed in this way. It is in this cultural setting that we, as music teachers, expect children to work as composers and to value their work.

Composing at different ages

Concepts of how composing happens, and what we might actually call composing, are related to the age of the composers. The context, whole-class, group, or individual, the nature of the composing task, and expectations about the process or the product, need to be appropriate to the skills, knowledge and understanding that the composers are able to develop in the course of the work, or draw upon from previous experience.

Swanwick and Tillman (1986, also in Swanwick 1988), in their study of children's composition, go beyond this and propose a 'sequence of musical development', linked to Piaget's theories of child development. In their famous 'spiral of musical development' (1986: 331, 1988: 76) development can be seen progressing upwards from a 'sensory' and then 'manipulative' relationship with musical 'materials' (sound and simple instruments) from 0–4 years old, to a period of 'expression' in the years from 4–9, starting with 'personal expressiveness' and developing so that expression becomes 'contained within established musical conventions', known as the 'vernacular' (1986: 332). This is followed by a developing relationship (10–15 years) with 'form', initially in an experimental and 'speculative', but then in an 'idiomatic' way, showing a growing awareness of musical styles, popular music or 'what children regard as a "grown-up" musical style' (1986: 333). The final turn of the spiral is concerned with 'value'. A 'symbolic' level, 'distinguished by the capacity to reflect upon musical experience and relate it to growing self-awareness and rapidly-evolving general value systems', can develop into a highly-developed 'systematic' relationship with music, in which the individual is able to engage with, reflect on and discuss music, in an 'intellectually organised way' (1988: 79/80). However, as Swanwick points out, some people may not achieve the 'symbolic' level, and fewer again the 'systematic'.

There are several aspects of this research that are open to debate; nevertheless, the sequence does provide a background on which we can map out curriculum activities against a broad, if not wholly satisfactory, concept of musical development.

How composing is organized, whole-class, group, or individual, also raises age-related issues. A typical model would suggest a move from whole-class, teacher-led composing with small children to teacher-led group composing; to pupil-led groups; with the emphasis moving to individual composing at GCSE. Paterson and Odam (2000) complain that pupils are not provided with enough opportunities for individual composing in Key Stage 3 and that this hinders the development of their individual skills and understanding. They point out the need 'to manage the process from dependence to independence, from directed work to autonomy' (2000: 26). They acknowledge a number of reasons for this:

- limited space and equipment;
- inadequate provision for ICT equipment preventing the realization of multi-layered pieces;
- group work being a way of dealing with classes where the range of abilities and experience is wide;
- for some teachers, a belief in communal music-making.

However, they point out that:

- group work enables some pupils to become skilled at 'coasting', or to hide their lack of experience;

- 'low levels of social skills can impede musical progress' (ibid: 24);
- it is hard to accurately assess the effort, or, I would suggest, the contribution, of an individual group member.

Whilst I accept these practical observations, I am less convinced by Paterson and Odam's statement that 'composers do not naturally form committees to compose, and there is very little evidence of such activity outside the restricted world of the pop group' (2000: 24). I would suggest that this view is fraught with unwarranted assumptions about what makes someone a 'real' composer, and, although they acknowledge that group composing does take place in popular music, the 'restricted world of the pop group' is a misleading phrase. It is either laden with value judgements about what constitutes 'proper' music, or implies that this way of working is only used by a few musicians. The latter is not true. It may well be that the majority of practising musicians in this country either compose, or arrange, 'by committee', and that this practice extends far beyond the 'pop group' to include rock, folk, jazz, reggae, and a plethora of other styles, including groups that gather specifically to compose together. It also ignores the development of the recording studio as an integral part of the composing medium in the second half of the twentieth century and into the future, in which not only musicians but also engineers interact as composers.

Rightly or wrongly, I have consciously not extended the debate to include composing in other cultural settings and any implications that might follow from this, as the topic, whilst fascinating, is huge. Suffice it to say that in some societies, music-making is almost wholly a communal activity. Those interested could read Small (1987) or Blacking (1976 and 1987), amongst others.

Paterson and Odam point out that if pupils do not gain experience of individual composing before Key Stage 4, they may feel 'abandoned and vulnerable' (2000: 26). However, perhaps it is the nature of the assessment of composing for GCSE that causes this. Although it is permissible to submit group compositions, it is hard to justify the award of anything other than a low mark, and the OCR syllabus clearly warns teachers that 'candidates can be disadvantaged by presenting joint compositions for assessment' (1998: 27).

The inevitable outcome is that teachers focus on individual work and, if they are not adequately prepared, pupils may well experience difficulties. What seems less clear is the rationale for the method of assessment. Is it not a distortion of the developmental model of music education which forms the basis of the National Curriculum and which GCSE is supposed to assess? Scant attention is given to consideration of the process. In the OCR examination, candidates are required to complete a 'Record of Candidate's Intentions'. It is claimed that this record is important, but for what purpose is not clear, for the mark scheme only considers the product. If the intention is that pupils should show that they have progressed 'from dependence to independence, from directed work to autonomy' (Paterson and Odam 2000: 26), then one would have to consider what this might mean. For I would suggest that high-quality group work would not demonstrate a lowly dependence, but rather interdependence, and that this is a truly musical attribute for which they should gain credit. Focusing exclusively on individual composing does make the assessing of composing simple. The candidate's contribution is clear. S/he did it all. However, surely it is the assessment that should be appropriate for the knowledge being assessed, not the knowledge for the assessment. Is this not making 'the measurable important rather than the important measurable'? (Rowntree 1977, from NACCCE 1999). Perhaps the rationale for assessing composing in this way goes unquestioned because it fits neatly with a traditional view of composing, reflected in Odam's statement that 'in the final analysis composing is an individual activity' (1995: 59).

What seems clear is that, as pupils progress through Key Stage 3 and beyond, some will learn best in individual composing activities, some through paired activities, and some through group activities. Most, I would expect, will benefit from the variety of different encounters, and may continue to do so into adult life. It is the teacher's responsibility to:

- offer pupils the opportunities that will enable them to learn best;
- provide them with composing activities that will help them to work towards the next stage in a sequence of musical development;
- have clear aims and expectations of what musical learning, skills, knowledge and understanding will ensue;
- take account of the previous learning pupils can draw upon.

What constitutes composing?

Although the use of the term 'composing', as opposed to 'composition', does focus attention on the activity rather than the product, it does not in itself help us to consider what the activity might involve.

In western society it is considered important that a composition should be original. Along with these notions of originality come more vague assumptions concerning the quality or value of work that is to be honoured with acceptance as a composition. The report by the National Advisory Committee on Creative and Cultural Education (NACCCE 1999: 30) is helpful in resolving these issues. First, it suggests that the value of a creative work is a judgement 'of some property of the outcome related to the purpose', i.e. it may be satisfying, tenable or effective; and second, it proposes that there are different categories of originality: individual, 'a person's work may be original in relation to their own previous work and output'; relative, 'it may be original in relation to their peer group'; and historic, 'the work may be original in terms of anyone's previous output'. It suggests that, in an educational context, 'originality in creative work will often be judged to be of the first two categories', and that instances of historic originality are more likely to emerge from a system of education which encourages the creative capacities of everyone.

In the context of the teaching and learning of music, rather than in considering whether the critics are right to proclaim a new masterpiece, it may be more useful to think about a range of 'composing activities' rather than compositions. Some activities might require pupils to add parts to a given template, maybe adding an additional percussion to a MIDI-file of a samba rhythm. Some might require pupils to learn and perform given parts and then to complete the piece. For instance, pupils could learn a given reggae ostinato bass-line and chord sequence, and then compose a song and instrumental sections to fit the backing. At the other end of the spectrum, the aims of the learning might require pupils to compose all the parts for their song, or to use an effects processor to create an evocative and imaginative soundscape in response to a non-musical stimulus. Paterson and Odam (2000: 38) point out that, in composing, 'learning by copying has a noble precedent'. Perhaps the copying of a stylish reggae bass-line, and using it as the foundation for a composing activity, might provide a valuable musical experience, and do more to teach pupils something real about the intricacies of this music than asking them to compose their own. Later, they might draw on this experience to help them compose their own.

By using a range of composing activities, the teacher is able to focus clearly on designing meaningful musical encounters that enable pupils to learn through producing work both of value and of individual and relative originality. Limited curriculum time can be used effectively as pupils are not being asked to reinvent the wheel, but rather are being given the opportunity to experience 'wheelness'.

What about creativity?

It would not seem contentious to consider music to be a creative art. Indeed most people happily associate the arts with notions of creativity, and it would seem sensible if the learning of music was closely allied with developing pupils' creative abilities. But Ross (1995), Spencer (1993) and Harland *et al.* (2000) complain that pupils do not perceive school Music as being creative or imaginative, despite the undoubted popularity of music as an 'out of school' activity. Nor should we assume that this activity is solely related to consuming music as a listener, for Ross identifies music-making and playing a musical instrument as among the most popular leisure pursuits (1995: 186), and Paterson and Odam state that 'about a third of all pupils claim to compose music outside school and the majority of pupils at Key Stage 4 do so' (2000: 11). However, as Swanwick writes:

> the oldest and best established theory of music education is that which emphasizes that pupils are the inheritors of a set of cultural values and practices, needing to master relevant skills and information in order to take part in musical affairs … The task of the music educator is primarily to initiate students into recognizable musical traditions.
>
> (1988: 10)

This, until now, might be a fair description of the underlying concept of musical learning at A level, with its focus on four-part harmony, counterpoint and art music, defined as 'the "proper music" of the Enlightenment tradition together with the work of contemporary maestros who have engaged seriously with it, extended to include – selectively – the subversives' (Ross 1998: 256).

The new specifications for the AS level in 2001 and A level in 2002 may do much to change this. Certainly there is the intention to provide a continuity from GCSE that was missing before. However, this concept of music education, which sees pupils as 'empty vessels' to be filled with the approved body of knowledge, has been the typical experience of those who have entered higher education in music, and it clearly does not aim to nurture creative and innovative ideas, and may well, in fact, suppress them.

Music teachers are in a difficult position. They are required to teach a curriculum based on a developmental model of active musical learning, but often their own experience is the antithesis of this. This leaves them with some difficult problems to resolve. What is the relationship between the acquisition of skills and the established canon of musical knowledge on the one hand, and the nurturing of creativity and a focus on acts of musical creation on the other? To compound this the developmental model that leads to GCSE, with its intention '(1.1) to encourage imaginative teaching in schools and foster a greater understanding of music through more direct experience of the creative processes involved' (DES 1985: 1), has ended there. For after GCSE the nature of the teaching and learning changes, as we have seen. Spencer points out that only a tiny minority take the A level examination and thus become the inheritors of the set of cultural values and practices to which Swanwick refers. It is hardly surprising that these people might see this as the basis for 'real' musical learning, and it is from this minority that music teachers are largely recruited. This would go a long way to explaining Spencer's complaint that:

> despite all the pioneering efforts of the past twenty-five years, there is still no ethos established at the grass roots of music education where both teachers and pupils are actually encouraged to *value* imagination, fantasy and adventurousness.
>
> (1993: 83)

These pioneering efforts that have, at least to some degree, come to fruition in the National Curriculum for Music and the GCSE may have done much to change the appearance of practice within the classroom, if not the deep-rooted values of many classroom music teachers. For it may well be that there persists an attitude that this developmental learning is 'all right' up to a certain point, but then pupils need to learn about 'real' music and acquire 'proper' musical skills. If outmoded views concerning the body of knowledge that constitutes 'real' musical learning and art music as 'real' music persist, music educators will continue to fail to grasp the true meaningfulness of music, and fail to teach aesthetic and creative elements with conviction. As Spencer writes, the system is, at present, self-perpetuating with 'grade' examinations and A level defining the path of 'real' musical learning, leading to higher education, and then, for many, the music teaching profession, where the established values are again disseminated to a new generation. Ross demands that 'the hegemony of a moribund Art Music Establishment must be subverted' (1998: 261). He suggests that music teachers have failed to make their subject a truly creative art because of the failure of serious music developed in the twentieth century to appeal to and convince the profession as a whole, to say nothing of the public. He claims that writers, painters and dramatists succeeded in doing so and goes on to write that:

> what is more, the essentially modern phenomena of jazz and rock music have not been seen as compatible with the serious aims of formal education: perhaps reflecting the more reactionary elements in public understanding and professional outlook. If the training of student teachers has done little or nothing to challenge and change their own tastes and practice then what hope when they become teachers in schools.
>
> (ibid: 260)

A new emphasis on creativity

Recently the use of the words 'creativity' and 'creative thinking' has been a feature of publications emanating from Central Government. The *National Curriculum Handbook for Secondary Teachers in England* (DfEE/QCA 1999) makes several references to creativity in its general requirements. Many of the subject-specific preambles make use of some form of the word 'creative'. In addition, the report of the NACCCE has suggested that creativity has a vital role to play in education. The argument is that the education system that was introduced by the 1944 Education Act was designed to 'provide a workforce for the post-war industrial economy' (NACCCE 1999: 18). However, the economic context has changed and increasingly the skills that are perceived as essential are creativity, innovation and communication. I would contend that school music and, in particular, composing activities in the curriculum are of vital importance in developing these skills. Far from presenting a case for the importance of music education on the grounds of transferable skills, I am suggesting that creativity is also vital to music education, that 'the heart of musical learning is musical creation itself' (Loane 1984: 227).

Teaching composing?

Ross writes that 'the rush to composition – and the elision of composition with participation as the answer to pupil alienation in music education – has been a completely false trail' (1995, p. 196).

Superficially this can be interpreted as a criticism of the inclusion of composing in the curriculum, but maybe the focus should be on the *rush* to composition. Unlike 'appraising' which needed to be thought about, music teachers had established, and maybe limited, views on what composing was. It may well be that insufficient thought has been given to what teaching composing entails. Ross even suggests that music cannot be taught and states that:

> Music teachers ... seem unable to imagine themselves – as *teachers* – in anything other than high-profile, managing all the classroom transactions from some central vantage point (phantom podium) and committed to

teaching a curriculum that issues in readily assessable outcomes, all of which have transparent relevance to music as a craft, a technical achievement rooted in its own technology and semantic system. So music teachers teach what can be taught ... They teach about music – they can't of course teach music, since music cannot be taught: not in any way that would tally with the normal understanding of what might be meant by 'teaching' – i.e. instruction.

(1995: 192)

Certainly this sort of teaching is going to do little to alleviate pupils' feelings of alienation and may do much to harm the case for music education. As Paynter points out, 'schooling seems to be about imparting and receiving knowledge, and in this we prefer conformity rather than discriminating between different ways of coming to know' (2000: 26), and this may lie at the heart of the problem. How should we teach composing? How can we help pupils to become better composers?

Paynter writes that it is natural for human beings to make up music and that only a small part of this 'daily outpouring is made by those we would call trained musicians' (2000: 6), and that this in itself causes problems. If it is so natural, why should we not just let pupils get on with it? They do not need to be concerned with concepts of 'form' and 'structure'. They respond imaginatively and intuitively, playing with the sounds they discover, making patterns and musical pictures.

Isn't it all a matter of feeling and emotion, not something a teacher should attempt to influence? ... but the mistake is to conceive of emotion and feeling as being entirely divorced from and in opposition to 'thought'. It has tended to make teachers of younger children wary of discussing musical details, on the grounds that what the children have made is simply 'what they feel'; whilst with older pupils the tendency is to avoid reference to what is felt by concentrating upon technicalities which are presented as 'rules'. Neither way are pupils helped to get better at inventing their own music.

Our feelings may appear to be involuntary and irrational but they are, of course, activities of the mind. Even the simplest intuitive piece made up by a very young child is recognised as music only because it is heard as music: that is, as a *process* which starts, goes on, and stops and in which sounds follow one other or are combined in various ways. Spontaneous and natural though the music may be, there are points where things change: some things happen that are not heard again; some things go on for a short time and others for much longer; some passages are *progressive*, so that we feel the energy and forward 'drive' of the music, others are *recessive* in effect, the music calming or becoming quieter or slower until it seems to want to stop of its own accord. These things are the result of decisions – not necessarily conscious decisions but decisions none the less – taken by whoever makes up the music, and the precise moments when changes occur are crucial to its success. Since – as I shall try to show – all musical expression, simple or complex and of whatever cultural background, behaves like this, we could conclude that the surest way to help pupils to get better at composing is to encourage them to think about the essentially *musical* process, not as abstract rules, but directly in relation to what they themselves create.

(Paynter 2000: 7)

In response to Ross's definition of teaching as instruction, Paynter points out the difference between 'instruction (*instruere* – to build into [the child's mind]) and education (*educere* – to lead out from [the child's mind]) (p. 7)'. He suggests that in music education both have a role. Instruction is a suitable basis for teaching someone to play an instrument, but composing is different because the teaching cannot take place until students present something they have made.

> The word 'composing' means 'positioning' [things] together, and when anyone has tried putting sounds together and is pleased with the results, enough to remember them, then the teacher can start to teach – mainly by asking questions about what is presented. It may be no more than a brief melodic pattern or a progression of chords … It does not have to be notated, and even if there were only two notes the teacher could ask, 'Why did you put that note there and the other one *there?*' We are not imparting received techniques because what is presented to us did not exist until the pupil(s) invented it. Of course, there are bound to have been influences – all the music the pupils have ever heard, and their musical preferences: what they think of as 'music' – but even if it is derivative, what they produce is *what they have made*, and to do that they had to take decisions. By focusing on those decisions, and by pressing students to discover as much as possible about why they have made the music as it is ('I just like it like that' is not good enough!), we start them on the path of asking the questions that every composer must ask about every piece: 'Where are these musical thoughts leading? What are the possibilities? Why should I choose that path rather than any other? How do I know when this piece is completed?'

(2000: 8)

Clearly this is teaching through 'leading out' rather than 'building into', '*educere*' rather than '*instruere*', but it is teaching none the less.

Creative thinking

Harland *et al.* remark that arts teachers rarely 'made mention of using imagination, self-expression, creativity or the development of ideas within the arts' (2000: 358). They go on to suggest that this may be because teachers see these as an 'innate feature of education in the arts' (2000: 358). However, Paynter's view that music teachers do not know how to help pupils get better at composing suggests that this assumption that work in the arts will involve creativity (merely because it *is* work in the arts) is not sufficient. Surely the 'innate' features of any subject should be central to the teaching of that subject. If this is the case, then the teaching of composition should include the teaching of creativity, if composition is to be taught in any real way. Put in these terms this is not helpful! How can you teach creativity? Some might even go so far as to suggest that it's something you're born with. You've either got it, or you haven't. If developing pupils' creativity is vital, then we need a clear understanding of what creativity is. It needs to be defined in a way that makes creativity something that can be taught.

Enabling creative development

Research into creativity has largely fallen into two categories: that which has looked at promoting creativity in a subject-specific context but which does not describe or define creativity itself; and that which has sought to describe it and define it. Typically, these studies become increasingly convoluted in their attempts to express their exact meaning, whilst avoiding the many pitfalls that surround research into such a seemingly elusive concept. Consequently they are of little use to the classroom practitioner. However, Webster (1988, 1990a, 1990b, and in Spruce (ed.) 1996) develops a useful and teachable model of creativity.

> The word creativity has been used in so many different contexts that it has lost much of its meaning and power ... In the educational context, it might be more prudent to use the term creative thinking ... By focusing on creative thinking, we place the emphasis on the process itself ... We are challenged to seek answers about how the mind works to produce creative results. This approach demystifies creativeness, places it in context with other kinds of abilities and external influences, and, perhaps most importantly, makes our job as educators much clearer.
>
> (Webster 1990a: 36)

The National Curriculum defines creative thinking skills as enabling 'pupils to generate and extend ideas, to suggest hypotheses, to apply imagination, and to look for alternative innovative outcomes' (1999: 24). However, this throws no light on the process. It tells us what the skills 'enable', without addressing what the skills might be or how they might be taught and learnt. Webster starts from the premise that creative thinking is not a mysterious process 'reserved only for those who are labelled genius. It can be defined and identified in us all' (1988: 34).

What makes his thinking significantly different is his focus on the roles of convergent and divergent thinking skills. Convergent thinking can be described as that which enables pupils to arrive at the one correct answer to a problem. This is the sort of thinking that is developed by an objectives-led curriculum that stresses factual content, and with a structure that aims to lead pupils through the mosaics of an increasingly complex and prescribed body of knowledge. Its apparent value is constantly reinforced by government requirements to have easily measurable standards that that can be compared through league tables and other comparative data. Divergent thinking is that which enables pupils to consider problems for which there is more than one answer, where any number of possible answers may be equally acceptable. Creative thinking occurs when:

> the search for aesthetically acceptable answers is made possible by strategies that include movement between convergent and divergent thinking skills – in other words, the ability to generate a number of possible solutions and then arrive at the single best,
>
> (Webster 1988: 34)

although perhaps 'single most pleasing' might be more appropriate.

This sort of thinking seems to be exactly what Paynter is intending to promote when he questions pupils about their composing. There may also be a significant link between this and Odam's (1995) ideas on right and left brain functions. He contends that it is vital that pupils must first engage with the music using the right brain, and then move to using the more analytical functions of the left brain.

Composing is characteristically a succession of divergent and convergent movements at varying levels. Each small decision requires its own divergent and convergent thought, whilst the balance of a sequence, the instrumentation, the dynamic shape, and decisions about the larger structure of the piece, all require the same process to be followed. The possibilities for planning meaningful composing projects and lessons that allow for these are limitless!

Adopting this approach does not ignore the acquisition of skills and knowledge. The stimuli, tasks or problems, and the information and techniques that the teacher provides will determine the focus for the skills which pupils will be developing. To this, as Loane (1984) describes, pupils will bring their previously-acquired skills; they may draw on techniques suggested by the teacher as the work progresses; and they may discover new techniques and adopt these as appropriate to their creative intent. Thus the curriculum that establishes the development of composing through creative thinking as its aim provides the context within which skills and knowledge can be learnt. It is important that skills and knowledge are acquired because, as Webster (1990b: 24) points out:

> divergent thinking requires the mind to survey its data banks for possible musical content, so that the more that is in those banks, the better. It is impossible to expect individuals to think creatively if nothing is there with which to think creatively.
>
> (1995: 196)

However, one should perhaps not forget that there is an important role for the 'imagined' solution that is then discovered through exploration.

A final note

Clearly music educators are presented with a difficult task as they attempt to unravel the complex web of inherited values, cultural assumptions and concepts of education that face them. Nor is the National Curriculum for Music entirely helpful. Despite its adoption of active approaches to the learning of music, Paynter writes that it also

> tends to support the belief that intellectual rigour is provided by histor-ical/cultural information, notation skills, and 'bar-by-bar' analysis. This ... appears to raise the status of Music by giving it parity with other subjects such as History, Mathematics and Languages, but does little to develop students' interests in their own creative efforts. Indeed, it may have the opposite effect, students being inclined to undervalue their composing because the approved curriculum appears to value other things more.
>
> (2000: 26/7)

In many ways it is also subject to the same confused thinking that we are trying to unravel.

> All too easily we may leave students with the impression that, whilst we believe it is good for them to 'have a go' at composing, that it is not on the same intellectual plane as learning about 'great' music.
>
> (Paynter 2000: 27)

Gammon sketches a delightfully simple model for the music curriculum, in which the central activity, composing, is 'stimulated by listening' and provides 'much of the material for performance, listening and appraisal'. (1996: 108)

> In this model the creative aspect (composing) has the dominant role but is fed by, and feeds into, the performative and responsive aspects (performing and listening). The functional aspect [rules, forms, elements, materials, how things work, causation, etc.] ... is a function of the three major areas of activity. The whole is surrounded by the amorphous realm of fact and context.
>
> (ibid.)

This, of course, requires that teachers are able to teach composing, and Paynter's and Webster's ideas on this may have much to offer in bringing this sort of curric-ulum model to fruition.

Harland *et al.* are overtly critical of music education in the schools that took part in the report. It is hard to discern precisely what it was about the teaching of Music in these schools that led them to conclude that 'music was the most problematic and vulnerable artform' (2000: 568). However, they highlight as good practice the importance of practical task-based activities ('doing'), and the enjoyment that pupils derive from 'learning through *doing their own thing*' (2000: 570). They also suggest that 'in view of the critical problems facing music, there is an urgent need to tackle the quality of teaching' (ibid.: 570). So it is clear that it is the teaching that they perceive as being at the root of the problem, and it may be that there are significant links between this and the issues covered in this chapter. For they comment that:

> the strong emphasis in music on knowledge and skill-based outcomes reflects a different type of perceived outcome in music compared with the other artforms. This was discussed in Chapter 4 as pupils perceiving their learning in music to be 'learning about' the rudiments of music … and comparatively little on 'learning how', to compose, for example … This linked very much with discussion in Chapter 6 on creativity, where, in general, pupils were found to talk about creativity in conjunction with composition only at a later stage in their secondary schooling.
>
> (ibid.: 269)

Whereas in a school where pupils' attitudes to music were more positive they report that 'the emphasis [was] on skills relating to creativity and composition, rather than learning the basics *per se*' (ibid.: 273).

The report clearly sees the importance of creativity, but comments that there seemed to be a lack of 'sequential and/or progressive development in creativity'. (ibid.: 112) They suggest that:

> in the light of pupils' very enthusiastic, if varied, descriptions of creativity as an effect of arts education and in the wake of the NACCCE report and the setting up of the QCA task force on creativity, it is worth asking whether the time has come for curriculum designers to offer teachers a more explicit model of development in creativity in all its various guises. Making the learning of thinking skills and creativity a much more transparent and overt part of the curriculum (and of teacher training) could offer many potential benefits for pupils .
>
> (ibid.:112)

It is to be hoped that this call will be heeded and that the pioneering efforts of the past thirty years of music education will be realized, and an ethos established where 'both teachers and pupils are actually encouraged to *value* imagination, fantasy and adventurousness' (Spencer 1993: 83). However, in the meantime, whilst we await these developments, there is much that can be done to make Music in the school curriculum a vital and meaningful experience that fosters creativity and innovation.

References

Blacking, J. (1976) *How Musical is Man?*, London: Faber.
—— (1987) *A Commonsense View of All Music*, Cambridge: Cambridge University Press.
Department for Education and Employment and the Qualifications and Curriculum Authority (1999) *The National Curriculum Handbook for Secondary Teachers in England*, DfEE and QCA.
Department of Education and Science, Welsh Office (1985) *The National Criteria*, HMSO.

Flynn, P. and Pratt, G. (1995) 'Developing an understanding of appraising music with practising primary teachers', *British Journal of Music Education*, 12(2):127–58.

Gammon, V. (1996) 'What is wrong with school music? – a response to Malcolm Ross', *British Journal of Music Education*, 13: 101–22.

Harland, J. *et al.* (2000) *Arts Education in Secondary Schools: Effects and Effectiveness*, National Foundation for Educational Research.

Loane, B. (1984) 'Thinking about children's compositions', *British Journal of Music Education* 1(3): 205–31.

National Advisory Committee on Creative and Cultural Education (1999) *All Our Futures: Creativity, Culture & Education*, DfEE Publications.

OCR, Music 2000 (1998) *General Certificate of Secondary Education, Syllabus*, OCR.

Odam, G. (1995) *The Sounding Symbol*, London: Stanley Thornes.

Paterson, A. and Odam, G. (2000) *Composing in the Classroom: the Creative Dream*, NAME.

Paynter, J. (2000) 'Making progress with composing', *British Journal of Music Education*, 17(1): 5–31.

Plummeridge, C. (1991) *Music Education in Theory & Practice*, London: The Falmer Press.

Ross, M. (1995) 'What's wrong with school music?', *British Journal of Music Education*, 12: 185–201.

—— (1998)'Missing solemnis: reforming music in schools', *British Journal of Music Education*, 15(3): 255–62.

Shepherd, J. and Vulliamy, G. (1994) 'The struggle for culture: a sociological case study of the development of a national music curriculum', *British Journal of Sociology of Education*, 15(1): 27–39.

Small, C. (1987) *Music of the Common Tongue*, London: Calder/Riverrun.

Spencer, P. (1993) 'GCSE Music: a survey of undergraduate opinion', *British Journal of Music Education*, 10: 73–84.

Swanwick, K. (1988) *Music, Mind, and Education*, London: Routledge.

—— (1996) 'Music education liberated from new praxis', *International Journal of Music Education*, 28: 16–24.

Swanwick, K. and Tillman, J. (1986) 'The sequence of musical development: a study of children's composition', *British Journal of Music Education*, 3(3): 305–39.

Walker, R. '1987) 'Musical perspectives on psychological research and music education', *Psychology of Music*, 15(2): 167–86.

Webster, P. (1988) Creative thinking and music education', *Design for Arts in Education*, 89(5): 33–7.

—— (1990a) 'Creative thinking, technology and music education', *Design for Arts in Education*, 94(5): 35–41.

—— (1990b) 'Creativity as creative thinking', *Music Educators' Journal*, 76(9): 22–8.

—— (1996) Creativity as creative thinking', in G. Spruce (ed.) *Teaching Music*, pp. 87–97, Milton Keynes: Open University Press.

13 Relevance and transformation

Roles for world musics

Malcolm Floyd

I finished writing this chapter on the day (10 October 2000) when it was announced that two-thirds of secondary school students thought that their Music lessons had either had little or no relevance for them, or had not taught them anything, depending upon the way particular programmes presented the news. Of course such headlines always miss out much of the interesting detail and paint a picture rather bleaker than is the case in reality. However, they do remind us to know why we construct curriculums and syllabuses in particular ways, and to be able to communicate the essence of that to those we teach at all levels of education. In the light of this, my basic premise is that music is a route to knowing the self, and simultaneously reifying senses of community. It is a way of giving substance to enculturation and empowerment in education. The discussion that follows looks at such issues through the example of 'world musics'. We have become very aware of 'world musics' in educational circles in recent years, with a great many *animateurs*, stimuli and learning materials appearing in many forms and guises, looking at musics from many parts of the globe. Some look at the music *per se*, in terms of its structures and modes of operation. This now seems to me to be insufficient, and allows for the unauthorized appropriation of techniques, timbres and, perhaps most perniciously, samples without acknowledgement. However, most of these resources do acknowledge an originating culture and attempt to provide a socio-cultural framework for understanding the music. Nevertheless, I think there are further steps that should, and could, be taken for schools and others to draw more fully on the significance of music in the lives of people.

The vast majority of these sessions and materials are aimed at children and their teachers in the West, and at the more-or-less defined curriculums which delineate or at least guide what actually happens in schools and classrooms. Of course this is the case – how could it be otherwise? People in other areas produce their own materials aimed at their own children and educational systems. The question of how things might otherwise happen arises because there appears to be little resolution or prospect of compromise between two positions held in this discipline, as is apparent in looking at volume 13 of the *British Journal of Music Education* (1996), which has interesting articles from both Elizabeth Oehrle (Oehrle 1996: 95–100) and Trevor Wiggins (Wiggins 1996: 21–9). Oehrle urges the importance of inter-cultural music in creating a culture of tolerance; Wiggins talks of the difficulties (even impossibilities) of realizing the inherent messages in somebody else's music.

Oehrle takes on Teilhard de Chardin's idea of divinely guided evolution: Part One – Diversity and Expansion – is to do with populating the earth and developing physical and cultural difference; Part Two – Unification – is about people coming back together through increased communication, and a psychological and spiritual consciousness of other (Speaight 1967).

The role of music in this, particularly the use of the music of others, is to develop consciousness and so Oehrle emphasizes the importance of 'education through music'. She says: 'Intercultural education through music could be the means of correcting ... "errant perceptions": a way of breaking down the barriers and prejudices that isolate one from the other ... a way of moving towards a culture of tolerance' (Oehrle 1996: 96), and she cites the supporting views of various musicians and educators including Elliott, McAllister, Nettl and Swanwick.

If this is at least one principle behind the current interest in world musics in education, what allows us to perceive that such music is accessible and available for use to these ends? Partly, perhaps, because that is what people have done with it so far. Field recordings have been selected, transcriptions made and at one time piano accompaniments would have been added (and I have to admit here that this includes a piano accompaniment set to a transcription I originally made of a Turkana song from Kenya). Parts for Orff instruments are created or adapted from original percussion, and carefully chosen, often dramatically sanitized, information on background has been included. This is published in a user-friendly format with appealing pictures. In some cases the original contributors are acknowledged, perhaps paid, and copyright issues have been fully discussed and resolved. However, questions remain: is this what the music is for? Who 'owns' the music and authorizes its transmission into this educational diaspora?

Trevor Wiggins in his article talks about ownership being established by usage, rather than being 'rights ... conferred by creation'. This implies, at least from within specific African contexts, that ownership can change. How far is this true? When school children in Winchester sing songs from northern Kenya, do they become co-owners through this usage? It may be the case that they are often only able to come to grips with the surface qualities of the song – their version of the transmitted sounds, with an approximation of 'expressive qualities'. Does music outside the place where it can legitimately be owned through informed usage have the potential to be owned without that depth of informed usage? And who is able to make that decision? Wiggins makes the point that music communicates more than form and feeling; there is other information in a range of levels of meaning, and these levels of meaning are, or can be, lost when music is used outside its own culture. The music also loses its ability to be used as a badge of identification. What will it take for the children in Winchester to have meaningful access to all of this?

The fundamental significance of this link between music and culture is of course important to Oehrle, and she cites Nettl: 'Music can best be understood as an aspect of the culture of which it is part, and understanding can in turn help us to understand the world's cultures and their diversity' (Nettl 1992: 6, quoted in Oehrle 1996: 98).

However, how can this understanding be realized? If I know a song, is it right for me to teach it to someone else? How may I teach it? Is there anything else that needs to be taught alongside the song? It appears from what has already been said that I must teach something of the culture, including the epiphenomena of the song; am I sufficiently aware of the culture to be able to do that? Is anyone else? Hood, talking about the music of Java, is encouragingly positive in his comment that: '[The] western ethnomusicologist, because of training, is capable of insights and evaluations, as a transmitter of a non-western music which no Javanese, even with training abroad in western methods, could ever duplicate' (cited in Nettl, 1992: 3). But are these necessarily the insights and evaluations which the informants would want to be transmitted? Perhaps the latter part of his sentence needs to be addressed, so that the enabling of those within a culture becomes a priority, and not through the assumption that only 'western methods' can have an impact and relevance for students in the West. To explore this further, I want to consider one particular example, the music of the Masai of Kenya and northern Tanzania. I have written about this in several contexts (see for example Floyd 1996, 1998, 1999, 2000a, 2000b) and that I am doing so again here is a reflection of the fact that I am still in the process of coming to grips with the Masai song repertoire, and its complex relationship between music and its context. It is important to say here that while I comment on my understanding of what I have gleaned from my generous Masai hosts, I cannot speak for them. However, what follows does contribute to the debate about who best communicates about one group to another; is it the person within the first group, who has the deep knowledge of what the group has to communicate, or the person within the second group, who has the deep knowledge of how best to communicate with their group?

Several authors, notably Geertz, have used the analogy of webs to describe the structure of cultures, and suggested that the quantity and quality of sharing between individuals, with negotiations around issues of 'self' and 'other', defined the edges of such structures. This complex set of inter-relationships is apparent intra- as well as inter-culturally. It is expressed, for example, in the diagram of Masai song repertoires in Figure 13.1.

Although the literature, and emic (the 'insider's', 'subjective') and etic (the 'outsider's', 'objective') perceptions, talk of an apparently coherent 'Masai' culture, this example of Masai cultural expression makes clear where differentiation happens within the culture, at least in this one way. It is partly age-related, in that changes occur over time, as infants become children and as people get married. It is also gender-related, as males move more slowly through the process than females. It is also function-related as the integration of song with ritual means that young girls are moving towards marriage, regarded as their immediate and final function, while young men are moving first to become *ilmurran* (warriors), and thence to marriage and elderhood. In addition to these internal cultural relationships the Masai have also to deal with the cultures of yet others. These include groups who have grown in strength as weapons are gradually traded into Kenya for food and provisions, and who thus feel capable of fighting those in their way. This is part of the explanation for the dramatic increase in banditry in Kenya in recent years. There is also an

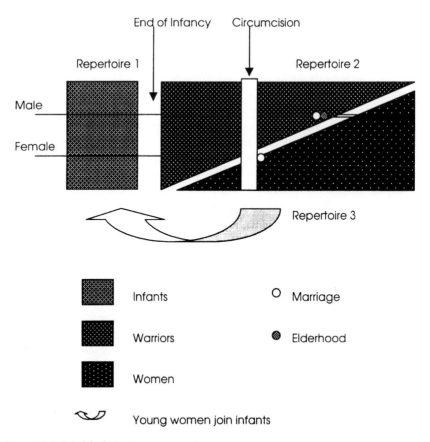

Figure 13.1 Model of Masai song repertoires

ever-increasingly demanding and still-forming national meta-culture, which is itself in relationship with a global mega-culture. Figure 13.2 is one possible model of how cultures work (drawn from Floyd 2000a: 29).

This model may be described thus: behaviours, stimulated by needs and problems, require an adaptive system which takes the form of 'expressive actions' (saying something about something, or trying to alter it), within a cultural and culture-specific response. Such a response may include provision of supplies and shelter, kinship, protection, activities, training and hygiene. These expressive actions, working as sign, symbol, signal and index, might be called communication, and this exists in two styles, universals and alternatives. Universals may include speech, material traits, art, mythology and scientific knowledge, religious practices, family and social systems, property, government and war, although the reifications will be various. Alternatives appear as the diversity of particular practices and habits. Individuals are most likely to function with alternatives, and the larger society with universals.

How does it relate to Masai reality? It is possible to identify some 'universals' such as the importance of cattle, the status of *ilmurran*, and the structures of social

Universals   Alternatives

\   /

Communication (society, group, individual)

Λ

Expressive Actions in Cultural Response

Λ

Adaptive System

Λ

Behaviours

Λ

Needs and Problems

Figure 13.2 Model of culture

organization. The fullest expression of 'alternatives' is to be found within the songs, where communication happens at the level of what is currently significant. This can happen because, although the songs generally follow audible formulae, the performers themselves construct both text and melodic realization. It would appear then that the model has some aptness for the Masai situation. However, this needs to be set beside the problem articulated by T.S. Eliot: 'The effective culture is that which is directing the activities of those who are manipulating that which they call culture' (Eliot 1948: 107).

The manipulators in Masai society are principally the elders, as this is fundamentally a gerontocratic society (as made clear by Spencer 1965), who maintain control through the allowing of 'rituals of rebellion' and through the management of cattle, through trading and marriage. However, conflict has the potential to become more significant with the strengthening of acculturative agencies, including formal education. The symbiotic relationship between culture and individuals is reified through the processes of enculturation. To show this a diagram of enculturation can be set beside Masai specifics (Figure 13.3).

The idea that socialization and learning take place in a continual process among the Masai gets its strongest support in the overview of ritual where stages are clearly marked throughout an individual's life, and in culturally helical patterns. This can be seen particularly in the recurring meat-feasts indicating progression through stages of social development, and in the relationships between age-sets and their elder patrons. Formal learning situations also exist, and are focused almost entirely on initiation. This is certainly a recognizable period with specific outcomes that are reinforced through a fear of failure and tested through ordeals. The songs themselves follow this pattern, corresponding closely with a period of infancy where there is no gender differentiation, through a formal period of initiation to a period of adulthood where there is a strong division between the musical practices of women and of married men.

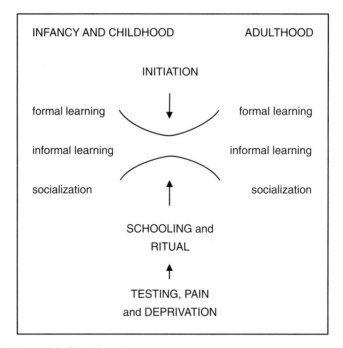

Figure 13.3 A model of enculturation

However, there is an additional phase for the Masai male, which comes between adolescence and adulthood, where physical adulthood is not recognized by marriage. This is at least partly to enable the continuation of polygny, as there are fewer males seeking spouses. The origination of this practice may be a result of being a warrior people, which had the inevitable result of there being fewer males anyway as a result of conflict. This is reinforced by the musical repertoire as well, as it shows this skewing of musical practices against a purely age-based pattern. Further, the element of formal learning for males relates strongly to this warrior phase, and less certainly to the period of marriage and elderhood. This also shows that the enculturative processes, particularly as observable in musical practices, exemplify and make real the relationships between Masai individuals and their common culture. It may be useful to spend some time exploring these musical enculturative practices in more detail.

Masai music

- *is understood and associated with behaviours and emotions.* There is a range of issues in the songs which fits these parameters, including social organization, social behaviour and punishment. Anger is the predominant emotion which can be discerned in the texts, related also to fear, criticism and praise.
- *is shaped by culture and is intentional.* This is apparent in the use of cultural icons, including cattle and warriors, and is intentional to the extent that people consider the songs to be human constructions, although song is so

common and persistent a feature of life that the actual occasions of song are not always deliberately pre-determined, and often arise spontaneously.

- is socially conditioned and conditioning. The repertoires indicate a close relationship between social structure and the music performed. This occurs along three interacting axes: gender, age and function.

- *involves all present in communal experience.* This does not mean to say that all within the culture are equally involved, but that all those Masai present at the event with music are involved, often as performers. Also, those 'present' may be wider than immediately apparent, as non-performing audiences are constructed, and construct themselves, in various sites that allow involvement at varying levels. This includes elders who move away from villages to allow for the singing of married women, and young boys who stay inside their homes when *ilmurran* are singing outside.

- *is group expression.* Most Masai music is performed by groups. However, there is much solo singing within pieces which depends upon individuals to construct text from personal experience, often emphasizing their particular skills and achievements, and melody from a range of appropriate genres and formulae.

- *is available for use within culture.* Songs are used to promote individuals' causes: in relationships, requests to authorities, to air grievances and so on, and performance is not restricted beyond what is considered appropriate in any particular situation. For example, *Laomon* (the prayer songs of women) have echoes within the new Christian songs appearing, sung by both men and women.

- *has specific functions, dictated by cultural needs and problems.* As a need or problem arises, texts will be created to address it within the supply of song frameworks. It is true to say that certain song-types are used consistently, if not exclusively, however, so that 'Ntinyakamba' is frequently part of the processes leading to male initiation.

- *may occur at specific times/seasons/places.* Songs are linked with time, season and place, as they relate to function. Initiation is the most obvious example, but a particular sense of place is created at times to allow rebellion to happen within acceptable parameters.

- *reveals social dynamics.* This works on at least two levels. Individuals have particular responsibilities and rights within a communal, gender-exclusive supportive framework. The model of repertoires given in Figure 13.1 reflects a wider social organization relating to gender, age and function.

- *leads to communal transformation.* Songs allow the exploration of issues which alert both individuals and the wider community to impending problems, and the testing of potential solutions. However, in many of these songs the eventual result is communal rather than personal transformation, as individual problems are raised in the context of wider issues of principle.

- *enhances consciousness.* There is some sophistication about this as consciousness is raised through practices that seem to eliminate the possibility of enhancing consciousness, for example the movement of elders away from the places where warriors' songs may include protest. The warriors have 'let off steam', the elders know that there has been protest and can deal with issues in a way that does not undermine their own individual authority, or the wider social structure, and without having to confront the warriors. Songs also pass on information about particular exploits, dangers, forthcoming events and so on.

Having brought together some of the principal issues around Masai culture, enculturation and music at the 'traditional' level, it is important now to put this into contemporary and potential contexts; to consider what spurs there are to adapt and change. National government has been a principal source of spurs since independence, with a strongly articulated policy of 'Nation-building', with an awareness of a wider economic and technological internationalism. This has led to consideration of ways of achieving a national consciousness in all parts and communities within this diverse country, which has resulted in a strong national focus on educational policy and implementation. How does this impact upon the Masai? Here is a summary of the thoughts of Paulo Freire on such issues, with interpolations applicable to the Masai:

> Provided with the proper tools [a dynamic and eternally (re-)creative musical practice, encouraging individual contribution within a communally supportive framework, which is determined along several possible axes] the individual can gradually perceive personal and social reality as well as the contradictions in it, become conscious of his or her own perception of that reality, and deal critically with it.
>
> (Freire 1970:14)

There are a few potential problems here for the Masai. For a warrior people the distinction between 'self' and 'other' is fundamental. Traditionally 'other' has meant 'not Masai', and this resistance to 'other' is clear in the large percentage of songs about war and so on, and the much smaller percentage referring to positive meetings. This then militates against an easily-adopted form of national unity, with concomitant difficulties for national development. However, the following passage suggests a route using music as a way of engaging with such processes.

• Music	*The songs of the Masai, which exist as structures to enable the daily creation of particular realizations,*
• as part of affective culture, through a dual commitment to art and society	*integral to socially functional cultural dynamics,*
• prepares individuals within a community	*support and require the contribution of individuals within specific communal song frameworks,*
• for life, including its uncertainties,	*to achieve enculturation, and to be aware of current realities and changes, which entail engagement with the debate on nationhood on their own terms,*

• in its capacity to act as a mode of discourse and communication through symbolic expression	*through the exploration of ideas within song text and musical manipulation,*
• in communal experience,	*in appropriately shared and situated events,*
• guiding choice in social action.	*enabling action either among those performing, or those affected by the discourse.*

It has become apparent that identity as a concept has lost its sense of cohesion and integration, and this has had a potential impact on identities at all levels: individual, communal and national. It allows the uncomfortable realities of discord and rebellion to be seen rather as processes reifying the dialectic of cultural dynamics. Through schism, new positions are found and fought for. The holding together of such various identities is exemplified clearly by the Masai. This is not to say that it happens easily, but that they are aware of it, and have prioritized a particular model of coalescence which can be summarized thus: the individual is valued as contributing to the local Masai community, which sees itself as integral to the wider collective of Masai peoples. In turn this acknowledges both the opportunities and constraints of the geographical 'nation', including its wider global relationships.

This is the particular message from the songs of the Masai. The commenting of song upon action, of song upon policy, and even of song upon song provides a model of creative critical reflexivity which is an encapsulation of a praxis-based socio-political methodology. Any mutuality of understanding, of expression, of reification of the intangible, occurs through our songs. My singing with the Masai has been not only a tool for examination but a location for a joyful encounter between our webs. They have always been willing to share their songs, in the knowledge that all song needs support. This is expressed in many of the songs themselves, where there is an enthusiasm for giving the support where it can be taken up willingly, and there is the recognition by the singer that support is needed: 'My fellow singers support me singing'.

But now for the tricky question: does the transmission of such songs have any importance? These songs may communicate in all the ways suggested above, but only within a particular context known to the enculturated user; they may 'give out some education as what did our parents do' (cited in Floyd 1998: 158) but not about the parents of those outside the culture. There may be a tangible link in the fact of the music making you 'comfortable, strong, and keeps your body constant, not too fat or thin' (ibid.), and Wiggins comes to this as one of his possibilities for working in this area (op. cit. 29).

But how might this happen as a process? Wiggins presents a dichotomy of transmission which is often formal in the West, while not so for aurally-transmitted music. In the West, he says, teachers analyse, present information in a conceptualized form and correct mistakes. In Africa, people perform and leave children to copy and understand in their own way. The conceptualization is done by the pupil and is unlikely to be verbalized (Wiggins 1996: 24).

I would like to suggest that we might develop the role of the originator in the pattern of originator (singer) – mediator – receptor (student), and that the media-tor's part be much more to bring originator and receptor together, to enable an empowering transformation, than to evaluate the one and transmit information to the other.

Let me try to answer my earlier questions in this light. 'If I know a song, is it right for me to teach it to somebody else?' Only if I know the song in such a way that I have ownership of it, through deeply informed usage. Otherwise it is much better for me to get out of the way of the potential originator–receptor sharing. 'How may I teach it?' Perhaps I should not teach it anyway, but rather allow others to join with me, in a process that may lead to transformative ownership for them. We tend to learn in the field from observation and doing over a period of time. Can we real-istically condense that into a transcription, even with a recording, sufficient to transform a class in two hours (a not uncommon situation)? 'Am I sufficiently aware of the culture to be able to teach something of it?' This is really the same as the first question, and the answer is yes, if I have sufficient informed usage to be an owner of songs.

The fundamental place of 'musicing' in British music education is now firmly established, although curriculums at present often only focus on the receptor's part in process and product in world musics. A role for music teachers, then, might be to facilitate this bringing together of 'authorial musicer' and 'receptor', so that the terms eventually become insubstantial, and all are musicing collaboratively, whether that leads to fusion or the holding together of two or more consciously different cultures.

In any case, perhaps a much better response to these questions might be to acknowledge the people who know best, and to devise ways of making direct connections. In this I do of course include the various individuals and groups who have a strong background in the music, and maintain their links with the commu-nities who have helped to build such backgrounds. But I think it is also time to develop this further, and find ways of collaborating with these African communi-ties themselves. This is potentially very problematic, and open to abuse and disrup-tion of what are initially good intentions, but it must be worth exploring, and is the aim of a research project currently being set up linking institutions and communi-ties in the UK, Kenya, Tanzania and Uganda. I want to finish by setting out some of the principles being applied in two parts of this project.

It was the problems of the Music Conservatoire of Tanzania (in Dar es Salaam) which started this process in the first place. Having been going for about thirty-five years, it has found that there are now not enough people who (a) want to have piano lessons leading to external examinations (b) could afford to pay for them anyway. On the other hand, a need has been identified for tuition in guitar, keyboard and choir-training, but there are (a) very few qualified competent tutors and (b) no current system to organize and fund such tuition anyway. My involvement followed from work I had done with the Kenya Conservatoire of Music from 1982–9, and two main lessons were brought from that to the Tanza-nian situation:

- while people from 'outside' may have particular expertise which can be drawn on, such projects require the primary commitment to come from those within the situation;
- this commitment, with appropriate negotiated support, then allows for the possibility of sustainability.

From this starting point discussions in Tanzania have led us to formulate a number of principles which underpin our future plans, and I hope resonances of the earlier exploration of the Masai and their music are apparent:

- music is intimately connected to, and part of, the people who create, recreate and receive it. Thus, to deal with it as an abstraction, as an autonomous entity to be dealt with solely at an intellectual or emotional level would be to deal with it incompletely;
- because of music's deep relationship with both individuals and communities, any project would have to engage with the actual priorities and needs of those individuals and communities involved, rather than working from a set of otherwise admirable targets that might only be viable in limited ways, and whose sustainability would be suspect at best;
- because of the insistence on relating to real and current issues, no prior favouring of particular styles or genres would be appropriate. This means that this is not a project which urges everyone to rediscover 'traditional' music, although there is a hope that those involved may wish to look to such music as part of a rich and dynamic repertoire from which to draw;
- while there is a strong move to sharing musics, this should be allowed to happen so that the experience is not limited merely to transmission, but is truly transformative.

We are also borrowing from some of the work done in 'Theatre for Development'. Robert Chambers (1983: 201), whose work remains an important guide to all work in this area, asserts that the fundamental point is that there must be 'reversals in learning'. He gives examples of the sorts of activities which would enable this:

- sitting, asking and listening
- learning from the poorest
- learning indigenous technical knowledge
- joint research and development
- learning by working
- simulation games

Perhaps activities such as these, realized through music, would be a way both of approaching various levels of meaning within music, and of contributing in concrete terms to the acknowledgement, recognition and understanding of others. There is considerable real potential for all those interested in how music helps us function, and how we individually and communally contribute to that, to work in the ways suggested here. I am urging contact, initially through competent media-tors, but eventually directly. This can be through personal meeting, video exchange, interactive websites, jointly producing and sharing materials and resources, enabling mutual access to archives and living performers, in short, demanding the transformation for ourselves and others that music has the power to deliver. Today's headlines can be seen as depressing and dispiriting, but perhaps they are, rather, a timely reminder of what our students are looking for, and I would argue that we all look for personal relevance in what we do. Surely the quest for transformation of ourselves and our world could make music relevant and worth learning for everyone.

References

Ampomah, K. (1997) 'A Ghanaian perspective on the changing role of traditional African music in a contemporary society', unpublished MPhil thesis, University of York.

Eliot, T. S. (1948) *Notes Towards the Definition of Culture*, London: Faber & Faber.

Floyd, M. (1996) 'Promoting traditional music: the Kenyan decision' in *World Musics in Education*, pp.186–206, Aldershot: Scolar.

—— (1998) 'Missing Messages: Lessons from Tanzania', in *British Journal of Music Education* 15(2): 155–60.

—— (1999) 'Warrior composers: Maasai boys and men' in M. Floyd (ed.) *Composing the Music of Africa*, Aldershot: Ashgate Publishing.

—— (2000a) 'Music in education and enculturation: a Maasai case study', PhD thesis, Birmingham Conservatoire.

—— (2000b) 'Maasai musics, rituals, identities' in G. Harvey (ed.) *Music in Traditional Indigenous Religions*, Aldershot: Ashgate Publishing.

Freire, P. (1970, repr. 1993) *Pedagogy of the Oppressed*, London: Penguin.

Geertz, C. (1973, repr. 1993) *The Interpretation of Cultures*, London: Fontana Press.

Merriam, A. P. (1964) *The Anthropology of Music*, Northwestern University Press.

Nettl, B. (1992) 'Ethnomusicology and the teaching of world music', in *International Journal of Music Education* 20: 3–7.

Oehrle, E. (1996) 'Intercultural education through music: towards a culture of tolerance', in *British Journal of Music Education* 13: 95–100.

Speaight, R. (1967) *Teilhard de Chardin: a biography*, London: Collins.

Spencer, P. (1965) *The Samburu*, London: Routledge

Wiggins, T. (1996) 'The world of music in education', in *British Journal of Music Education* 13: 21–9.

14 Instrumental teaching as music teaching

Keith Swanwick

Learning to learn

On the surface, and compared with general music teaching, instrumental instruction appears to be relatively uncomplicated by considerations of knowledge and value. I play an instrument; therefore I can show you or anyone else how to play it. But life is not quite so simple, and there is a great deal involved in any educational transaction. In many ways instrumental teaching seems a very haphazard affair with idiosyncratic extremes, depending on the individual teacher who can be somewhat isolated in the confines of the music room or studio. We may think that the instrumental student simply wants to learn to play an instrument, but what does that mean? There are ways of teaching the trombone or the bass guitar that open up the way into musical playing and musical understanding more effectively than others, that are either a part of an initiation process into musical discourse or are not.

Getting people to play any instrument without musical understanding – not really 'knowing music' – is an offence against human kind. It denies both feeling and cognition and under such conditions the world becomes meaningless. Discourse is stripped of significance, shorn of quality; intuitive understanding is driven out and the knife of technical analysis cuts away to the bare bone. Some of the most disturbing teaching I have witnessed has been in the instrumental studio, where – in a one-to-one relationship giving the teacher considerable power – a student can be confronted simultaneously by a complex page of notation, a bow in one hand and a violin in the other, along with exhortations to play in time, in tune, with a good tone. On the contrary, however, some of the very best teaching has been by instrumentalists. For example, take this case study, a description by Christine Jarvis of children at work as part of the Tower Hamlets project in London primary schools.

> The violins were tuned by the teacher while each child bowed the open-strings. This prepares children for the time when they are able to tune their own instruments, familiarizing them with both the sound and the process, though in most group lessons violins are pre-tuned to save time. The teacher then distributed 'practice sheets' with four tunes written out in note names or Sol-fa.

The lesson proceeded with a revision of the bow-hold, and attention to general posture, followed by a performance of 'Hoe down', which was played once more. 'Cowboy, chorus' was then performed several times, the children walking round in a circle as they played, three or four being invited to improvise answering phrases between each performance of the tune. The leader then introduced a sight-reading game, 'spin-a-tune', and a few minutes were spent reading through a piece, examining the rhythm and naming the notes before playing it.

The lesson continued with work on the D-major scale, first singing it to Sol-fa, then playing it using rhythms chosen by the children based on short sentences including colour, animal, action, place. Some amusing sentences were produced, making quite long rhythms. Posture and bow-hold were checked again, and the lesson concluded with 'Ringing bell' played with varied bowings, including tremolo and spiccato.

The pace was fast, with active involvement and lively participation of the children throughout. Teaching was very child-centred and made technical work fun by using a variety of games. The teacher always found things to which they could relate.

Group Lessons: the third and fourth years (ninety-two children in all) are usually divided into two groups for simultaneous lessons in the two school halls. On this occasion, with a Christmas concert looming, the morning began by rehearsing Christmas songs. The teaching team was present, as were all the class teachers involved. Eight songs were practised, some in a less traditional version, the words of one or two being adapted. For example, in 'The twelve days of Christmas', five gold rings became five ripe mangoes, and so on. Other songs included two rounds and three other seasonal songs, two of which were sung as a duet. Attention was directed to intonation, and there was some rhythmic practice. The project teacher was helping to prepare all the classes in the school for the Christmas concert and was observed in a lively session with infants and nursery children in the afternoon, all class teachers being present.

Following the morning singing session, they divided into two string groups. The smaller group (seventeen violins and three cellos) were given a lesson centred on bowing technique in two pieces. Some time was spent practising slurred bowing in preparation for one of these pieces. Notation was also revised and fingering sung before playing pieces through. This lesson was more technical than the average large group session.

Meanwhile, the noticeably less-advanced large group (fifty-two children) rehearsed some items for the school Christmas concert. These included 'Hoe down' and open-string versions of both 'Jingle bells' and 'Silent night' with the melody played on the piano. A Bengali teacher learns the violin with the group, and one or two other class teachers were present, including the deputy head. This group do not have back-up lessons. The emphasis in this lesson was essentially on the enjoyment of the musical experience.

(Swanwick and Jarvis 1990: 27–8)

The teaching and learning described in this passage were fairly typical of sessions in the Tower Hamlets String Teaching Project, now unfortunately closed down through a policy of removing education budgets from town halls and putting money directly into schools. This remarkable scheme achieved an international reputation. The essence of the project was to bring a team of musician-teachers into regular contact with unselected classes of children in primary schools – mainly in the East End of London – and to make music a constant feature in the life of the school. The main lessons with whole classes of around twenty-five unselected children were backed up by work in smaller groups where there was a more technical focus. The complexities of playing a stringed instrument were not tackled by narrowing down attention to one way of approaching music or by confining activities to one style of practising or to hacking through a tutor book page by page. Musical learning in these schools took place through multi-faceted engagement: singing; playing; moving; listening to others; performing in different size groups; and integrating the various activities we associate with music. Those teachers responsible for bringing this about saw their job as teaching Music through an instrument, not just teaching the instrument. They understood that musical knowledge has several strands, different levels of analysis; and they left space for intuitive engagement – where all knowledge begins and ends.

Even at the level of 'knowing how' – the psycho-motor technical management of an instrument – there are insights to be won into how we actually learn complex skills and sensitivities, gaining control over sound materials. The simple view of what happens would be to assume that a skilled action – say playing 'Hoe down' on a violin – is the result of tying together into one bundle a number of smaller technical bits into a larger whole, rather like making a broom or a peg rug. But do we really build up a technique from individual bristles, from atoms of muscular behaviour? The element of truth in this is rather small and needs a massive correction. Above all the performance of a skill requires a plan, a blueprint, a *schema*, an action pattern.

When I run towards a moving tennis ball – hoping to hit it back over the net – I am not just stringing together a number of totally separate physical movements of legs, arms, hand and so on. I am co-ordinating hand, eye and body into a unique variation on a known theme, called 'getting the ball back'. When I play a piece on the piano or trombone I am not only drawing on specific bits of knowledge but will be executing a plan, a blueprint, managing the piece in accordance with a set of requirements 'in my head', which unfolds and to some extent changes as we go along. Once I lose the thread of the plan – perhaps by getting behind in my musical thinking – or perhaps too far in front of the unfolding moment – then things tend to fall apart.

Building up a representation or *schema* seems to be facilitated by varied practices. For instance, I might stand in front of a dart-board or archery target practising hitting the bull's eye. But if I always stand in exactly the same practice position with the same weight of arrow or dart and then eventually test myself with a fixed number of tries I am likely to be less successful than if I had the same number of practice shots from different distances, perhaps with differing weights of projectile. I am forming a *plan*, an image of how to throw at a dart-board or shoot at a target, not acquiring a set of automated muscular tricks from a fixed position. In any case, it is impossible to perform any action twice in exactly the same way. Seeing the target and feeling the action from differing perspectives helps me to get the plan in better shape; there seems to be more of the mind at work. Variable practice has been shown to be important in *schema* formation (Schmidt 1975). When teaching music, educators have always suspected this to be true and good instrumental teachers have found ways of getting their students to play the same material – perhaps scales or pieces – slowly, quickly, detached, legato, in dotted rhythms, with accents falling in different places, using alternative fingerings or hand positions and so on. This variety and depth of approach was characteristic of the Tower Hamlets project, where children clapped, moved, played, sang and listened to music.

We are also helped to form plans by the use of metaphors, mental images, mind pictures of the action. For example, I want to take hold of a cello bow in a way that conforms both to the shape of my hand and the stick and allows me maximum flexibility and control in action. One fairly common approach seems to be to try to sort out the position of each finger in turn, perhaps having a teacher move my hand about or place appropriate fingers at the right angles and in the right places. But that would be the teacher's plan, not *mine* and things are likely to go wrong when I am left on my own. Alternatively, I could put my hand in a 'pretend' bucket of water and shake off the drops – now the hand and arm are free and loose. Then – following an idea of Phyllis Young – I might imagine that I take up a fairly soft strawberry between thumb and second finger, applying this 'plan' to the bow itself (Young 1978). Through a series of metaphors and drawings on an existing repertoire of movements, I come to be in control of my own bow-hold and will have begun to generate a *schema* or plan of my own – a mental picture which can be refined and further developed. In developing images of action a student is learning how to manage music, becoming autonomous, learning how to learn. How different all this is from a teacher pushing my fingers around – something that is done to me rather than anything that I am doing. Unfortunately it seems that much instrumental teaching tends not to be informed by this realization.

Fiona Pacey studied the effect of introducing varied practice over an eight-week period, during which a number of young string players between the ages of 8 and 12 were asked to work with their teachers to test out the strength of the hypothesis (Pacey 1993). In one of a number of experimental projects the particular set of sound materials to be brought further under control concerned loudness levels: the ability to play a passage quietly or loudly, a skill in string playing which depends crucially on the movement and weight of the right arm, the speed and amount of bow and, of course, the monitoring ear. After some weeks of 'normal' teaching, the teachers moved to a more intensive variable practice schedule, where, during three sessions, they had the students use a great variety of bowing actions using several parts of the bow. In organizing practice towards this end the teachers did not limit themselves to practising only the required simple forte and piano difference. That would be rather like always standing at the same position during target practice.

Before and after this intervention, each pupil was recorded on tape playing the tune 'Lightly Row' (see above), a relatively easy piece marked with required changes of loudness level indicated by *f* and *p*, in basic notation which they all understood.

Altogether there were forty-seven instrumentalists playing violin, viola or cello and these were taught by nine different teachers in small groups. The project was organized within an overall time schedule that randomized the placing of the intervention of variable practice. So group 'A' began to work in this way after the third observation (recording); group 'B' after the second; and group 'C' after the fourth observation. Thus, although the whole project spanned eight weekly sessions, students from any single group were recorded in only six performances, the 'observations' – 'O'. For example, the schedule for Group 'A' was as follows.

$$O^1 \quad O^2 \quad O^3 \quad \text{INTERVENTION} \quad O^4 \quad O^5 \quad O^6$$

The research design is a time series based on product analysis – judges listening to the playing of the students. Repeated observations over a time series are a more ecologically sensitive way of gathering data than 'one-shot' testing. The situation is quite complex though and, as we might predict, there is a good deal of variance between individual pupils, those playing different instruments and groups with particular teachers. Seven independent observers – all teachers and members of performing groups – were asked to assess on a low to high continuum the level of success in playing forte and piano. Six performances of every student were presented to them on tape-recordings – in random order of course – with no prior knowledge of which student was which. The assessments of these 'judges' were then averaged to help us look for estimated change over time.

As expected, there is a general upward trend over the six occasions of measurement. We always tend to optimistically assume that playing improves over time and with teaching. Taking all three groups together there was a suggestion that the slope

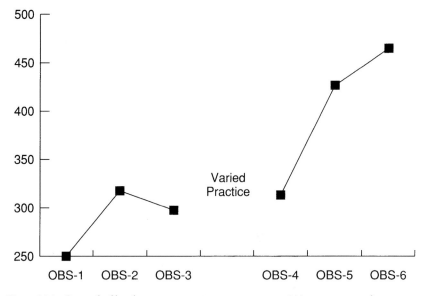

Figure 14.1 Control of loudness on string instuments: group 'A' – seventeen players

of the upward trend increased slightly after the intervention point, though because of the relatively small numbers involved and the complications of pupil, teacher and instrumental variables this cannot be confirmed to a level of statistical significance.

It is worth looking more carefully at one of the larger groups – the seventeen pupils in group 'A'. With this group the introduction of varied practice began at the end of the third session, just following the third observation (recording). The next session included quite a range of varied practice with different bow lengths and this was continued into the fifth session, at the end of which the fourth observation took place. Figure 14.1 shows the pattern of change for students in this group.

Inspection of these data suggests a fairly sharp increase in the upward slope after the intervention with the varied practice programme. Looking a little closer at the data, we can also see a difference between those students whose earlier performances of 'Lightly row' were rated by the expert judges to be on the low side in terms of loudness control and those whose performances from the start were already perceived to demonstrate control of the bow to produce different loudness levels. Figure 14.2 shows this pattern. It is interesting if not surprising to notice that those students given initial high ratings by the teacher-judges appear to change little over time. There is obviously a limit to the amount of improvement to be expected beyond what is already a good performance. After a time any task gets to be insignificant in its level of challenge. However, the ten students with first-time lower ratings produce a steep climb in managing changes of loudness level following the intervention, as can be seen in Figure 14.2.

Variable practice in this case really did seem to pay off, though mostly for those students who initially were not able to manage control of loud and soft playing so very well, while the more advanced students appeared to improve hardly at all. This

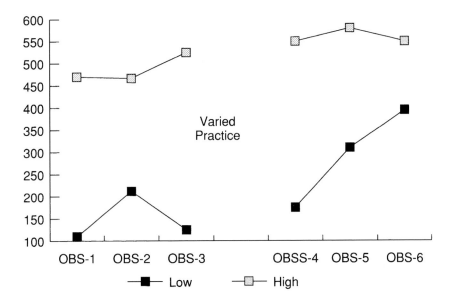

Figure 14.2 Control of loudness on string instuments: high and low starts

is not so surprising; we are hardly likely to become more fluent in a skill which is already well under control. Such results are encouraging, an analysis of what we already intuitively suspect to be true, carried out as far as possible under research conditions. Approaching technical control from several different angles facilitates learning. It makes sense. If I can play a piece in only one way – perhaps at one speed with one level of articulation – then things are like to go adrift fairly easily and the whole thing can break down when something untoward happens. But if I have prac-tised altering the expressive character by adjusting speed, accentuation and relative loudness levels, then not only is my technique likely to be improved but the chances of an interesting performance are raised. Musical decisions are being taken.

Giving time to experiment with music in various ways does two things. First, it lets in the prospect of intuitive insights, unconsciously coming to new ways of approaching the performance; second, it supplies alternative slices of analysis, bringing to consciousness a broader repertoire of expressive possibilities. Often it seems that instrumental students are confronted with one technical hurdle after another with little musical gratification on the way, no sense of accomplishment and hardly any chance to make performance judgements for themselves. Playing becomes mindless and routine, and musical knowledge is neither gained nor projected to an audience. Two educational settings are especially likely to produce this unhappy state of affairs: one is the individual lesson and the other the very large group with one instructor. In the first there is a tendency to be pushed mainly into technical mastery to the exclusion of musical judgements; in the second it is all too easy to become another cog in a machine.

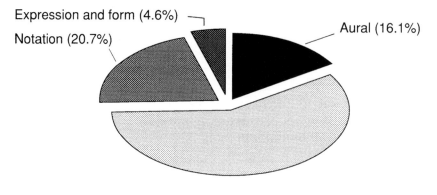

Expression and form (4.6%)

Notation (20.7%)

Aural (16.1%)

Technical (58.6%)

Figure 14.3 Use of time in instrumental lessons: four teachers observed four times

An account by Kevin Thompson of his study of instrumental teachers at work suggests that attention tends to be focused on aural, manipulative and notational skills and on teaching technical terminology. Figure 14.3 shows the proportion of time spent by four fairly typical teachers in various ways during weekly lessons over one month. These students were aged between 9 and 12 years and they were playing wind, brass and string instruments.

The emphasis within instrumental teaching that we see here is pretty clear. Technical work and technical talk seem to be the order of the day and there may be good reasons for this. Sessions are often short and teachers want to be sure that students are getting into 'good habits'. Without technique nothing is possible. Since technique itself appears to be enhanced by varied practice, we need to be sure that we are not just grinding away within a narrow set of routines. Playing passages in one way may not be the best way to meet even the limited aim of acquiring a manipulative skill. In general, it would be better to have students play more pieces in different ways and at lower levels of manipulative difficulty than always to press on relentlessly with the next exacting assignment, a strategy which leaves no time for intuition or analysis and keeps the discourse in the studio fixed on the level of mastery of materials.

Group interaction

One way of broadening the instrumental teaching agenda is through work in groups. I ought to make it clear that I am not advocating group teaching exclusively, nor am I denigrating the private teacher. I simply want to draw attention to some of the potential benefits of group teaching as just one valuable strategy in instrumental instruction. To begin with, music-making in groups has infinite possibilities for broadening the range of experience, including critical assessment of the playing of others and a sense of performance. Music is not only performed in a social context but is learned and understood in such a context. Music and music learning involve building up plans, images, *schemata*, through ways of thinking, practising, playing and responding; learning by imitation of and comparison with other people. We are strongly motivated by observing others and we strive to emulate our peers, often with a more direct effect than being instructed by those persons designated as 'teachers'. Imitation and emulation are particularly strong between people of similar ages and social groups. The basic requirements for anyone playing an instrument are careful listening and perceptive watching. A group with a good teacher is an ideal circumstance for the development of these attitudes. We might think of 'master-classes' where everyone present can learn something. Giving attention to someone else's sound, posture, style of playing and technical achievement is all part of group motivation; so is the stimulation of other people's triumphs and the consolation of recognizing their difficulties. There is here scope for intuitive knowledge, learning by osmosis.

Group teaching is not at all the same as teaching individuals who happen to be scheduled in a group, giving attention to each of them, say, on the basis of ten minutes each over half an hour. Working with a group is a totally different form of educational endeavour. To start with, the teacher has to be especially alert. There can be no casual drifting into lessons without previous preparation. There can be no listening with half an ear whilst looking out of the window, consulting the diary of engagements or attending to the length of one's fingernails. There are constant questions to be addressed. What is the next stage of development and where do we go from here? How do we involve all students at all times?

Involvement does not mean only the physical activity of playing the instrument. In a group, an important activity will be listening and diagnosing, discussing and trying-out. One of the most striking things about good group teaching is the degree and range of participation of all group members. Every teacher will remember the kind of experience where we feel, 'If only so-and-so were able to hear this', or 'How much time might be saved if I could get all these people together'. Group teaching does not exclude individual help and is certainly not 'anti-technique'. Kevin Thompson observed his four teacher-colleagues at work with individual students and also with groups of up to eight people. By systematically observing an individual in each group who was 'matched' as closely as possible with a student having individual lessons, Thompson found that:

> individual and group-taught students received more or less the same spread of time to the various aspects of learning in music, with the exception of notational skills. In spite of group-taught students having received less time in this category, their level of achievement in fluency of notation was disproportionately high. Perhaps teachers made fewer repetitive statements in group settings and saved instructional time. This, coupled with the possibility of learning from others, may account for the alacrity with which the group-taught students acquired notational skills.
>
> (Thompson 1984: 168–9)

No more time was spent 'off task' or setting up equipment in group settings than in individual lessons, and Thompson observed that, while students in groups seemed

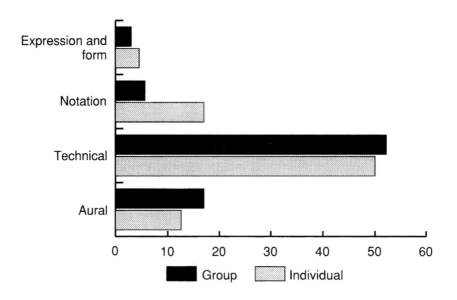

Figure 14.4 Group and individual teaching focus of attention

to be acquiring a wider range of skills in more varied musical and social conditions, the teachers behaved very differently when working with groups, with positive changes in levels of preparedness, interaction and personal dynamism. From interviews he conducted with fourteen experienced group instrumental teachers, he concluded that they saw instrumental groups as educationally valuable rather than as an economical necessity and that working with groups was the preferred mode of teaching, though they recognized the necessity at times for individual instruction.

Resistance to instrumental group-teaching most often comes from those who have come through music schools and conservatoires where the one-to-one ratio is jealously preserved and no other alternative seems feasible. Yet we recognize that people can learn a great deal by sitting next to other players in a brass band, guitar class, a rock group, or as a member of a chorus. There is an obvious example here in the school and college bands of North America. In these essentially large-scale teaching groups of mixed instruments, people learn much of their playing technique and stylistic understanding from within the group itself. I would not advocate this as necessarily the best way of organizing instrumental learning but refer to it merely in order to point out that the one-to-one way of working is an extreme at the opposite end of a spectrum.

How much time in lessons is spent on common problems? Is there anything to be learned from regular participation in a small ensemble? Are there not dull lessons when both teacher and pupil feel lethargic, tired, uninspired and might not a group even out the ups and downs of personal temperament and present a constantly stimulating challenge to teachers who are really interested in teaching?

It is unwise to teach individuals on a kind of deficit model; they bring along their mistakes to the lesson and we try to sort them out. This is neither possible nor desirable in a group setting. Good group teachers know how to structure sessions to avoid mistakes and misunderstanding from the outset. A group should be large enough to be a potential music-making ensemble but small enough for any individual to play a distinctive part. A number somewhere between six and fifteen tends to be seen as optimum by those who work with groups. The major requirement is that the teacher has to prepare beforehand; the major benefit is that – under the cover of a group environment – the pupil can be learning on the intuitive side as well as taking part in a range of analytical work that will lead towards student autonomy – freedom from the teacher.

Literacy or fluency?

Staff notation seems to have a curious effect on musical behaviour and it certainly has a strong influence on instrumental teaching and playing. The greatest virtue of written signs is their potential for communicating certain details of performance that would easily be lost in aural transmission, just forgotten. Imagine what would happen if the production and preservation of any large-scale classical symphonies had been entirely dependent on the collective memories of composers and performing groups. It is inconceivable that many if any of these works could have been composed at all without the visual maps and designs that constitute the making of a score. But imagine also what happens if these scores are converted either by machine or by mechanical playing into sound, as for example, in the distinctive regularity of fair-ground organs. Without aural performance traditions, most expressive and structural shaping is missing. Worse, imagine the consequences of insisting on notating jazz, rock, a raga improvisation or almost any folk music *before* performance. Such a needless exercise would impede fluency and stifle creative thought. Yet, in instrumental teaching within the western classical tradition, notational 'literacy' is thought to be essential and thus notation is often central to instruction and is frequently the starting point,

   This apparent tension between improvisation and notation has bothered educators for some time. Consider Kodály: 'millions are condemned to musical illiteracy, falling prey to the poorest of music' (Kodály 1974: 119–204). He thought that every child by the year 2000 should be able to read music and every detail of his *Choral Method* leads towards this goal. On the other hand, for Dalcroze, music reading came second to feeling music in movement. Orff considered notation to be important but his emphasis is on making music rather than reading it. Although Kodály advocated improvisation we hear very little about it in the *Choral Method*. For Dalcroze, improvisation had a very important function, to awaken the 'motor tactile consciousness'. For Orff, the central principle of his *Schulwerk* was not the performance of written music with ready-made accompaniments but, as he said, a 'continuous inventing', though imitation is the 'beginning of improvisation'. Orff is looking for a 'spontaneous art of discovery with a hundred ways and a thousand possible structures' (Thomas in Keetman 1974: 13).

   Music educators and other musicians do seem to agree that one goal of music education should be to help people to develop what is sometimes called the 'inner ear', a 'dynamic library' of musical possibilities which we draw on in performance. Jazz musicians certainly have strong views on improvisation. I made notes at a conference I was chairing in London, where jazz players extolled the virtues and essential nature of improvisation. In brief summary, the collective wisdom of this group appeared to be as follows:

- everyone can improvise from the first day of playing;
- the basic principle is to have something fixed and something free, the fixed including scale, riff, chord, chord sequence and – crucially – beat;
- it is possible to make great music at any technical level;
- use systems but beware of fixed, rigid teaching strategies;
- imitation is necessary for invention and copying by ear is a creative effort;
- improvisation is characterized by problem-solving and a high level of personal interaction;
- there is no consensus as to how people can be helped to practise improvisation – commitment leads to self-tuition and the motivation is 'delight';
- improvisation is self-transcending, not self-indulgent, and the product matters, we make contact with something beyond our own experience, it makes demands upon the way we listen;
- the secret of playing jazz is the aural building of a 'dynamic library'.

There is no mention of notation here, yet once again we can identify the intuition/analysis dialectic. Improvising is the development and demonstration of a retrieval system and intuition is its essential process. The spotlight of the mind that searches what we already know for what is relevant *at this time* is guided, not by conscious thought, but by intuitive scanning. But as we know, intuitive knowledge can only grow if it is complemented by analytical mapping, and this includes identifying the 'something fixed', both channelling and extending the way we listen. 'Copying', imitating, are themselves acts of analysis where we sift out certain elements for attention – those things we want to emulate. Varied practice is also analytical, a way of consciously extending the dynamic library, cataloguing, classifying, building up a *schema*, an action pattern.

The 'inner ear' is essentially the forming of music images and this faculty is developed through the interaction of intuitive musical expression and analytical sifting. All musical performance is inevitably 'playing by ear' and an astute analysis of this curious term by Philip Priest brings out clearly the diverse educational activities that fall under the common terminology. His definition of 'playing by ear' is comprehensive: 'all playing that takes place without notation being used at the time' (Priest 1989). The categories below point to some of the various possibilities:

- memorized signs, where the player's memory of the notation from which the music has been learned is used as a visual aid;
- imagined signs, where the player constructs such signs for the first time as an aid to finding pitch notes;

- imitation of a model (seen and heard), where both the physical actions and sounds they produce are observed and copied;
- imitation of a model (heard only), the copying of a pattern or tune based on what is heard – whether live or recorded;
- imitation of imagined sound, where the player attempts to reproduce remembered tunes or patterns;
- improvised variation, altering the original music (read or remembered) by elaboration but keeping to the structure;
- invention within a framework, playing from a sketch (chord symbol or figured bass) in the prevailing rhythm and style;
- invention with no framework, sometimes called extemporization, the player being free to choose every aspect of the music;
- experimental invention, discovering sounds and nuances new to player and perhaps to music.

(Priest 1989: 1)

Priest derives a pedagogical model from this – seen in Figure 14.5 – an analysis which greatly assists us to envisage a range and depth of teaching possibilities.

Musical activities often involve more than one of the processes shown in Figure 14.5 at the same time and any player may be more or less conscious of them – more or less intuitive or analytical. Analysis takes place whenever we stop to think, sort out a fingering or choose to separate out a strand or section for practice. Using notation of any kind is always a form of analysis; certain elements of music are abstracted, taken out of the dynamic library for inspection and given special attention, perhaps pitch or rhythm relationships or chord sequences. As Priest says, it has been assumed among music educators that skill with musical notation with its implicit underlying analysis is essential for an 'understanding' of music. The concept of 'musicianship' in music curriculums is often closely tied in with notational skills and certain limited kinds of aural tests. Yet the value of notation as a remembering and transmitting device is not always needed and is now more than ever under question, thanks to micro-technology and especially sophisticated recording techniques. In much music-making it is no longer essential. As an analytical performance and compositional tool, it can have value but only if the analysis is in the first place and ultimately aural. Priest again:

> Naming notes and recognizing signs are *ancillary skills* for a player, not essential to performance nor to understanding if by understanding we mean *thinking in sounds and being able to appreciate and convey artistic expression through music.*
> (Priest 1989: 175; italics in original)

The alternative may be that students just 'bark at print' – a phrase used to refer to reading out aloud without any real sense of meaning. Listening to some students practising the piano is rather like have me read Mandarin from a phonetic transcription. I would have no idea what it means and must sound dreadful. There must be better ways.

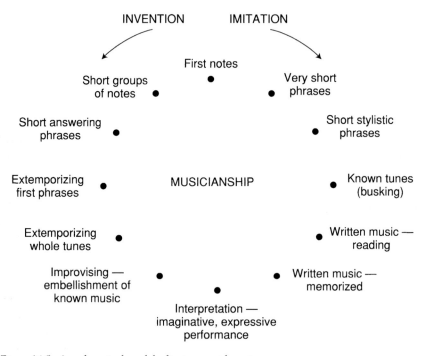

Figure 14.5   A pedagogical model of instrument learning

Source: Priest (1989).

The fourth finger on the a string

Daniel is seven. He now has a half-size cello which not only looks wonderful but can – in the right hands – sound well too. Why a cello? Someone came to his school and played one. Thereafter he wanted to play 'a big instrument like the cello'. When taken to the first half of a concert which included Strauss's *First Horn Concerto* and seated on the front row, he resolutely ignored the horn soloist in front of his nose and scrutinized the celli. Why this should be is hard to know. Visual and aural images of instrumentalists playing seem to linger in the memory and perhaps there are ranges of instrumental sonority that seek out particular people as if to say 'Hi! You're on my wavelength, my sound spectrum coincides with your way of taking the world'. Sound materials are wonderfully compelling, even before the music starts. They are the beginning and the end of musical experience.

We have a recommended tutor book but, when getting him started at home, I am puzzled by the titles of the pages: 'fourth finger on the A string', and by the captions within pages: 'the bow-hold', 'ledger lines', 'basic knowledge' (which turns out to be about the notation of the bass clef), 'the minim', 'the semibreve rest'. This particular slice of musical analysis fails to captivate Daniel and it worries me.

I do not even play the cello beyond the most elementary level, but I have worked intensively with string players and I think I know what matters. They care about the sound they make, they know that string sonorities can be powerfully evocative and that the instruments have all sorts of potential (how near the bow is to the bridge or fingerboard, which part of the bow is appropriate, off or on the string) and they like their playing to be coherent, structured. Just wandering through a piece is no way to play it.

So we begin. 'Pluck each string in turn four times – yes, anchor your right thumb lightly against the side of the finger-board'. Now let's get the bow to work. 'Try pulling it across the C string and then pushing it back again' (first getting the fresh strawberry hold) and 'feel the sound in your chest'. 'Now the next string.' I am soon becoming a pianist expert in vernacular patterns based on the open strings of the cello, and these figures organize our music-making. They include horn calls, dramatic tremolo, flowing divisions of the beat that lead us on to the next change of string and Latin American rhythm patterns (especially the habanera or tango) that seem to fall under the bow so effectively. We are making music and it is the first lesson. In time we shall explore other sets of sound, including the up and down patterns of left-hand fingers on the A string – especially the difference between C and C# which so strongly affects expressive character.

This personal account – a small case study description, a thumb-nail sketch of an encounter with music – serves only to press the point that instrumental teaching must be *musical* teaching, not merely technical instruction on the instrument. There is no point in teaching music at all unless we believe that it is a form of human discourse and that the beginner instrumentalist is being initiated from 'day one' into this discourse and not into 'the semibreve rest'. Analysis on only a narrow technical level and without intuitive response leads nowhere. Perhaps this is why so many instrumental students give up. In *Music, Mind and Education* I characterized the apparent analysis/intuitive rift as a tension between instruction and encounter:

> this tension between instruction and encounter is both inevitable and fertile. These apparently contradictory aspects of human learning are the positive and negative poles between which the electricity of educational transactions flow. Encounter and instruction correspond with the left and right of the musical spiral, with the natural ebb and flow of musical experience. To some extent, it is possible to proceed by instruction in the acquisition of manipulative skills, vernacular conventions, idiomatic traditions, systematic procedures. Here, learning can be more easily structured and sequenced. But it is encounter that characterizes the left-hand side: sensory impression, personal expression, structural speculation and symbolic veneration. Here, the student needs to be left alone with possibilities, many of which will exist thanks to some instructional framing. Theories and practice of music education that fail to

acknowledge a dynamic relationship between left and right, leave us trying to clap with one hand.

(Swanwick 1988: 135)

Rule number one: no lesson is in order without music and music means delight and control of materials, heightened awareness of expression and whenever possible the delight of good form. A session without music is time wasted and the wrong message is taken away – that it is sometimes in order to play unmusically. It is *never* in order.

Rule number two: always go for intuitive fluency before analytical literacy. In the early days at least, music should be articulated freely before sorting out notation. We do not need the limited analysis of a printed copy in front of our faces *every* time we play. Aural awareness precedes and is the foundation, the real 'rudiments of music'; it is also the end-game of musical knowledge.

Rule number three: by all means push but also pull. Students can be drawn into what they sense to be worthwhile. How well do we and other people play for and with the student? Is music an invitation? Students need to feel that what they do contributes to sustaining human minds; we all do.

Instruction without encounter, analysis without intuition, artistic craft without aesthetic pleasure: these are recipes for educational disaster. Meaningless action is worse than no activity at all and leads to confusion and apathy, whereas meaning generates its own models and motivation and in so doing frees the student from the teacher. Thus we take charge of our own learning; there is no other way.

References

Keetman, G. (1974) *Elementaria: First Acquaintance with Orff-Schulwerk*, London: Schott.

Pacey, F. (1993) 'Schema theory and the effect of variable practice in string teaching', *British Journal of Music Education* 10(2).

Priest, P. (1989) 'Playing by ear: its nature and application to instrumental learning', *British Journal of Music Education* 6(2): 173–91.

Schmidt, R. A. (1975) 'A schema theory of discrete motor skill learning', *Psychological Review* 82(4).

Swanwick, K. (1988) *Music, Mind and Education*, London: Routledge.

Swanwick, K. and Jarvis, C. (1990) *The Tower Hamlets String Teaching Project: A Research Report* London: University of London, Institute of Education.

Thompson, K. (1984) 'An analysis of group instrumental music teaching', *British Journal of Music Education* 1(2): 153–71.

Young, P. (1978) *Playing the String Game*, Austin: University of Texas.

15 The art of improvisation and the aesthetics of imperfection

Andy Hamilton

Miles Davis's *Kind of Blue*, from 1959, is one of the most famous recordings in jazz. The pianist on the date was Bill Evans. In his sleevenote to the album, Evans drew a comparison with a Japanese school of painting on parchment, where change or erasing is impossible without damage to the parchment:

> the artist is forced to be spontaneous ... These artists must practise a particular discipline, that of allowing the idea to express itself in communication with their hands in such a direct way that deliberation cannot interfere. The resulting pictures lack the complex composition and textures of ordinary painting, but it is said that those who see well find something captured that escapes explanation.[1]

These procedures are, he continues, echoed in the 'severe and unique disciplines of the jazz or improvising musician'. According to Evans, Miles Davis conceived the sketches for *Kind of Blue* only hours before the date, and the musicians were not shown them until they turned up at the studio – yet most performances were completed satisfactorily on a first take. 'Therefore, you will hear something close to pure spontaneity in these performances,' Evans wrote. This is especially remarkable because, as he says, the pieces represented a particular challenge – Davis's settings pioneered a new style of modal as opposed to chord-based improvisation in jazz.

Evans thought deeply about improvisation and was totally committed to it. But unusually, he had a thorough grounding in classical repertoire and technique. Some listeners, hearing only this influence, regarded his style as effete, cocktail piano dressed up as Debussy-Ravel impressionism. More recently an equally questionable adulation by classical writers has appeared; a sophisticated version is found in Peter Pettinger's excellent recent biography.[2] Pettinger is right to argue that Evans generated his deep emotional expression from a classical 'singing tone'. But he neglects Evans's commitment to improvisation, and takes classical masterpieces as the touchstone of artistic excellence.

On this kind of view, it is hard to explain why improvisers should not write out their 'improvisations' in advance, improving and perfecting them – that is, composing them. Improvisation is a near-universal tendency in music and really needs no defence. But from the aesthetic viewpoint of western art music it appears to have the deficiencies highlighted by Ted Gioia:

> Improvisation is doomed, it seems, to offer a pale imitation of the perfection attained by composed music. Errors will creep in, not only in form but also in execution; the improviser, if he sincerely attempts to be creative, will push himself into areas of expression which his technique may be unable to handle. Too often the finished product will show moments of rare beauty intermixed with technical mistakes and aimless passages. Why then are we interested in this haphazard art?[3]

Gioia is concerned to show why we are, nonetheless, interested in the 'imperfect art' of improvisation. His defence he labels 'the aesthetics of imperfection', in contrast to 'the aesthetics of perfection' which takes composition as the paradigm. In this essay I will argue that the contrast between composition and improvisation proves more subtle and complex than Gioia and other writers allow. The focus is principally on jazz and related popular music, but much of the discussion is, I think, applicable to other kinds of improvised music.

Aesthetics of perfection and imperfection

The dichotomy between improvisation and composition is rooted in historical circumstance and lacked its present meaning, or perhaps any meaning at all, before the musical work-concept achieved hegemony – a process of increasing specificity of the score that was completed during the nineteenth and early twentieth centuries. As Lydia Goehr writes, 'By 1800 … the notion of extemporization acquired its modern understanding [and] was seen to stand in strict opposition to "composition" proper.'[4]

Philosophers, mesmerized by the vision of the scored musical work, mostly do not think enough about improvisation and its implications. In Roger Scruton's *The Aesthetics of Music*, for instance, the work-concept dominates and an improvisation is treated as a work that is identical with a performance – an attitude that reflects the hegemony of western art music. George Lewis rightly argues that since 1800 there has been an 'ongoing narrative of dismissal' of improvisation by western composers, though like Scruton he rather neglects the historicity of the concept of improvisation.[5] That narrative expresses an aesthetics of perfection which arose with the work-concept, and which is opposed by an aesthetics of imperfection associated with improvisation.

This opposition concerns, in the first instance, whether composition should be privileged over improvisation, or vice versa. But it offers a fruitful framework for looking at certain aesthetic questions in the performing arts – questions that turn out to be fundamental to the nature of music. It is illustrated by the debate between Busoni, the defender of improvisation, and Schoenberg, the compositional determinist.[6] Schoenberg emphasized the autonomy of the composer-genius in the creation of masterworks, which, he insisted, required the complete subservience of the performer; Busoni found virtues in improvisation and in the individual contribution of the performer-interpreter.

Busoni writes:

> Notation, the writing out of compositions, is primarily an ingenious expedient for catching an inspiration, with the purpose of exploiting it later. But notation is to improvisation as the portrait is to the living model … What the composer's inspiration necessarily loses through notation, his interpreter should restore by his own.

He defends his practice of transcription – the arrangement of a composition for a medium different from the one for which it was originally composed – and argues that 'Every notation is, in itself, the transcription of an abstract idea. The instant the pen seizes it, the idea loses its original form'. The purity of the improvisation is one step less removed from the locus of artistic inspiration.

For Schoenberg, in contrast, there is only gain in the working-up of an improvisation into a crafted composition. He rejects Busoni's claim that improvisation has artistic priority: 'the portrait has higher artistic life, while the model has only a lower life'. The interpreter is the servant of the work: 'He must read every wish from its lips'. Interpreters' attempts to express their own individuality are regrettable: 'And so the interpreter mostly becomes a parasite on the exterior, when he could be the artery in the circulation of the blood'.

The aesthetics of imperfection thus focuses on the moment or event of performance, while its rival emphasizes the timelessness of the work. The rival aesthetics is tendencies in the rather complex thought of Busoni and Schoenberg, and the dichotomy, as will become clear, implies others: process and product; impermanence and permanence; spontaneity and deliberation. A contemporary expression of an aesthetics of perfection is found, for instance, in comments by British composer Thomas Adès, who is evidently more interested in product than process: 'I'm trying to fix something … I don't know how a jazz artist or improviser goes about their work, it's a mystery to me. And I would think that what I do is rather a mystery to them'. Adès is not tempted, like Mark-Anthony Turnage, to incorporate passages of improvisation in his compositions. Revealingly, he says that if he did, 'in 70 or 80 years' time there'll be this very weird situation where you'll have these scores with holes in them, and the people won't be there to fill the holes in'.[7]

To some readers the idea of an 'aesthetics of imperfection' will be overly paradoxical, its connotations too negative: how could imperfection possibly be an aesthetic value? But 'perfection' and 'imperfection' have a descriptive sense close to their Latin derivation: '*perficere*' means 'to do thoroughly, to complete, to finish, to work up'; '*imperfectus*' means 'unfinished, incomplete'. The aesthetics of imperfection finds virtues in improvisation which transcend the errors in form and execution acknowledged by Gioia. Indeed, it claims, these virtues arise precisely because of the 'unfinished state' of such performances.

While acknowledging the unique value of improvisation, the argument of this essay consists of a progressive qualification of the rival aesthetics, and in particular a rejection of its common assumption that improvisation is a kind of instant composition. The rival aesthetics offers an account of both interpretation and improvisation. Here I focus on the latter, but an essential part of my argument is that there is in important respects a fluid contrast between a composed work and an improvisation. Their exemplars stand in a continuum, and 'improvisation' and 'composition' denote ideal types or interpenetrating opposites. The latter term derives from Hegel – interpenetration of opposites is a law of Hegelian logic – and I hope it is not too pretentious to regard the argument in the present article as a kind of dialectic. A feature that seems definitive of one ideal type also turns out to be present, in some sense, in the other – or so I will argue with regard to preparation, spontaneity and structure.

The continuum can be illustrated as follows. Pre-realized electronic music stands at the far end of the pre-structured spectrum since, although possibly possessing spontaneity at the level of composition, at the level of performance – strictly a misnomer – it is fixed. Composers such as Bach who leave much to the performer, and trial-and-error compositional efforts of students in a recording studio, contrast with the organic, motivically developing, through-composed works of composers such as Schoenberg. Within the improvised sector, pre-performance structuring ranges from the work of jazz composers such as Ellington and Gil Evans to the very loose frameworks brought along by Miles Davis to the *Kind of Blue* recording session. At the furthest 'improvised' limit of the continuum stands free improvisation, a development of 1960s free jazz, which dispensed with recurring harmonic sequences and an explicit metre.

Thus the aesthetics of perfection and imperfection applies not just at the level of performance, but within the process of composition also. Or rather, there is a sense in which these levels overlap; there may, for instance, be little difference between a loosely constructed studio composition and the recording of an improvisation. It may, for some purposes, be useful to divide the continuum in two, with works on one side and improvisations on the other, but this glosses over continuities and similarities.

The rival aesthetics extends into other aspects of artistic production. With recording, for instance, the arena of debate is shifted onto new ground, again with a contrasting focus on the moment of performance (imperfection) or the timelessness of the work (perfection). Recording offers new possibilities of vindicating an aesthetics of perfection, since allegedly contingent conditions of live performance can be screened out – an approach expressed most thoughtfully in the creative recording techniques of pianist Glenn Gould. The imperfectionist view, in contrast, is that recording should be treated as a transparent medium giving a faithful representation of a particular performance, with only the grossest imperfections eliminated.[8]

Although an aesthetics of perfection seems to demand absolute fidelity to the composer's intentions – or rather, it has a very narrow and stringent conception of what such fidelity involves – it should be separated from a commitment to authentic performance in its present-day sense. The aesthetics of perfection perhaps implies a Platonist conception of the musical work as a timeless sound-structure detachable from its original conditions of performance – instruments as well as locations. The implication from Platonism to perfectionism is stronger, as Glenn Gould's remarks illustrate:

> Music need not be performed any more than books need to be read aloud, for its logic is perfectly represented on the printed page; and the performer ... is totally unnecessary except as his interpretations make the music understandable to an audience unfortunate enough not to be able to read it in print.[9]

The recent concept of authenticity, in contrast, is more ambivalent between perfection and imperfection. It has been argued that it rejects the 'portability of music' in favour of an ideal of acoustic interdependence of composer, ensemble, and environment.[10] But it may also be regarded as a confused expression of a timeless conception – a preservation in aspic. But the issue of musical Platonism requires development elsewhere.

It is necessary at this point to say a few inadequate words about terminology. Just as 'composition' is not a unitary phenomenon, neither is 'western art music'. The concept of an 'art music' requires more than an article in itself; jazz, for instance, may now be an art music in its own right. Most people know what is being referred to by the term 'classical music', but its drawbacks are manifest. In the other arts the term refers to a period of particular excellence or influence. Only in music is it ever simply equated with 'serious', signalling the museum of musical works which constitutes the modern concert repertoire, an end-product of post-Romantic historicism. So here I stick with 'western art music'.

Instrumental impulse and individual tone

The idea that improvisation involves 'pure transmission of the musical idea' is emphasized by many proponents of an aesthetics of imperfection, including Busoni and Bill Evans. W.F. Bach wrote of his father:

> his organ compositions were indeed full of the expression of devotion, solemnity and dignity; but his unpremeditated organ playing, in which nothing was lost in the process of writing down but everything came directly to life out of his imagination, is said to have been still more devout, solemn, dignified and sublime.[11]

The view is echoed by Leo Smith, avant-garde trumpet-player and ideologist of free jazz:

> Improvisation ... is not like composition ... [where an] idea [is conceived] at one instant, only to be funnelled at a later time through a standard system of notation onto paper as merely a related idea, and finally interpreted and performed ... as an idea removed at least three times from the original.[12]

These writers regard improvisation as a kind of instant composition, a natural picture which the present essay is concerned to undermine. I will do so indirectly at first, by exploring the immediacy which arises from the improviser's close relation with their instrument, then directly by looking at the spontaneity present in improvised performances.

Proponents of an aesthetics of imperfection such as Derek Bailey have maintained that there is an 'instrumental impulse' which improvisation encourages, and which is much stronger than among interpreters. For the improviser the instrument is 'a source of material, and technique is often an exploitation of the natural resources of that instrument'. Saxophonist Steve Lacy writes: 'The instrument – that's the matter – the stuff – your subject.'[13] Bailey could have cited Beethoven's riposte to Schuppanzigh, when the violinist complained about a difficult passage in the Violin Concerto: 'Do you believe I was thinking of your wretched fiddle when the Spirit spoke to me?'[14]

But perhaps even Beethoven was not always so confident about the Spirit's lack of concern with mundane technical matters. Many improvisers see the instrument as musical material, but so also do many composers. Where they are not performers of the instrument they are writing for, such composers sensibly learn about its possibilities from those who are. A contemporary example is Luciano Berio's virtuoso *Sequenze* for solo instruments, which explores new sonorities and effects, many of which are now passing into mainstream tradition.

However, Bailey's remarks about the instrumental impulse highlight a significant contrast between improvisers and interpreters. In improvised music, instrumental timbre and instrumental technique are non-standard and more individual. Jazz saxophonist Sam Rivers provides an uncompromising instance: 'I listened to everyone I could hear to make sure I didn't sound like them. I wasn't taking any chances; I wanted to be sure I didn't sound like anyone else.'[15] Classical saxophonists, in contrast, seem to subscribe to a standard of correctness involving a plummy tone and string-style legato, evolved to blend with the rest of the section and orchestra, and resulting in stylistic anonymity.

Classical saxophone is an extreme case. But in western art music there is, within a particular period and within broad parameters, at least the concept of a standard of correct technique and tone – though authorities may differ over the nature of rubato, the desirability of vibrato, and so on. Individualities of tone are narrower, if still important and inevitably subject to fashion. (To the extent to which this no longer applies in contemporary western art music, there is a break-down of barriers between composed and improvised music.)

The jazz ethos of freedom has led to a marked variety of timbre and tone in certain instruments, notably trumpet, saxophone and string bass, while in other cases, for instance piano, jazz has been less innovative in comparison to classical music. But it is hard to see how the concept of a standard of correctness has application anywhere in jazz. A jazz saxophonist who resorted to the vaudeville technique of slap-tonguing, or the classical player's woodwind tone, would be unfashionable but not 'incorrect'. (Wynton Marsalis's aspirations towards a jazz academy are peripheral to the main development of the music.)

Although the need for orchestral homogeneity is a factor, the contrast in individuality follows principally from the fact that classical players are interpreters of a composed work to which they must strive to be faithful – a requirement understood differently depending on whether the interpreter agrees with Busoni or Schoenberg, but one that inevitably imposes limits on tonal idiosyncrasy. Moreover, the whole interpretative enterprise is underwritten by the authority of the art music. Denigration of more individual, unschooled techniques by proponents of an aesthetics of perfection is an expression of classical authority, in the sense found in John Potter's recent book *Vocal Authority*. Potter is concerned to explain, in ideological terms, how one variety of singing, 'that used for what we in the West call classical music, appears to have a uniquely authoritative status relative to all other possible kinds'.[16]

A subtle illustration of the operation of authority is found in Peter Pettinger's discussion of Bill Evans, who developed an individual timbre for jazz piano precisely by drawing on the classical model. Pettinger's musical thesis is that from classical arm-weight technique Evans created an apparently understated but powerful emotional expression unprecedented in jazz, wresting a singing tone from what is essentially a percussion instrument. What attracted him was that Evans 'sounded like a classical pianist, and yet he was playing jazz ... it was the very idea that one style of music could be played with the skills and finesse normally only brought to another'. Sonny Clark, a possible influence on Evans, is described as

> one of those pianists who feel, and show, respect for the instrument; one who collaborates with it rather than acts the aggressor upon it. Such a player is immediately in a position to judge and vary sound quantity (while maintaining quality), and thereby to control tonal nuance within a line.[17]

Pettinger's subtext is an expression of classical authority over keyboard technique. His implication is that great jazz pianists such as Ellington, Bud Powell, Thelonious Monk and Cecil Taylor fall short. It is true that in earlier jazz, pianists had to play on substandard instruments where an attempt to extract a singing tone would be futile; Evans's style is possible only on a grand piano of superior quality. But there are other timbral effects to be gained from a piano than a singing tone, and it would be more correct to say that it was a concern with classical tone which most jazz pianists lacked.

Consider Cecil Taylor's description of being influenced by Horace Silver, who played 'the real thing of Bud [Powell], with all the physicality of it, with the filth of it, and the movement in the attack', which Taylor at that time called 'the Negro idea'. Visceral energy, funk and bluesiness are unlikely to be obtained with classical arm-weight technique, and they are not qualities associated with Bill Evans.[18] But his lines exhibit a lean rhythmic vitality lacking in the Evans transcriptions played 'perfectly' but unidiomatically by classical pianist Jean-Yves Thibaudet.[19] Thibaudet is typical of classical pianists who try to play jazz, putting effort into irrelevant expressive effects while neglecting the crucial improvised feel. Pettinger is wrong to privilege one kind of technique over another. The prescriptions of the authoritative art music are not universal; good technique must be characterized with reference to the kind of musical effects the performer is trying to achieve.

I claimed earlier that improvisation and composition constitute interpenetrating opposites. This is illustrated by the way in which both composers and improvisers use the instrument as musical material; the creation of an individual timbre in improvised music is matched by a more circumscribed tonal individuality in great classical soloists. But the dialectic of interpenetration is more clearly observed in respect of the alleged unique spontaneity of improvised music.

The concept of improvisation: improvised feel and intentional fallacy

'You will hear something close to pure spontaneity in these performances,' Evans wrote of *Kind of Blue*. This claim is an essential element of an aesthetics of imperfection, but it has not always been the improviser's ideal. According to a report of the 1760s, Austrian composer and violinist Carl Ditters von Dittersdorf performed a violin concerto followed by an encore of brilliant 'improvised' virtuosity which, he later admitted, had been prepared in advance.[20]

This attitude to improvisation persists after the development of the work-concept. Most jazz musicians up to the Swing Era would have felt no compunction in rehearsing and working-up their solos. Billie Holiday was one among many whose performances of the same song varied only in minor details, though her interpretations evolved over time.[21] Harry Carney from the Ellington orchestra rarely varied his solos on given numbers at all. The influence of Charlie Parker in the artistically self-conscious modern jazz of the 1940s was paramount in generating an ideal of genuinely spontaneous creation. But performers with his genius, where alternative takes of the same song at the same recording session will be radically different, remain very rare.

What does spontaneity amount to in improvised performances? And how does it matter aesthetically? These questions bring us to the heart of the concept of improvisation. A useful case study is the contemporary von Dittersdorf observed by a journalist from *Downbeat* magazine:

> How much is improvised? Tonight, [Ray] Bryant played 'After Hours' in a note-for-note copy of the way he played it on the Dizzy, Rollins and Stitt album on Verve some fifteen years ago. Was it written then? Or worse. Has he transcribed and memorised his own solo, as if it were an archaeological classic? It was fine blues piano indeed, but it was odd to hear it petrified in this way.[22]

If it was 'fine blues piano', would it matter that it was 'petrified'?

Writers who adopt a purely genetic or causal account of the concept of improvisation imply that its presence is of little aesthetic consequence. Stanley Cavell claims that the standard concept of improvisation 'seems merely to name events which one knows, as matters of historical fact … independent of anything a critic would have to discover by an analysis or interpretation … not to have been composed'. And Eric Hobsbawm writes: 'There is no special merit in improvisation … For the listener it is musically irrelevant that what he hears is improvised or written down. If he did not know he could generally not tell the difference.' However, he continues, 'improvisation, or at least a margin of it around even the most "written" jazz compositions, is rightly cherished, because it stands for the constant living re-creation of the music, the excitement and inspiration of the players which is communicated to us'.[23]

Of course, the concept of improvisation has an essential genetic component. Although it glosses over crucial complexities, a succinct definition would be 'not written down or otherwise fixed in advance' – Ray Bryant's performance was apparently fixed though not written down. A purely genetic account claims that whether a performance is improvised is not usually apparent merely by listening to it. It suggests, furthermore, that the mere fact that a performance is improvised is not an aesthetically or critically relevant feature. (There will be several variations on the latter claim.) This amounts to the formalistic claim that there is an 'intentional fallacy' concerning improvisation – reminiscent of the suggestion that extraneous knowledge of authorial intention is irrelevant to critical evaluation.

The genetic account exaggerates the extent to which improvisation is undetectable, I would argue. There is a genuine phenomenon of an *improvised feel*, gestured at by Hobsbawm's comments on what improvisation symbolizes. Curiously, the best description of it is found in a book aimed at the few remaining improvisers in the organ-loft. In *The Art of Improvisation* from 1934, T. C. Whitmer offered a set of 'General Basic Principles' which included the following description, one which justifies the term 'aesthetics of imperfection':

> Don't look forward to a finished and complete entity. The idea must always be kept in a state of flux. An error may only be an unintentional rightness. Polishing is not at all the important thing; instead strive for a rough go-ahead energy. Do not be afraid of being wrong; just be afraid of being uninteresting.[24]

From this feel, I think, arises the distinctive form of melodic lines and voicings in an improvised performance. The qualities Whitmer cites are salient features, present to varying degrees. Although Bill Evans's beauty of tone seems in conflict with a 'rough go-ahead energy', there is an understated tensile quality in his work. Jean-Yves Thibaudet's performances of Evans transcriptions, in contrast, do not sound improvised.

One might say of a purported improvisation – 'That couldn't have been improvised' – meaning, for instance, that the figuration is too complex, the instrumental voicings too clear to be created under the constraints of an improvised performance (although one might consider that J.S. Bach was able to improvise music of such complexity). The converse claim – 'That couldn't have been composed' – sounds odd, because the features which justify it are more elusive. But it is often possible to justify the claim, 'That *wasn't* composed'.

It is true, however, that an improvised feel might be present in music which takes improvisation as its model – Ray Bryant's example might be a case in point – and possibly even where a composer is looking to create an improvised effect. Would the fact that the performance was not improvised 'matter aesthetically'? One might justifiably alter one's view of the skill of the performer; but there is a more elusive sense in which it matters. The sense of disappointment on discovering that the performer was a von Dittersdorf belongs to an interesting family of responses to what appears to be extraneous knowledge that some artistic ideal has been transgressed. The listener is surprised and disappointed to discover that an enjoyable piece by John Cage was created randomly using chance operations based on the *I Ching*; that a classical recording was constructed from tape-extracts of many separate takes, that an art photographer's work involves superimposition of figures or objects not in the original scene; that a putative abstract painting is in fact a piece of discarded interior decoration; or – a more extreme case – that a favourite painting is a fake. (Improvisation used to be called 'faking', hence 'fake books', collections of melodies and chord sequences of standard songs for improvisation; the idea, presumably, was that the player would be 'faking' that they were playing something composed.)

In the case of improvisation, the artistic ideal is part of what separates art from entertainment.[25] Ray Bryant's performance, for all its skill, seems indebted to the routine that wows the audience. (Oscar Peterson might be a better example of this approach.) A routine is something perfected by the performer, who knows it works and sticks with it. In so far as improvisation is present, it involves a 'bag of tricks' model. Routines are just what are avoided by the 'modernists' who reject the culture industry – Bill Evans, Paul Bley, and all those who despise flashy virtuosity. There are obvious parallels here with the development of western art music.

So there are various senses in which improvisation matters aesthetically. Claims of an intentional fallacy are not vindicated, even assuming that there is a viable notion of 'extraneous' knowledge. The role of preparation further undermines such claims. Cavell and Hobsbawm seem to subscribe to the 'instant composition' view of improvisation. In my criticism of this view I will develop the negative definition of improvisation, and the beginnings of a positive one in terms of improvised feel. The idea of a continuum of composition and improvisation has been rather neglected in the preceding discussion, but it reappears in the idea of different kinds of preparation for performance.

Spontaneity and the aesthetics of perfection

The view of improvisation as instant composition is a characterization shared both by an aesthetics of imperfection with its ideal of complete spontaneity, and by the aesthetics of perfection which denigrates improvisation. These positions are, in a way, mutually dependent; the difference is that one eulogizes instant composition while the other declares it hopeless. Later I will criticize the first position. Here I will argue against the first, which claims that all improvisers, precisely because of their aspiration to complete spontaneity, are really like von Dittersdorf; improvisation is a barrier to individual self-expression, not a way of realizing it. Modernist composers are almost unanimous in this view. (The positions of Stockhausen and, if it is possible to extend the debate to other art forms, Jackson Pollock are ambivalent.)

Elliott Carter, for instance, argues that improvisation allows undigested fragments of the unconscious to float to the surface. Since he is not an Expressionist, he does not approve:

> carefully written scores produce the most unroutinized performances because, in preventing performers from playing in their usual way, they suggest another kind of spontaneous reaction – to the musical concepts underlying the music –which has greater potential for liveliness than is usually the case with improvisation.

His conclusion is that 'improvisation is undertaken mainly to appeal to the theatrical side of musical performance and rarely reaches the highest artistic level of … western [art] music'.[26]

Pierre Boulez questions the more radical chance or aleatoric techniques deployed during the 1960s by Stockhausen and others, which leave much to the performer's decision:

> If the player were an inventor of primary forms or material, he would be a composer … if you do not provide him with sufficient information to perform a work, what can he do? He can only turn to information he has been given on some earlier occasion, in fact to what he has already played.[27]

The criticism is that familiar patterns of notes are embedded in the performer's muscular memory as a result of countless hours spent with the instrument, and regurgitated when there is no restraining score. Improvisers express themselves less than they think because so much of what they play is what they are remembering, including things they do not even know they are remembering. This, at least, is the Carter-Boulez line.

Carter, like Adorno earlier, neglects those modernists in improvisation who do not just appeal to the 'theatrical side of musical performance'. Boulez's statement clearly begs the question against improvisation. It amounts to an assertion of the classical hegemony expressed by the honorific title 'composer'. Improvisation precisely constitutes a denial of the view that if the player were an 'inventor of primary forms or material', he or she would be a composer. (What the force of 'primary' is remains unclear.) It is true that the improviser has less chance than the composer to eradicate cliché in their work – as the aesthetics of imperfection recognizes. But there are various ways in which the critique may be addressed. One is to view the improviser's successive performances of a song or a number as constituting a developing work, incrementally altered and never wholly spontaneous. I am not sympathetic to this view, which could not cover all cases, but will return to it in the final section.

Here I want to argue that Carter and Boulez neglect the fact that the improviser's preparation and practice are precisely intended to 'keep [them] from playing what [they] already know'. Saxophonist Steve Lacy, one of the most thoughtful improvisers in contemporary jazz, argues that:

> [There] is a freshness, a certain quality that can only be obtained by improvisation, something you cannot possibly get by writing. It is something to do with the 'edge'. Always being on the brink of the unknown and being prepared for the leap. And when you go on out there you have all your years of preparation and all your sensibilities and your prepared means but it is a leap into the unknown.

LaMonte Young, the pioneer of minimalism, commented:

> There's a very fine balance between structure, preparation and control, and letting things come through. When I play *The Well-Tuned Piano*, even though I've practised and have a great deal of information under my fingers and running through my head … I totally open myself up to a higher source of inspiration and try to let it flow through me. I play things that I could've never played, that I couldn't imagine.[28]

Other improvisers, instead of talking mystically of a 'higher source', will appeal to the unconscious as a fertile source of musical ideas, in a way which Carter rejects.

Thus there is a relation between performance and pre-performance activity not envisaged by Carter and Boulez – nor by the polar opposite of their view, the pure spontaneity of an aesthetics of imperfection. Interpreters think about and practise a work with the aim of giving a faithful representation of it in performance. Improvisers also practise, but with the aim of being better prepared for Lacy's 'leap'. Many improvisers will formulate structures and ideas, and at an unconscious level these phrases will provide openings for a new creation. Thus there are different ways for a performer to get beyond what they already do, to avoid repeating themselves.

For the improviser, the performance must feel like a 'leap into the unknown', and it will be an inspired one when the hours of preparation connect with the requirements of the moment and help to shape a fresh and compelling creation. At the time of performance they must clear their conscious minds of prepared patterns and simply play. Thus it makes sense to talk of preparation for the spontaneous effort. This is the limited truth in the claim that improvisation is valuable because it is closer to the original idea.

These are elusive claims, and they can be vindicated only by looking at actual cases. For instance, the contrast between relatively mechanical and spontaneous deployment of prepared ideas is illuminated by Carl Woideck's excellent book on Charlie Parker. A central claim is that Parker's creativity declined after 1950, for health and drug-related reasons. His huge repertoire of motifs was deployed increasingly mechanically – though still with a brilliance his peers could not match – and no longer developed, Woideck argues. This does not mean that Parker was reproducing practised solos; indeed, part of the problem seems to have been that he ceased practising from the late 1940s onwards. Here we have a case of pre-existing structures being employed in progressively less spontaneous ways.[29]

Free improvisers, interpreters and 'improvisation as a compositional method'

Proponents of a radical aesthetics of imperfection can also be criticized for neglecting the connection between preparation and performance. Some free improvisers claim to go beyond even Charlie Parker-like standards of freshness and improvise, in Ornette Coleman's words, 'without memory'. Leo Smith writes that 'at its highest level, improvisation [is] created entirely within the improviser at the moment of improvisation without any prior structuring'. Derek Bailey advocates 'non-idiomatic improvisation', apparently without a personal vocabulary; I also recall an interview on BBC Radio 3, where pianist Keith Tippett told how in his practising and performing he attempted to exclude phrases he had played before. This aspiration is surely unattainable and fortunately so. An improviser's individuality precisely resides in, among other things, their creative development of favourite stylistic or structural devices, without which they risk incoherence and non-communication. Bailey's ideal paradoxically ends up as impersonal improvisation; the guitarist himself, whatever he may think, is a highly idiomatic and individual improviser.

It is important to realize that both imperfectionists and perfectionists share similar misconceptions concerning the interpretation of a work. Many proponents of an aesthetics of imperfection believe that interpreters simply 'reproduce the score'. The dialectic here is the counterpart of that concerning instant composition: imperfectionists condemn interpretation as mere reproduction, while perfectionists praise it for the same reason, since a reproduction allows no corrupting role for the performer's individuality. (These are extreme statements of the rival positions; the views of Busoni and Schoenberg are more subtle.)

It is true that commentators from various traditions have criticized the increasingly uniform and soulless perfection of classical performances.[30] But it is the achievement of the greatest interpreters to produce the illusion of spontaneous creation.[31] When artists of the stature of Lipatti or Brendel or Furtwängler perform or conduct, and the circumstances are propitious, the work is heard new and fresh, in a way it never has before. There is a genuine phenomenon here as well as an artistic illusion. In the sense of spontaneity as freedom to reconceive something at the moment of performance, there is a micro-freedom for interpreters, involving many subtle parameters such as tone and dynamics, in contrast to the macro-freedom of improvisers. So as interpreters get to know a work intimately, a certain freedom can develop; a performance will then feel like a 'leap into the unknown' and have, in a sense, an improvised feel. Performers make the work their own, they internalize it; just as actors do not merely recite the lines of a play, but become the part. But great performances can illuminate a truth about the work; the performer does not simply strive to 'do something different'. George Lewis is therefore wrong to contrast composition with 'real-time music' – interpretation occurs in 'real-time' too.

However, an aesthetics of perfection also misunderstands the process of interpretation. A well-rehearsed performance of a familiar work will, after all, involve something that the performer has already played, and this could become stultifying. So interpreters must strive for that improvisational freshness which gives the illusion that they are not playing 'what they already know' – that is, a pre-existing work. (The quotation from Carter does acknowledge that scores 'suggest another kind of spontaneous reaction'.)

Improvisation makes the performer alive in the moment; it brings one to a state of alertness, even what Ian Carr in his biography of Keith Jarrett has called the 'state of grace'.[32] This state is enhanced in a group situation of interactive empathy. But all players, except those in a large orchestra, have choices inviting spontaneity at the point of performance. These begin with the room in which they are playing, its humidity and temperature, who they are playing with, and so on Thus interactive empathy is present in classical music too at a high level, for instance in the traditional string quartet. Again, the rival aesthetics fail to recognize that improvisation and composition are interpenetrating opposites – features that appear definitive of one are found in the other also.

It remains finally to consider the view put forward by writers from various standpoints, that improvisation should be regarded as a variety of composition – where this does not mean 'instant composition'. Now there is a sense in which recordings convert improvisation into composition. They can be subject to critical analysis, enter a canon and help to establish art music status – all this is found in jazz.[33] Thus improvisations can perhaps become works from the viewpoint of their reception. But it has also been argued that, from the viewpoint of their production, improvisations can count as compositions. There may be an immediate practical impetus behind such claims. The Arts Council of England and Wales, for instance, operated a *de facto* policy that was product-based, funding composers but not improvisers – hence a profusion of uninspired 'suites' by jazz musicians.[34]

Jazz writer Sidney Finkelstein wrote in 1948:

> Improvisation is a form of composition. Improvisation is music that is not written down, composition is music that is written down … The ability to write music makes possible a bigness of form and richness of expression that is beyond the limits of improvisation … [But the] slow creation of a great jazz solo [from performance to performance] is a form of musical composition.[35]

I think that Charlie Parker was not unique in transcending Finkelstein's analysis, but his central claim has been echoed in different ways by later writers.

Roger Scruton, writing from a western art music perspective, maintains that an improvisation is a work that is identical with a performance, while apparently suggesting that there is a stricter sense in which the work-concept supersedes improvised music:

the distinction between work and performance grows spontaneously in the practice of acousmatic hearing ... [involving] a peculiar experience of 'same again ... There could not be meaningful improvisation without this experience, and the emergence of 'works' from a tradition of spontaneous performance is exactly what we must expect when people listen, and therefore recognise what they hear as 'the same again'.[36]

Scruton fails to recognize that the concept of improvisation, in its present-day sense, precisely arose as a reaction to the emergence of works; there is plenty of scope for 'playing it again' in the way that jazz utilizes the standard songs of Tin Pan Alley.

Some improvising musicians put a very different slant on this kind of claim. Evan Parker, one of the leading free improvisers, advocates 'improvisation as a compositional method', and describes his piece 'De Motu' as 'an improvisation composed uniquely and expressly during its performance in Zaal de Unie in Rotterdam on Friday May 15th 1992'. He continues: 'In the period of preparation I made notes of ideas and patterns ... in a method that can be seen as analogous to a painter's sketchbook where fragments of what might become the final work are treated in isolation from one another.'[37]

Possibly with Parker's view in mind, George Lewis objects to the claim that 'any kind of generating music is a kind of composing':

the problem is not just taxonomical ... what you're doing is placing yourself under the hegemony of composers, or people who call themselves composers ... Once you decide you don't *need* to be accepted as a composer, then you should be accepted as doing what *you* do. You should be accepted as an improviser.[38]

Lewis is right: the issue is not taxonomic. But both his attitude and Evan Parker's can be seen as contesting the western art music hegemony, possibly with equal effectiveness. They are right to give weight to the ideological import of the traditional vocabulary, and either view is defensible; what is essential is that the picture of instant composition is avoided.

It would be wrong to give the impression that improvisers and composers are in two mutually uncomprehending camps; this no longer reflects the situation on the ground, at least among the avant-garde in America. But there are many pervasive misunderstandings of improvisation which I hope this essay helps to correct. Despite the qualifications of it presented here, I believe that the aesthetics of imperfection is right to focus on music as event. This position perhaps points to the primacy of the performance over the work, subverting the standard account whereby works are exemplified in performance. But that is material for another occasion.[39]

Notes

1   Miles Davis, *Kind of Blue* (New York: Columbia, 1959), sleevenote. Reprinted as 'Improvisation in jazz'. in R. O'Meally, *The Jazz Cadence of American Culture* (New York: Columbia University Press, 1998).

2   Peter Pettinger, *Bill Evans: How My Heart Sings* (New Haven, CT and London: Yale University Press, 1998).

3   E. Gioia, *The Imperfect Art* (Oxford: Oxford University Press, 1988), p. 66.

4   L. Goehr, *The Imaginary Museum of Musical Works* (Oxford: Clarendon Press, 1992), p. 234 – a brief account of the changing concept of improvisation is found at pp. 188–9 and 232–4. Goehr is possibly influenced by Adorno's insistence on the historicity of the concepts of improvisation and composition, discussed in Max Paddison, *Adorno's Aesthetics of Music* (Cambridge: Cambridge University Press, 1993), pp. 192–8.

5   R. Scruton, *The Aesthetics of Music* (Oxford: Clarendon Press, 1997); George Lewis, 'Improvised Music after 1950: Afrological and Eurological Perspectives', *Black Music Research Journal*, vol. 16, no. 1 (1996), pp. 91–122.

6   The 'debate' consisted of Schoenberg writing marginal comments in his copy of Busoni's book; subsequent quotations are from P. Busoni, 'Sketch of a New Aesthetic of Music', in *Three Classics in the Aesthetic of Music* (New York: Dover, 1962), p. 84, and H. H. Stuckenschmidt, *Arnold Schoenberg: His Life, World and Work* (London: John Calder, 1977), pp. 226–7.

7   A. Hamilton, 'Thomas Adès: Sleaze Operas', *The Wire*, issue 176 (October 1998), p. 13.

8   I discuss later the sense in which recordings convert improvisations into works; and address the issue of recording in a sequel to the present essay. My inadequate first thoughts on the general issue appeared as 'The Aesthetics of Imperfection', *Philosophy*, vol. 65, no. 253 (1990), pp. 323–40.

9   Quoted in Kevin Bazzana, *Glenn Gould: The Performer in the Work* (Oxford: Clarendon Press, 1997), pp. 20–21.

10 This is the view of Robin Maconie, *The Concept of Music* (Oxford: Clarendon Press, 1990), pp. 150–51.

11 Quoted in 'Improvisation' by Eva Badura-Skoda, in S. Sadie (ed.), *The New Grove Dictionary of Music and Musicians* (London: Macmillan, 1980).

12 L. Smith, *notes (8 pieces) source a new world music* (creative music, USA: Leo Smith, 1973 – the pamphlet has no page numbers or capital letters).

13 Quoted by Derek Bailey, *Improvisation: Its Nature and Practice in Music* (Ashbourne, Derby: Moorland, 1980; 2nd edn London: British Library, 1992), pp. 92, 94 (1st edn). This groundbreaking book is an invaluable resource for discussion of improvisation.

14 Or words to that effect – for a less pithy version, see I. Crofton *et al.* (eds), *A Dictionary of Musical Quotations* (London: Routledge, 1988), p. 15.

15 Sam Rivers, *Dimensions and Extensions* (New York: Blue Note, 1986), sleevenote.

16 John Potter, *Vocal Authority: Singing Style and Ideology* (Cambridge: Cambridge University Press, 1998), p. 1.

17 Pettinger, *How My Heart Sings*, pp. ix, 72. The cantabile style appeared during the nineteenth century – it was clearly not possible on the fortepiano – though Bartok was not the only classical composer who later rejected it. No one has explained how its production is physically possible, even with the mechanism of the modern piano.

18 Quotation from J. Collier, *The Making of Jazz* (London: Granada, 1978), p. 456. One irony is that Taylor is also conservatory-trained; another is that Evans himself always cited Bud Powell as his key jazz influence. The interesting case of Thelonious Monk is discussed in T. Fitterling, *Thelonious Monk: His Life and Music*, trans. R. Dobbin (Berkeley, CA: Berkeley Hills Books, 1997), pp. 99–104.

19 Jean-Yves Thibaudet, *Conversations with Bill Evans* (London: Decca, 1997).

20 Badura-Skoda, *Improvisation*, p. 43.

21 We know this from alternative takes of the same song. On improvisation in early jazz, see G.

Schuller, *The Swing Era* (New York: Oxford University Press, 1989), pp. 162n. and 307n.; and Conrad Cork, *Harmony with Lego Bricks* (Leicester: Tadley Ewing, rev. edn 1996), pp. 81–6.

22 *Downbeat* report from May 1978, quoted in Gioia, *Imperfect Art*, pp. 52–3. How did Hollenberg, the journalist, know the solos were note-for-note the same – he wasn't taping without the artist's permission by any chance? Even von Dittersdorfs have performing rights.

23 S. Cavell, 'Music Discomposed', in his *Must We Mean What We Say?* (Cambridge: Cambridge University Press, 1976), p. 200; Hobsbawn quote from *The Jazz Scene*, first published 1959 under the pseudonym of Francis Newton, quoted in R. Gottlieb, *Reading Jazz* (London: Bloomsbury, 1997), p. 813. Cavell offers a more elusive sense of 'improvised' on pp. 200–201.

24 Quoted in Bailey, *Improvisation*, p. 48.

25 I owe this suggestion to Max Paddison.

26 E. Carter, *Collected Essays and Lectures, 1937–95*, ed. J. Bernard (Rochester, NY: Rochester University Press, 1997), pp. 324–5. Carter's music has been much-influenced by jazz rhythms – maybe he just prefers his jazz well-rehearsed, like Jelly Roll Morton's.

27 P. Boulez, *Orientations* (London: Faber & Faber, 1986), p. 461. Lukas Foss says that in improvisation 'one plays what one already knows', while John Cage, who is not a modernist and so might be more sympathetic, agrees; see Lewis, 'Improvised Music after 1950', p. 106. Aleatoric music is in fact only marginally influenced by improvisation – an issue discussed in A. Hamilton, 'Undercurrents # 5: Music of Chance', *The Wire*, issue 183 (May 1999), pp. 42–5.

28 B. Case, 'Steve Lacy', interview in *The Wire*, issue I (Summer 1982), pp. 6–7; M. Webber, 'LaMonte Young meets Mark Webber', *The Wire*, issue 178 (December 1998), p. 44.

29 C. Woideck, *Charlie Parker: His Music and Life* (Ann Arbor: Michigan U.P., 1996), pp. 175–6, 199–200, and *passim*. The distinction between creative and non-creative use of motifs is also well discussed by Lewis Porter, *Lester Young* (London: Macmillan, 1986), and Cork, *Harmony With Lego-Bricks*. Lewis, 'Improvised Music after 1950', pp. 106–7, discusses the 'motif theory' proposed by cognitive psychologists.

30 Roland Barthes comments that with recording 'the various manners of playing are all flattened out *into perfection*' ('The Grain of the Voice, in his *Music, Image, Text* [London: Fontana], 1977, p. 189); and see, for instance, Adorno's discussion of Toscanini in 'The Mastery of the Maestro', in his *Sound Figures*, trans. R. Livingstone (Stanford, CA: Stanford University Press, 1999).

31 Stressed by Gunther Schuller in 'The Future of Form in Jazz', in his *Musings* (New York: Oxford University Press, 1986), pp. 24–5. Despite the illusion of spontaneous creation, the sad truth is that my article has been reworked to death with almost all traces of the original idea completely obliterated – so in answer to the repeated and irritating question: 'No, it wasn't improvised.'

32 I. Carr, *Keith Jarrett: The Man and his Music* (New York: Da Capo, 1992) Jarrett's 'state of grace' makes frequent appearances, on pp. 67, 72, 92, 104, 131, 151, 159, 163. Indeed it is sometimes described as 'the usual state of grace' – 'it is uncanny how often [Jarrett] manages to achieve the inspired state' (p. 104).

33 The point is made by W. Brooks in 'Music in America: An Overview (Part 2)', in D. Nicholls (ed.), *The Cambridge History of American Music* (Cambridge: Cambridge University Press, 1998), p. 269.

34 I owe this point to Conrad Cork, who was a panel member in the 1980s.

35 S. Finkelstein, *Jazz: A People's Music* (New York: Citadel Press, 1948, repr. London: Jazz Book Club, 1964), pp. 109, 111.

36 Scruton, *Aesthetics of Music*, p. III; *idem*, 'Reply to Hamilton, "The Aesthetics of Western Art Music"', *Philosophical Books*, vol. 40 (1999), pp. 157–8.

37 Quotations from a manuscript written to accompany the performance at the Zaal De Unie, and donated to the Rotterdamse Kunststichting.

38 Interview in sleevenote to George Lewis and Miya Masaoka, *Duets* (Berkeley CA: Music & Arts, 1998).

39 I am grateful for discussion of these issues over some years with Conrad Cork and David Udolf, and more recently Max Paddison, Ben Watson, Evan Parker, Berys Gaut and Gary Kemp. Thanks also to Peter Jones and Derek Bailey for the initial inspiration, and to the anonymous referee and editor of this journal.

Index